RACE FOR JUSTICE

The struggle for equality and inclusion
in British and Irish churches

Edited by Richard S. Reddie

MONARCH
BOOKS

Dedication
To Noel and the late Lucille Reddie, my parents, who taught me the
importance of justice.

This edition copyright © 2022 Lion Hudson IP Limited

The right of Richard Reddie, Rosemarie Mallet, Inderjit Bhogal, Wale Hudson-Roberts,
Edwina Peart, Paul Parker, Richard Zipfel, Sandra Ackroyd, Mark Sturge, Arlington
Trotman, Mandy Ralph, Aled Edwards, Damian Jackson, Jonny Smith, Richard Daly, and
Sivakumar Rajagopalan to be identified as the authors of this work has been asserted by
them in accordance with the Copyright, Designs and Patents Act 1988.

Published by **Monarch Books**
www.lionhudson.com

Part of the SPCK Group
SPCK, 36 Causton Street, London, SW1P 4ST

ISBN 978 1 80030 010 1
eISBN 978 1 80030 011 8

First edition 2022

Acknowledgments
Unless otherwise state, Scripture quotations are taken from the Holy Bible, New
International Version Anglicised. Copyright © 1979, 1984, 2011 Biblica, formerly
International Bible Society. Used by permission of Hodder & Stoughton Ltd, an Hachette
UK company. All rights reserved. "NIV" is a registered trademark of Biblica. UK trademark
number 1448790.

A catalogue record for this book is available from the British Library

Produced on paper from sustainable sources

Printed and bound in the UK, July 2022, LH26

Contents

About the Authors

Richard S. Reddie

Richard Reddie is a writer, researcher, cultural and religious commentator, and broadcaster. He has written for various publications and taken part in a number of television and radio programmes. He is the author of several books, including the groundbreaking *Black Muslims in Britain* (Lion Hudson, 2009), which was the first scholarly research into this growing phenomenon and was subsequently turned into the documentary *Young, Muslim and Black* by BBC Radio 4. Richard is currently the Director of Justice and Inclusion at the leading ecumenical body, Churches Together in Britain and Ireland.

Rosemarie Mallett

The Right Revd Canon Dr Rosemarie Mallett was born in Barbados but has lived most of her life in the UK. She has worked in West and East Africa as well as back in the Caribbean as an academic and researcher. She returned to the UK to study for her PhD. After working as an academic sociologist for twelve years, she trained for ordained ministry. Since 2005, she has served in various roles in the Diocese of Southwark, based in south London and East Surrey, as parish priest, diocesan director, and archdeacon, and is presently the bishop of Croydon.

Inderjit Bhogal

Revd Dr Inderjit Bhogal OBE is a leading theologian and Methodist minister. He is founder and President of City of Sanctuary, a former President of the Methodist Conference, and a former Leader/CEO of the Corrymeela Community. His work in interfaith relations was recognized with an OBE in the 2005 New Year's Honours list. Inderjit is recipient of the 2018 World Methodist Peace Award.

Wale Hudson-Roberts

Revd Wale Hudson-Roberts is the Baptist Union of Great Britain Justice Enabler, with responsibilities for racial justice. He is also the Pastor of John Bunyan Baptist in Oxfordshire and is married to Christine.

Edwina Peart

Edwina Peart is the Diversity and Inclusion Coordinator for Britain Yearly Meeting. In post since 2018, she works with Quakers (the Religious Society of Friends) to remove barriers to wider participation, deepen the spiritual life of the community, and strengthen its witness. She favours an intersectional approach that prioritizes lived experience while recognizing the constraints of structures and institutions that regulate and mediate modern life.

Paul Parker

Paul Parker was appointed in 2011 as Recording Clerk of Britain Yearly Meeting, the most senior staff position in the Religious Society of Friends (Quakers) in Britain. He is responsible for the Quakers' national organization, supporting around 460 local Quaker communities around Britain, and taking forward their work for peace, social, and climate justice in the world. He worships in Saffron Walden, where he first became a Quaker in his early teens. He believes Quakerism is poised to go "Whoosh!" in the twenty-first century.

Richard Zipfel

Richard Zipfel began life in the USA, where he was involved in the Catholic Worker Movement, the Civil Rights Movement, and the Peace Movement. He came to the UK in 1972, worked for the Student Christian

Movement for a few years, and then worked for thirty years as Policy Adviser on Race and Community Relations for the Catholic Bishops' Conference of England and Wales. Since retirement, he has served as a trustee for the Catholic Association for Racial Justice (CARJ).

Sandra Ackroyd

Sandra Ackroyd belongs to the United Reformed Church and has been active in racial justice advocacy for more than thirty years at all church levels and ecumenically. She has written a number of resources for the church, and has led training sessions and established projects to address inequality and racism.

Mark Sturge

Mark Sturge was the General Director of the African Caribbean Evangelical Alliance from 1996 to 2004. He was also the Head of England (London) for the international non-governmental organization Christian Aid. He is the author of the book *Look What the Lord Has Done!* (2005), which explores Black Christian faith in Britain. He is currently a doctoral student at Durham University.

Arlington W. Trotman

The Revd Arlington W. Trotman is a supernumerary Methodist minister and former Commission Secretary at Churches Together in Britain and Ireland's Churches Commission for Racial Justice. He is also a former moderator for the Churches' Commission for Migrants in Europe. He is a racial justice researcher, educator, trainer, conference speaker, and systematic theologian.

Mandy Ralph

Revd Mandy Ralph is a Church of Scotland minister serving at Annbank and Tarbolton Parish Churches in South Ayrshire, Scotland. She is the

Convener of the Equality, Diversity, and Inclusion Group, Racial Justice Priority Group, and the Research on Ethnic Minorities Project Group of The Church of Scotland.

Aled Edwards

Canon Aled Edwards OBE is Chief Executive of Cytûn: Churches Together in Wales, and Secretary of the Interfaith Council for Wales. He is a trustee of Displaced People in Action and Deputy Chair of the Brecon Beacons National Park Authority. He is a member of the Independent Advisory Group for Gwent Police. Aled is also a keen runner and has completed several marathons and ultra-marathons.

Damian Jackson

Damian Jackson is General Secretary of the Irish Council of Churches, the national inter-church ecumenical organization for the island of Ireland. His main areas of work include facilitating churches' work on migration and asylum issues, climate justice, housing insecurity, and community reconciliation. He has a PhD from the Irish School of Ecumenics in Trinity College, Dublin, examining the drivers of Irish Christians' attitudes toward undocumented migrants. He is married to Diane, has three teenage daughters, and lives in Dublin.

Jonny Smith

Jonny Smith has been a Salvation Army officer for more than eighteen years. In that time, he has led various London churches and is now the intercultural mission enabler for the Salvation Army. Jonny is passionate about this and strives to not only preach and teach, but also to live it out in the ordinary everyday of life. Jonny is married to Catherine, who is also a Salvation Army officer, and they have two boys. In his spare time, Jonny is a keen long-distance runner and Ironman triathlete.

Richard Daly

Dr Richard Daly has been in full time ministry for over twenty-five years and is currently the Pastor for the Brixton Seventh-day Adventist Church. He has a passion for working within the community and in doing so has served in local community initiatives and leadership projects. He has extended his ministry outside of the church as a hospital, prison and university volunteer chaplain, and has served as an Olympic Games chaplain working with athletes. Richard Daly is an avid reader and the author of sixteen books. He is married to Maxine and together they have three young adult boys.

Sivakumar Rajagopalan

Revd Sivakumar Rajagopalan is a first-generation Indian immigrant, whose experience of unearned caste privilege led him to abandon Hinduism for atheism, and later to become a Christian. He is an evangelical who believes that to proclaim the gospel of reconciliation with credibility we must first practise it. This has led him to be a passionate advocate for racial justice within the local church and community and during his tenure as Regional Minister for Racial Justice with the London Baptists from 2003 to 2018.

Foreword

Four decades ago, the then Churches Together in Britain and Ireland (CTBI) General Secretary, Philip Morgan, wrote to the churches regarding the 1981 Brixton Riots. In that document he hoped that "these events may prove to be a turning-point in race relations in Britain". One of the most disturbing aspects of our current context is that what was written forty years ago seems just as applicable today. The statement by the Brixton Council of Churches, produced at the time, highlighted the role of police and the media. It shone a spotlight on institutional racism at almost every level and demanded a response rooted in justice and peaceful co-existence. So what happened?

Well, if we reflect on today's context, working out of the COVID-19 pandemic, we can see that the need to challenge racial justice and race-related inequality is as urgent an imperative as it was forty years ago. In terms of jobs and who is losing them, in terms of lives being saved and who is losing them, in terms of communities getting justice and those who are crying out about justice denied, it seems it is always the Black, Asian, and Minority Ethnic communities that still today remain the worst served and the most marginalized. Issues of poverty, of discrimination, and of blatant racism too often wear the mask of authority and respectability. The response to the global Black Lives Matter movement has brought into stark relief the ways in which racism can still hide in plain sight and shames those of us who sit back and do little or nothing. As the Brixton Council of Churches wrote in April 1981, "We believe that the offering of constructive criticism can be a truer contribution to the good ordering of our society than unquestioning assent."

This book, highlighting the concerns and work of many people, is not offered as a retrospective "well done" but as a catalyst and call to action to bring justice to our own streets and workplaces. Over these last four decades, CTBI has sought to provide a space in which churches could be at once both challenged and supported to reflect on their role and contribution to the work of racial justice. An important element of that is sharing the practical examples that can inspire action. The women and men featured in this book show us what is possible, and what some of the paths might be. The experiences shared also serve to remind us why this work is so important and are an urgent imperative for those of us who seek to live out the Christian call to love our neighbour in contemporary society.

Bob Fyffe,
Former General Secretary, Churches Together in Britain and Ireland (2006–21)
Nicola Brady,
General Secretary, Churches Together in Britain and Ireland (2022 – present)

Introduction

The year 2020 was noted for a couple of phenomena that turned the world upside down. One was the outbreak of a pandemic that wreaked havoc throughout various societies, having a disproportionate impact on Black, Asian, and Minority Ethnic communities in particular. The other was the killing of George Floyd, a middle-aged African American, on 25 May 2020 in Minneapolis, USA. This tragedy sparked massive outrage and the resurgence of the Black Lives Matter movement, which saw protests on both sides of the Atlantic and in many other countries in which racism and inequality was evident.

That latter event also coincided with the twenty-fifth anniversary of Racial Justice Sunday (RJS) in Britain and Ireland.[1] RJS was established at a time when Britain experienced overt and covert forms of racism, and the tragic killing of Black teenager Stephen Lawrence in Eltham, southeast London, in April 1993 formed the backdrop to its emergence.[2] This murder and other racist attacks characterized the struggle of many Black, Asian, and Minority Ethnic people to obtain justice and equality in the criminal justice system, employment, education, (mental) health, and other public policy-related areas.[3] Moreover, the preponderance of far-right/extremist groups at the time led to high levels of race-related hate crime, which often went unaddressed by the forces of the law.[4] As we drew to the close of a millennium, Britain saw the publication of the Macpherson Report into institutional racism within the Metropolitan Police (1999) and the enacting of the Race Relations Amendment Act 2000. Equally, the noughties witnessed urban disturbances between White and Asian youths in the northwest (of England) and West Yorkshire and the rise of Islamophobia as a result of 9/11 and 7/7.

Yet, a decade and a half after Stephen Lawrence's murder, some commentators saw the election in 2008 of Barack Obama as US President as a sign that we were now living in "post-racial" societies. The evidence for this in Britain was groundbreaking legislation and anti-discrimination laws to curtail racism. Similarly, there was an increasing number of interracial relationships that suggested greater acceptance and tolerance of difference,[5] and a rising number of people from Black, Asian, and Minority Ethnic backgrounds obtaining important positions in society.

However, by the advent of the twenty-fifth anniversary of Stephen Lawrence's killing, all talk of a post-racial society had dissipated. Britain's decision to leave the European Union (Brexit) on 23 June 2016 saw an immediate spike in reported religious and race-related hate crime.[6] Brexit also came on the back of the then Conservative-led coalition Government's "Hostile Environment" in relation to immigration which, some argued, created an atmosphere of distrust and discrimination toward those not deemed to have the right to live in this country.[7] The "Hostile Environment" was at the heart of the subsequent Windrush scandal, which saw Black Britons who had lived in this country for decades losing their livelihoods and threatened with deportation.[8] In between those incidents, the country witnessed the Grenfell Tower fire tragedy in west London in June 2017 in which seventy-two people, many of whom were from Minority Ethnic communities, lost their lives.[9]

Race for Justice explores the responses of individual church denominations, parachurch groups, Minority Ethnic Christian congregations, and churches collectively in Wales, Scotland, England, and Ireland to address racism within their structures, as well as efforts to be prophetic in tackling inequality in society over the last twenty-five years. Over this expanse of time, many of these churches appointed Racial Justice Officers whose role it was to challenge the church on issues of equality and diversity, and to make sure they implemented all conference resolutions and report recommendations. Others have produced reports that assessed racism and inequality within their structures. Likewise, such reports made their way to conferences and resulted in resolutions that condemned racism in churches (and society) and called on them to tackle it immediately.

This book will explore the extent to which these initiatives have been successful in making their denominations better places for Black, Asian, and Minority Ethnic congregations to worship and have fellowship.

The book's contributors are all experts within this field; some are their religious denomination's racial justice, equalities, diversity, or inclusion officers. Others are key personnel within the ecumenical movement or scholars with an outstanding record of work in the area of racial justice. Each chapter therefore explores the churches' successes and failures over a quarter of a century (and more in many instances), and addresses what challenges they now face and their hopes for the future.

As well as individual denominations, *Race for Justice* features contributions from those who represent particular groupings and movements, and includes chapters on Black Majority Churches, British Asian Christian congregations, and ecumenical church-related engagement.

The book also includes contributions from Wales, Scotland, and Ireland, which, as a result of migration (that is also linked to refugees and asylum seekers), have become increasingly diverse, and thus face the challenges that were previously the preserve of England. As a result, this book will explore what this means for their nations going forward.

Race for Justice is an essential read for anyone with an interest in racial justice. It is also the first scholarly work to provide a thorough examination of what is taking place in all the historic denominations and churches in Britain and Ireland. Finally, as this book features contributions written by individuals inextricably linked to their denominations, groupings, and organizations, its contents are an authoritative and accurate view of the churches themselves.

Richard S. Reddie

Notes

1 The CTBI website explains, "Racial Justice Sunday is an occasion for
   Christians in Britain to collectively focus on racial justice. It began in
   1995, and generally took place on the second Sunday in September.
   In 2017, a decision was taken to move the date to the second Sunday
   in February (a direct swap with Education Sunday, which was then in
   February)." Churches are encouraged to "Remember the importance of
   racial justice; Reflect on human diversity and thank God for it; Respond
   by working to end injustice, racism and ignorance through prayer
   and action." "Racial Justice", CTBI, ctbi.org.uk/category/witnessing-
   together/racial-justice (last viewed 12 May 2022).
2 "Stephen's Story", Stephen Lawrence Day, stephenlawrenceday.org/
   stephens-story (last viewed 21 April 2022).
3 "Race report statistics", Equality and Human Rights Commission, 15

October 2020, www.equalityhumanrights.com/en/race-report-statistics (last viewed 21 April 2022).

4 Sarah Isal, "Preventing Racist Violence: Work with Actual and Potential Perpetrators – Learning from Practice to Policy Change", Runnymede, 2005, assets-global.website-files.com/61488f992b58e687f1108c7c/617bfb 10d1849afb49e1f0bc_PreventingRacistViolence.pdf (last viewed 12 May 2022).

5 "2011 Census analysis: What does the 2011 Census tell us about Inter-ethnic Relationships?" Office for National Statistics, 3 July 2014, www. ons.gov.uk/peoplepopulationandcommunity/birthsdeathsandmarriages/ marriagecohabitationandcivilpartnerships/articles/ whatdoesthe2011censustellusaboutinterethnicrelationships/2014-07-03 (last viewed 12 May 2022).

6 David Brown, "UK 'more racist after Brexit'", *The Times*, 12 May 2012, www.thetimes.co.uk/article/uk-more-racist-after-brexit-qb7hd7xl7 (last viewed 21 April 2022).

7 Amelia Gentleman, "Home Office told of Windrush errors five years ago, experts say", *The Guardian*, 8 May 2018, www.theguardian.com/ uk-news/2018/may/08/home-office-told-of-windrush-errors-five-years-ago-experts-say (last viewed 21 April 2022).

8 "The Hostile Environment Explained", The Joint Council for the Welfare of Immigrants, undated, www.jcwi.org.uk/the-hostile-environment-explained (last viewed 21 April 2022).

9 Jonathan Prynn, "Revealed: 'Chimney' Grenfell Tower cladding is used on blocks across London", *Evening Standard*, 15 June 2017, www.standard.co.uk/news/london/revealed-chimney-grenfell-tower-cladding-is-used-on-blocks-across-london-a3565786.html (last viewed 21 April 2022).

Chapter 1

Race, Ethnicity, and Participation in the Church of England: A Testament to Staying Power and Resilience

ROSEMARIE MALLETT

From the Communion to the Mother Church – Coming into the Cold

I was born in the Caribbean, in Barbados, baptized, and raised in the Anglican Church. I look back on sunny journeys through cane fields to get to church with brothers and cousins, trailing behind the adults, worrying about dirtying up my Sunday-best clothes or losing my pocket book, squirming through the formal service and looking forward to Sunday school classes afterwards. Church and Sundays were an integral part of the rhythm of life. If I thought anything of the church in England, the "mother church" as we were taught, I suppose I would have imagined similar style churches and services – quiet and formal, with children seen and not heard. The portrayal of the church in popular Agatha Christie, G. K. Chesterton, James Runcie, and Richard Curtis books, television dramas, and comedies very much concur with my sepia-tinted childhood memories.

That idealized representation of the Church of England as the hub of the community, as mother church, and as national moral compass had been in a steady decline in the imaginations and lives of White British nationals, certainly since the end of the Second World War.[1] The newly arriving migrants from former British colonies did not share their perspective.[2] Many of those arriving from the Caribbean as part of the Windrush[3] generation thought they were coming to help rebuild the "Mother Country", and that they would be able to join and attend the mother church, in the same way as they had done in their home countries.[4]

Those who had served in the Second World War knew quite a bit about racism, but they and the other migrants of the post-war era rapidly fell out of love with the concept of "Mother Country" and mother church when they realized the scandalous extent of the lack of welcome that would be given to them in Britain.[5] Despite the picture-postcard images shown on recruitment drives, the snow did not cheer, the sun did not warm, and the pavements did not glisten with gold. Instead, the general atmosphere was dismal, cold, and frosty toward these people of colour who arrived in British cities, communities, and churches. In too many instances, neither the "Father in God" nor the people of the mother church opened wide the doors in gestures of welcome and hospitality, nor did they attempt to heal the wounds of racialized rejection that had been meted out in workplaces and public spaces, on the buses, on the wards, in shops, and on the shop floor.[6]

Despite the centrality of Anglicanism in the former British colonies, David Haslam,[7] Glynne Gordon-Carter,[8] Kenneth Leech,[9] Mukti Barton, and, more recently, Azariah France-Williams[10] have well documented that this familiarity did not accord Black, Asian, and Minority Ethnic folk a favoured place around the communion table of parish churches in the established Church of England.

For me, as for most migrants, coming from my home country to this new home in England was a difficult transition to make, and home life and church life did not have their former rhythmical beat. Shift work realities often meant that parents could not attend church with the children, and the hospitality offered did not feel like a homecoming. Indeed, my stepfather stopped attending after the parish church turned him away when he first moved to the area. Church now felt like something to be endured rather than enjoyed, our colour and accents setting us apart until or unless we adapted, assimilated, or departed.

For us, as for so many other people of Caribbean heritage coming to England and desirous of continuing to place faith and worship at the heart of our lives, the Church of England became a contested space to be part of. Many turned to other denominational churches, in particular to the growing number of independent and Black

Evangelical, Pentecostal, or culture-/language-specific churches. Mark Sturge's book exploring Black Christian churches documents their growth and rise to prominence, particularly among the Caribbean and African communities.[11] Sadly, many others did not stay, like my father and then my brothers, as they became part of the growing numbers of the disaffected and de-churched. I too moved away from the Church of England as a centring place for my faith. It took me a long time to return.

Staying Power: Building Visibility, Presence, and Influence

In spite of the coldness of the welcome, many of the first-generation migrating Minority Ethnic Anglicans stayed with the Church of England.[12] However, few made it into the front pews or parochial church leadership, lay or ordained, never mind into senior leadership roles in the deanery, diocesan, or national levels of the established church. For those who stayed, it was a long time before they could see people who looked like them leading their churches, although numbers of UKME[13] clergy did start to grow, primarily of clergy members born overseas and trained both overseas and in the UK.

It was almost four decades after the *Windrush* docked at Tilbury, when in 1985 the church appointed a senior Black cleric to the top echelons of leadership in the UK.[14] After serving in the diocese for eleven years (three of those as an archdeacon), Wilfred Wood was appointed as an assistant bishop in the Diocese of Southwark, in Croydon, as the first Black Bishop in the Church of England, the mother church.[15] Very few, if any, of the Black African, Caribbean, Asian, or White church members would have heard of his Anglican Communion predecessor of 120 years earlier, Bishop Ajayi Crowther, a former enslaved African who was ordained as the first African Anglican bishop, consecrated as Bishop of West Africa in 1864.[16] It would not have surprised him, however, to hear of the racism subsequently faced by this pioneering bishop, and the growth of indigenous African churches half a century before the same movement started in Britain.[17]

Bishop Wood brought to his new appointment his very public ministry of the social gospel, championing racial justice, and proclaiming justice and equity to the disadvantaged, disenfranchised, and downright discriminated against.[18] However, he found himself fighting what must have seemed a lone cause, as very few other senior clerics espoused his advocacy for a more equitable church and a greater place for Black African, Caribbean, Asian, and other Minority Ethnic people in the structures of the church.[19] When he retired after all his years of service, Bishop Wood had not seen the progress and change he had hoped for within the church.[20] While hope remained, it was tinged with disappointment and a certain amount of disillusionment.

I want to also mention another determined Black Caribbean clergyman, whose inspirational work made a real contribution to the education of UKME ordinands, through the Simon of Cyrene Theological Institute which was established in 1989 in the Diocese of Southwark. The specific remit of the college was to promote pre-theological training for ordinands and lay workers specially designed to serve Anglicans from minority communities in the UK, and Sehon Goodridge was its first principal. Even at that time, Canon Goodridge was calling, along with other institutions in an Equal Partners Network, for the development of a programme of ministerial training aimed specifically at UKME people which would also support them through the training and into ministry.[21]

It was acknowledged by this network, as by Glynne Gordon-Carter, that the survival rate for ministers from ethnically diverse communities in majority church institutions was an issue that needed to be addressed urgently, to ensure a minimum level of representation of clergy from Minority Ethnic groups and to more genuinely reflect the multicultural reality of communities and church congregations. The Institute did not survive as the training institution, but was in many ways the precursor to much of the work being carried out today at the Centre for Black Theology at Queen's College, Birmingham, and the Whitelands Centre for Pentecostalism and Community Engagement at Roehampton University, London, under the leadership of Dr David Muir.

It was nine years until the next significant senior UKME appointment in the church. In 1994, Pakistan-born Michael Nazir-Ali was consecrated as Bishop of Rochester, and in 1999 entered the House of Lords as one of the Lords Spiritual, owing to his seniority in episcopal office. He was the first religious leader from Asia to serve there. In 2002, he was also one of the final two candidates considered for the position of Archbishop of Canterbury.[22] Dr Nazir-Ali's appointment as bishop was followed a couple of years later by the consecration of Ugandan-born John Sentamu as Bishop of Stepney in 1996. Six years later, in 2002, Sentamu was appointed Bishop of Birmingham, following Nazir-Ali to become the second UKME cleric to become a diocesan bishop. A very short three years later, in 2005, the prime minister's office announced Sentamu's translation to York as the ninety-seventh archbishop.[23] It would be another twelve years before another UKME bishop would be appointed in the church, when, in March 2017, Karowei Dorgu was consecrated as Bishop of Woolwich in the Diocese of Southwark. In 2022 the Revd Canon Arun Arora was appointed Bishop of Kirkstall.

Women were not able to be ordained to the priesthood in the Church of England until 1994, so there are fewer Minority Ethnic women in leadership in the church upper echelons. However, a trailblazing person to mention is Rose Hudson-Wilkin, who served as a Queen's Chaplain in 2008, as Chaplain to the Speaker of the House of Commons between 2010 and 2019,[24] and who now serves as the Bishop of Dover – the first Black woman of African heritage to hold such a senior role in the church.

Hudson-Wilkin is another Minority Ethnic clergyperson who has spoken out on the issue of racism within the church. She worked with the Committee on Black Anglican Concern (CBAC) and later served as chair of the Committee for Minority Ethnic Anglican Concerns (CMEAC), the two committees established by the Archbishops' Council of the Church of England to deal with issues of racism and equality of access.

However, Bishop Rose was not the first Minority Ethnic clergywoman to be consecrated as a bishop, as Dr Guli Francis-Dehqani, who is of Persian heritage, was, in 2017, consecrated Bishop of Loughborough with a focus on supporting Black, Asian, and Minority Ethnic clergy, lay workers, and congregations in the county. In 2021 she was consecrated as Bishop of Chelmsford, the first Minority Ethnic woman to hold such a position.

There were a number of other senior UKME clergy appointments in the new millennium. In 2001, Danny Kajumba, a Ugandan priest, was made Archdeacon of Reigate in the Diocese of Southwark. He remained the only Minority Ethnic archdeacon until 2013. A prominent South African Asian priest, Rogers Govender, was appointed as Dean of Manchester in 2006. He is still England's first and only Black cathedral dean.

There are now a number of Minority Ethnic archdeacons. In 2013, Mina Smallman was appointed Archdeacon of Southend, in the Diocese of Chelmsford, as the Church of England's first female archdeacon from a Black, Asian, and Minority Ethnic background. She was appointed together with Dr John Perumbalath, of Indian origin, who was appointed as Archdeacon of Barking. In 2018, Perumbalath was consecrated as Bishop of Bradwell, in the Chelmsford Diocese. In 2015, Liz Adekunle was appointed Archdeacon of Stepney in London, Karen Lund was appointed Archdeacon of Manchester in 2017, and Dr Rosemarie Mallett and Javid Iqbal were both appointed in 2020 as Archdeacon of Croydon and Archdeacon of Sheffield. Dr Mallett has since become the Bishop of Croydon.

Despite the flurry of appointments, little has changed since Dr John Sentamu stated in early 2005, "The Church of England is infected with institutional racism and is still a place of "pain for many Black Anglicans," and used the foreword to Mukti Barton's book to implicitly criticize fellow church leaders for failing to deal properly with discrimination in the organization. He referred to his role as a member of the Macpherson Inquiry into the death of Stephen Lawrence, which branded the Metropolitan Police as "institutionally racist", and said that institutional racism was also found in all churches to some degree.[25] This was echoed fifteen years later by Dr Justin Welby, Archbishop of Canterbury, at the General Synod (GS) meeting of February 2020,[26] when he apologized and said that he was ashamed that the Church of England is "still deeply institutionally racist".[27] As we have tried to show all along, it has not been the lack of will from senior Black clergy to call for changes to the racialized systems and structures of the Church of England.

Concerns, Commissions, Committees – Unfinished Business

From the Windrush years until today, awareness of continuing un/conscious bias in church institutions has grown and continues to provoke calls for far-reaching change. Added to this is the enduring impact of the church's history of involvement in the Transatlantic Slave Trade, colonization and colonialism, and the way that affected the hostile welcome given to many of the Windrush generation. In 2020, the General

Synod members backed the Private Member's Motion of the Southwark delegate, the Revd Andrew Moughtin-Mumby,[28] to apologize for racism in the Church of England, and also voted to "stamp out conscious or unconscious" racism. A cynic might be tempted to say, "Plus ça change," in recognition of the hard work put in by Bishop Wood in the 1980s to get Synod to establish a commission to look into such concerns.

In the same year as Bishop Wood's consecration, the Church of England published the controversial "Faith in the City" report (FITC) which, together with sixty other recommendations for government and church action on poverty, marginalization, and exclusion, called for action from the church on issues of racial exclusion and inequality within the church. Despite accepting the FITC report, General Synod did not approve the establishment of the recommended Black Anglican Concerns Commission, with its potential for far-reaching investigative powers across General Synod and Archbishops' Council. However, it did in the end agree to set up a Committee for Black Anglican Concerns (CBAC), with a part-time staff member to undertake this work across all forty-two dioceses of the Church of England.[29] Bishop Wood served as the first chairman and, despite the initial setback, continued to work to encourage inclusion and participation of Minority Ethnic Anglicans.[30]

From 1985 to 2015, the House of Bishops, General Synod, and the CBAC/CMEAC committees produced more than sixteen papers with a variety of recommendations to encourage and include UKME members into the church, into vocations, into clergy roles, and on to Synod. The first of those papers, published in 1991, entitled "Seeds of Hope", aimed to identify good practice and encourage dioceses to think theologically about racial justice issues and to give this priority in relation to the church's mission. Some twenty years later, in 2010, it was clearly necessary for the House of Bishops to make a theological statement entitled "Affirming our Common Humanity"[31] concerning the church's teaching on racial equality and its abhorrence of all forms of racism. Despite the setting-up of yet another committee in 2012 to "Turn up the Volume"[32] on senior appointments in the church, by 2015 it was clear that the recommendations had made little impact on diocesan or national church practice. In that year, the CMEAC published yet another report, titled "Unfinished Business", and the then Adviser to the Church of England on Minority Ethnic Anglican affairs, Dr Elizabeth Henry, wrote:

For more than 3 decades there have been numerous calls for the full representation of minority ethnic (ME) people at all levels of diocesan and national structures in the church... Sadly, there remains "unfinished business" concerning the inclusion and representation of ME people in the Church... As a consequence, the presence of ME people in the Anglican Church is largely invisible to wider society and the next generation of church members.[33]

On her departure from her position in the national Church in 2020, Dr Henry said:

I believe there is a willingness in principle, but not in practice, to tackle racism, increase representation, and genuinely work to achieve a greater sense of belonging for UK minority-ethnic people in church and society; and thus, sadly, progress is painfully slow.[34]

The history of the efforts of the various committees, the staff and board of CBAC and CMEAC members, and the outputs of their work has been well documented by the indomitable Glynne Gordon-Carter, the first appointed (lay) National Adviser to CBAC.[35] Her book, *An Amazing Journey*, records the story of institutionalized racism in the Church of England and questions whether the church was really committed to encouraging and enabling UKME clergy to find a welcoming place in serving the church. Ben Lindsay's 2019 book, *We Need to Talk about Race*, explored the Black experience in White Majority Churches and provoked great interest in the challenge the church still finds with racism.[36] A panel discussion on the same topic held later that year at St Paul's Cathedral in London attracted almost two thousand participants.[37]

In 2020, a Black Anglican priest, Azariah France-Williams, answered Gordon-Carter's question in his powerful book, *Ghost Ship*, which documents the continuation of a hostile environment within the church and challenges it and its hierarchy to step out of complacency and begin to dismantle the structures of racism that continue to exist. France-Williams calls for the church to begin the real work not simply of the reimagining but also of the renewal of the church.[38] This will mean not only apologizing for and lamenting what has happened, but also taking courageous action to dismantle structures of White privilege, power, and patronage to build a truly anti-racist church.[39]

Being anti-racist is not the same as simply not being racist. It is not a static rhetorical description but describes the active work that is being taken to counter, disrupt, and oppose racial injustice, to focus on reparation, reconciliation, and healing and to be repairers of the breach. This is not an easy task; it takes introspection as well as continued intentional action. So there must be urgency to the actions of the church, and whatever is done must have real outcomes with positive and intentional actions to redress inequities.

So, Are We There Yet?

There is little doubt that 2020 was a seismic year in many ways. The worldwide COVID-19 pandemic wreaked havoc upon the health and economic well-being of people, in ways that will be felt for years to come. It also highlighted the structural inequalities that exist between and within countries, as poorer and more marginalized communities have been disproportionally affected by the impact of the virus. At the same time, the spectre of racism and racial injustice was horrifically displayed on TV screens throughout the world in late May 2020, as viewers watched the callous murder of African American George Floyd at the knee of a White Minnesota policeman. The cruelty of the policeman and the lack of action from those around clearly demonstrated viscerally the racism that still pervades our world.

The General Synod motion in February 2020 and Azariah France-Williams' *Ghost Ship* published later that same year reminded us that racism also lurks dangerously within the church. But while UKME people have kept faith with the Church of England, have stayed, and indeed are growing in number in congregations, especially in urban centres, we are not there yet.

However, in June 2020, after almost thirty-five years, the House of Bishops finally backed the formation of the Archbishops' Racism Action Commission. The Commission began its work in late 2021, under the chairmanship of Lord Paul Boateng. The brief for the Commission is simple and far-reaching: on the issue of race to implement "significant cultural and structural" change within the Church of England. As Dr R. David Muir asks, "Is it Bishop Wood's dream coming to fruition after over three decades?"[40]

Without a doubt, the church has come a long way since the cold welcome given to many Caribbean Anglican Windrushers. However, that does not take away from the continuous criticism from those within and outside the church that recent advances made by women since the ordination of women in 1994 have not been mirrored by similar opportunities for male and female Minority Ethnic clergy in the Church of England, the mother church. The fact is that, despite high-level appointments, especially since 2017, there are still too few UKME clergy leading our churches, and even fewer in positions of responsibility, lay or ordained. This does not chime well in a church where a growing number of members are from Minority Ethnic backgrounds, from Asia, the African continent, the Caribbean, and new arrivals from Latin America and Hong Kong. Despite our Christian injunction to believe and behave as if we are all one in Christ, the deep inequalities that exist between and within groups of people of different colours, cultures, and ethnicities persist, and persist within churches, and UKME church members are still seeking to see their visible and cultural differences being acknowledged and welcomed.

After many years away, I finally rejoined the Anglican Church in England, because I felt called to witness and serve in the church that shaped my early life. I quickly realized that, along with my interest in work on social justice, there was still much to do on issues of racial justice, equality, and inclusion within the church: our governance structures, our liturgy, our preaching and teaching, our prayers, and our everyday actions as we live out God's love in the world. Despite the destructive power of the health pandemic, 2020 helped to reshape the direction of travel for many in the world, as we all have been seeking to find our way to the "new normal". I hope that the new normal for the church will mean that the reset button has truly been pressed on the way we journey together as the Body of Christ. I fully expect that the road map will be set for us to journey to be an anti-racist church, and that the direction of travel will at last be drawn up by those who most keenly feel the pain of racism.

I do pray that those who currently hold the reins of power will accept the necessary challenges and changes, and that we can all work to bring into being a shared covenant to dismantle racism and racialized inequality, to rebuild a truly radical, welcoming, and inclusive church, and to make our diversity our strength.

Notes

1 Grace Davie, *Religion in Britain Since 1945: Believing without Belonging* (Oxford: Blackwell, 1994).

2 Clair Wills, *Lovers and Strangers: An Immigrant History of Post-War Britain* (London: Penguin, 2017).

3 The Windrush generation describes those who arrived in the UK from Caribbean countries between 1948 and 1973. They came after recruitment drives in the Caribbean to join the nascent National Health Service, transport, and other sectors affected by Britain's post-war labour shortage. The name "Windrush" comes from the HMT *Empire Windrush* ship, which brought one of the first large groups of Caribbean people to the UK in 1948. As the Caribbean was then a part of the British Commonwealth, those who arrived were automatically British subjects and free to permanently live and work in the UK. See Thomas William Heyck, "The Decline of Christianity in Twentieth-Century Britain", *Albion*, Vol. 28, No. 3 (Autumn, 1996), www.jstor.org/stable/4052171 (last viewed 21 April 2022).

4 Donald Hinds, *Mother Country: In the Wake of a Dream* (Hertford: Hansib, 2014).

5 Sam Selvon, *The Lonely Londoners* (Harlow: Longman, 1956).

6 "Tears shed at Anglican service as public apology for historic racism is made", *The Voice*, 27 October 2020, www.voice-online.co.uk/faith/2020/10/27/tears-shed-at-anglican-service-as-public-apology-for-historic-racism-is-made (last viewed 21 April 2022).

7 David Haslam, *Race for the Millennium: A Challenge to Church and Society* (London: Church House Publishing, 1996).

8 Glynne Gordon-Carter, *An Amazing Journey: The Church of England's Response to Institutional Racism* (London: Church House Publishing, 2003).

9 Kenneth Leech, *Race: Changing Society and the Churches* (London: SPCK, 2005).

10 A. D. A. France-Williams, *Ghost Ship: Institutional Racism and the Church of England* (London: SCM Press, 2020).

11 Mark Sturge, *Look What the Lord Has Done! An Exploration of Black Christian Faith in Britain* (Milton Keynes: Scripture Union, 2005).

12 General Synod, "How We Stand: A report on black Anglican membership of the Church of England in the 1990s", 1994, https://www.

churchofengland.org/sites/default/files/2021-02/how_we_stand_1990s.
pdf (last viewed 21 April 2022).

13 Please note the move away from the acronym BAME to UKME, which
is more inclusive of colleagues who did not see themselves as falling
within a Black or Asian categorization. This term (unlike BAME)
has come into usage as it recognizes that people coming from global
majority ethnic heritages and living in the United Kingdom are
only Minority Ethnic in that context. The term "people of the global
majority" acknowledges that Black, indigenous, and people of colour
represent more than 80 per cent of the world's population and points
to the demographic inaccuracy of the "minority" terminology. The
2020 #BAMEOver survey looked into the terms that are most often
used to refer to Black or Brown people from Africa, the Caribbean,
and the Indian subcontinent and found that "BAME" is not only no
longer unreservedly accepted but in many academic papers it is being
vigorously contested as it assumes and confers a shared homogenous
identity and history for people coming from a wide range of ethnic and
cultural backgrounds and history. It is important also to note that this
discussion on ethnicity, colour, culture, and nomenclature is evolving.

14 It must be noted that by this time a number of indigenous senior
clerics had been appointed to lead provincial regions in the Anglican
Communion.

15 Wilfred Wood, *Faith For a Glad Fool: The Church of England's First
Black Bishop Speaks on Racial Justice, Christian Faith, Love and
Sacrifice* (London: New Beacon Books Ltd, 2010).

16 In the same year he was also given a Doctorate of Divinity by the
University of Oxford.

17 For much of the nineteenth century, the Church Missionary Society
(CMS) recognized the skills and abilities of Africans and missionaries
and evangelists of the faith. Sadly, less than twenty years after
Crowther's consecration, the attitudes of European missionaries
changed and started to concur with the racist attitudes held by many
colonialist traders and administrators at the time of the colonial
partition of Africa and the land grab by European countries. In 1890,
two European missionaries accused a number of African pastors of
fraud, ignorance, and immorality and held Crowther responsible
for their alleged behaviour. As a consequence, Bishop Crowther was
pressured out of the Niger mission and his bishopric was placed under

the supervision of European secretaries. This treatment of Crowther led to the formation of independent African churches. See Dr Katharina Oke, "Samuel Ajayi Crowther, Black Victorians and the Future of Africa", Faculty of History, University of Oxford, undated, www. history.ox.ac.uk/samuel-ajayi-crowther-black-victorians-and-the-future-of-africa (last viewed 21 April 2022).

18 Wood was a one-time president of the Institute of Race Relations. In 1992 he co-sponsored with David Sheppard, the then Bishop of Liverpool, a new set of race equality principles for employers, which became known as the "Wood–Sheppard Principles". He was Moderator of the Southwark Diocesan Race Relations Commission, the first of its kind in the Church of England, from its foundation. He served as Moderator of the World Council of Churches' Programme to Combat Racism, from 1977 to 1980. He was also Vice-Chair of the Archbishops' Commission on Urban Priority Areas, which undertook two years of explorations of the conditions in inner cities and deprived outer estates and published the explosive report, "Faith in the City", in 1985.

19 He did work closely with Canon Ivor Smith Cameron, one of the few other UKME Southwark senior clerics.

20 Wilfred Wood, *Keep the Faith, Baby! A Bishop Speaks on Faith, Evangelism, Race Relations and Community* (London: The Bible Reading Fellowship, 1994).

21 "Five Per Cent: A Report of two conferences sponsored by the Equal Partners Network", *British Journal of Theological Education*, Vol. 6, Issue 3 (1994), www.tandfonline.com/doi/abs/10.1080/1352741X.1994.11 674032?journalCode=yate19 (last viewed 21 April 2022). The conference was held at Queen's College, Birmingham.

22 Rowan Williams was instead appointed to the position by Tony Blair. Previously, Nazir-Ali had served as the first Bishop of Raiwind in West Punjab (1984–86), in the Anglican Communion.

23 It is important to note that Sentamu did not only serve in the church but also was a senior leader on key race relations issues in the wider community. He served as an advisor to the Stephen Lawrence Judicial Inquiry, dealing with a racist attack against a young Black man, and in 2002 he chaired the Damilola Taylor Review, dealing with serious youth violence. Both of these enquiries took place in the Diocese of Southwark.

24 Bishop Rose has been followed by another Minority Ethnic woman in

this position, as Canon Tricia Hillas was appointed Chaplain to the Speaker in 2019.

25 Barton, Rejection, Resistance and Resurrection, p. vii.

26 The General Synod is the national assembly of the Church of England. It came into being in 1970 under the Synodical Government Measure 1969, replacing an earlier body known as the Church Assembly. The General Synod considers and approves legislation affecting the whole of the Church of England, formulates new forms of worship, debates matters of national and international importance, and approves the annual budget for the work of the Church of England at national level.

27 In 2006 the General Synod of the Church of England issued an apology, acknowledging the part the Church itself had played, through the actions of individuals and agencies, in perpetuating and profiting from historic slavery and the exploitation of and discrimination against people based on the colour of their skin. The General Synod voted in February 2020 to apologize for racism experienced by UKME people in the Church of England since the arrival of the Windrush generation. Speaking to the General Synod, the Archbishop of Canterbury, Justin Welby, said there was "no doubt" that the Church of England was still "deeply institutionally racist".

28 Father Andrew Moughtin-Mumby, "General Synod: Windrush Commitment & Legacy", January 2020, www.churchofengland. org/sites/default/files/2020-01/GS%202156A%20Windrush%20 Commitment%20and%20Legacy.pdf (last viewed 21 April 2022).

29 In their books, Glynne Gordon-Carter and Azariah France-Williams both describe the differences between the reach of a Commission and the capacity of what essentially became a subcommittee. However, Bishop Wood and his small team worked to encourage each diocese to establish a diocesan Minority Ethnic Anglican Concerns (MEAC) committee or to at least have a link officer championing Minority Ethnic issues. The Diocese of Southwark, perhaps because of the presence of Bishop Wood as one of the area bishops, has become the lead diocese on this issue. In 1991 it established a Race Relations Commission and employed three area-based staff officers in the first instance to undertake the work of converting good intentions on paper into actions that would encourage and enable more UKME people to join and lead the church. They worked in parishes and schools, and with ordinands, curates, and clergy. The Commission created a Black

Forum to bring together lay and ordained church members to discuss issues of relevance to UKME people. In 2000, Southwark established an internal report on institutional racism, and consequent to that employed a CMEAC adviser and established not only the diocesan CMEAC committees but also MEAC committees in each of the three episcopal areas. Along with publishing a number of booklets, papers, and reports on the progress toward becoming a more equitable diocese, Southwark commissioned an independent consultancy in 2015 to see how much had changed. In 2015, a UKME Director of Social Justice was appointed with oversight of diversity and inclusion. In March 2021, in recognition of the work yet to be done on racial inequality, the diocesan synod voted to embed an anti-racism charter as part of the diocesan governance and parochial structure.

30 Gordon-Carter, *An Amazing Journey.*

31 "GS Misc 972, Affirming Our Common Humanity: A Theological Statement by the House of Bishops", 2010, https://www. churchofengland.org/sites/default/files/2017-10/affirming%20our%20 common%20humanity.pdf (last viewed 21 April 2022).

32 The House of Bishops initiated Turn Up The Volume (TUTV) to increase the number of Black, Asian, and Minority Ethnic clergy in senior appointments within the Church of England by helping UKME clergy prepare for posts of wider responsibility through leadership development and increased understanding of the local and national contexts of senior roles.

33 "GS Misc 1108, I too am C of E: A follow up to Unfinished Business-matching words with action", www.churchofengland.org/sites/default/ files/2017-12/gs%20misc%201108%20-%20cmeac%20presentation.pdf (last viewed 21 April 2022).

34 Chine McDonald, "Is the Church of England Racist?" *Church Times*, 3 July 2020, www.churchtimes.co.uk/articles/2020/3-july/features/ features/is-the-church-of-england-racist (last viewed 21 April 2022).

35 Gordon-Carter retired from the post of National Adviser for CMEAC in 2002 and was followed in post by Sonia Barron, who left the post to train for ordination. She was followed in 2013 by Dr Elizabeth Henry, another lay woman, who brought with her with a vision to engage with race awareness issues in the church and in society at large. Dr Henry retired in 2020 and has been followed by Dr Sanjee Perera as Archbishops' Adviser on Minority Ethnic Anglican Concerns.

36 Ben Lindsay, *We Need to Talk About Race: Understanding the Black Experience in White Majority Churches* (London: SPCK, 2019).

37 "We Need to Talk About Race Black Experience In White Majority Churches (2019)", St Paul's Cathedral, 29 October 2019, soundcloud. com/st-pauls-cathedral-london/we-need-to-talk-about-race-black-experience-in-white-majority-churches-2019 (last viewed 21 April 2022).

38 France-Williams, *Ghost Ship*.

39 R. David Muir, "Brexit, Englishness, Ethnicity and Race", in Jonathan Chaplin and Andrew Bradstock (eds), *The Future of Brexit Britain: Anglican Reflections on National Identity and European Solidarity* (London: SPCK, 2020).

40 Muir, "Brexit, Englishness, Ethnicity and Race".

Chapter 2

The Methodist Church and Racial Justice: A Task for All

INDERJIT BHOGAL

Introduction

This article offers a personal reflection on racial justice in British Methodism. For rigorous academic research on this important theme in the Methodist Church, I refer you to scholars such as Professor Anthony Reddie. The purpose of this article is not to give a comprehensive history of racial justice work but to outline the path to the establishment of Racial Justice Sunday in the Methodist Church.

Racial Justice Sunday was first marked in the Methodist Church in September 1995. However, in contemporary Methodism, the origins of Racial Justice Sunday lie deeper in history. Going back to the "Uniting Conference" of 1932, the Methodist Church engaged with matters of social justice through its Department of Christian Citizenship, and then through succeeding agencies such as the Division of Social Responsibility. In the Methodist DNA, social justice and social holiness are interrelated.

At the core of the work of the Department of Christian Citizenship was the plight of Jewish refugees, even before war broke out. By 1939, forty thousand refugees had left Germany and Austria. Some seventy-five thousand adult refugees, children, and young people were left stranded in Britain. The Citizenship Department, through its Secretary, the Revd Henry Carter, asked Methodists for financial support for work with refugees.

After the Second World War, during which countless numbers of loyal subjects from British colonies died in the cause of the Allies, many people termed "coloured" started to arrive in the UK. Many of those who came here from the Caribbean and India came at the invitation of British agencies to "help build the motherland". There was for example, Sybil Phoenix (née Marshall), who later told the story of listening to Enoch Powell MP in British Guyana when he spoke appealingly about working in Britain. I arrived in the UK in September 1964, aged eleven, with my Indian parents, from the newly independent Kenya, with the status of "British subject".

Black Methodists: A Tree God Planted

Black Methodists, particularly from the Caribbean islands, were beginning to worship in congregations in Notting Hill, Brixton, Birmingham, and Leeds. Though they were not always readily welcomed, without their membership, gifts, and contributions, many inner-city congregations would have been depleted and even closed. These were the days when many mainstream congregations told Black Christians, "Your church is down the road", pointing, for example, to the New Testament Church of God.[1] Nonetheless, in 1985 around sixteen thousand Black people were worshipping in Methodist churches and were contributing as Sunday school teachers, council members, local preachers, and church stewards, though many were reluctant to take up leadership roles for various reasons, not least because of the racism of White people.[2]

In 1977, a youth club run by Sybil Phoenix was burned down by the National Front. Sybil stood on the ground later and declared, "My name is Phoenix, and so help me God, out of the ashes I will rebuild."[3] In 1978, the Methodist Conference held in Bradford adopted a report, influenced by Sybil Phoenix, which declared racism a "sin" and "a direct contradiction of the Gospel of Jesus".[4] The 1978 Statement on racism was followed by the pioneering development from 1981 of racism awareness training, founded and led by Sybil Phoenix and the Revd Vic Watson, and delivered through the Methodist and Ecumenical Leadership Racism Awareness Workshops (MELRAW). The 1978 Statement had appealed for Methodists to participate in "constructive programmes for racial justice and the building of compassion and goodwill", but did not say what it meant by "racism" or "racial justice", nor did it outline any comprehensive plans for action. The focus of MELRAW was specifically to address and challenge the prevalence of racism in churches. The training was delivered ecumenically.

The 1980s saw the establishment of the Methodist Community and Race Relations Committee (CRRC) which came under the governance of the newly created Division of Social Responsibility. The early 1980s saw rising anger in Black people, particularly at racism in policing, criminal justice, education, housing, and immigration.[5] The anger at this injustice, like a voice crying in the wilderness, was expressed in the street uprisings that came to be termed "riots" – for example, in Brixton, Handsworth, Wolverhampton, Tottenham, and Toxteth.

In July 1981, I stood with Black and White young people who were literally fighting with police in Handsworth with bricks and sticks. I spent three days and nights (with a colleague) around Lozells Road, Handsworth. I sensed a deep and seething anger in the young people at police racism and violence.

I attended the Methodist Conference as a local delegate for the first time in 1983 and made a number of speeches on matters related to civil disobedience (which led to a major report on challenging injustice) and interfaith relations (which helped to establish the Methodist Committee for Interfaith Relations, with me as a joint secretary).

Following this Conference, I served on many Methodist committees, including the CRRC which I joined in September 1983. The Committee supported the appointment of a Methodist Secretary for Race and Community. In 1984, Mr Ivan Weekes took up this role, and he worked with and serviced the CRRC for the following ten years.

Ivan Weekes developed and promoted racial justice work with unrelenting passion and professionalism. He worked closely with Black Methodist leaders to develop constructive ways forward. He became an inspiration, mentor, and role model for many, and promoted Black leadership. Ivan was succeeded in his role by Naboth Muchopa, Jennifer Crook, and then, in 2018, Bevan Powell. Each brought their own passion, professionalism, experience, and wisdom to the task.

The Community and Race Relations Committee became the Committee for Racial Justice (CRJ) in 1995. In 2014, subsequent to the Equality Act 2010, working with all nine protected areas in matters of justice, the CRJ became the Committee for Equality, Diversity and Inclusion (EDI). The EDI came to an end in 2021 with a Methodist Conference strategy toward what was termed the Implementation of the Inclusive Church, addressing injustices and inequalities related to all the characteristics protected in the Equality Act 2010. The Methodist

Conference 2021 adopted this strategy under the title of Justice, Dignity and Solidarity. The changes in the names of the committees and work focusing on racial justice reflect the developing and broadening agenda.

The first meeting of Black Methodist Ministers took place on 29 May 1985. The meeting was supported by Ivan Weekes and was held in his office in Westminster Central Hall. The attendees were: Hewie Andrew, Inderjit Bhogal, Kingsley Halden, Herbert McGhie, Charles Watson, and Robinson Milwood. In attendance also were Ivan and a student minister, Wesley Daniel. The agenda of the meeting read: Black Leadership Experience; Stationing of Black Ministers; Black and Asian Contribution to British Methodism; Education of Superintendents and Chairmen; Recommendation to the Authorities. We were few, and we met as people engaged in ministry, under enormous pressures, in danger of exhaustion and burnout.

We committed ourselves to meet regularly for mutual encouragement and education in order to play an effective role in the life of the Methodist Church. And with this the Black Methodist Ministers' Group was founded. Ten years later, on 28 May 1995, at an anniversary service held in Wesley's Chapel, London, one of the last actions of Ivan Weekes in his role as Secretary for Race and Community was to lead us into being a Black Methodists Group, embracing lay and ordained Black leaders. This Group has continued to evolve, becoming the Belonging Together Ministers' Group (2009) aimed at helping the Methodist Church to fulfil its mission and ministry through its diverse membership.

The Community and Race Relations Committee, with its Ethnic Minorities in Britain Working Group within the Division of Social Responsibility, was the think tank that initiated racial justice work in the 1980s. It commissioned the research on the experiences of Black Methodists that resulted in the publication of Heather Walton's *A Tree God Planted* in 1985, with a set of recommendations. This report informed our thinking and work.

Two years on from this, the Methodist Conference (1987) adopted a seminal report, "Faithful and Equal",[6] and adopted a programme for tackling racism and action for racial justice. This included: all ordinands to undertake racism awareness training; encouraging all Black Methodists to offer themselves for all the ministries of the church; every church council to consider what action it has taken or will take to combat racism.

The 1990s saw the development of access courses encouraging more Black Methodists to offer and train for leadership, lay and ordained. Wesley Daniel and I persuaded the Methodist Conference to ensure that Black Theology was on the curricula of theological colleges. We wanted students to go beyond racism awareness training in preparation for ordination and ministry. We encouraged and promoted Black leadership. Within racism awareness training, we highlighted the need to address Whiteness and power issues.

Sybil Phoenix used to say, "Racism is prejudice plus power",[7] and these words are incorporated in the report Faithful and Equal (1987). Sybil insisted that while we all have our prejudices, the difference between Black people and White people is that invariably power is in the hands of White people. This is how the world is structured. White people needed to address this colour inequality as integral to addressing racism.

What was becoming clear was that tackling racism required more than awareness workshops offered by individuals. Greater stress was being placed on the need to engage the whole church in the work. The task of racial justice could not be left to individuals and groups. Racial justice is a task for all members, and it had to be embedded in worship and prayer. Racial Justice Sunday was adopted by the Methodist Conference, and it was agreed that it would be held on the second Sunday of September each year from September 1995.

The CRJ began to concentrate on the task facing the whole church, in all settings, and to work with ecumenical partners. We found strength in ecumenical partners through the British Council of Churches Community and Race Relations Unit (CRRU), which later became the Churches Commission for Racial Justice and brought Racial Justice Sunday to all denominations. Considerable strength in the struggle for racial justice came internationally from the World Council of Churches Programme to Combat Racism. The Kairos Document (1985) from South Africa, with its critique of State and Church Theology, challenged us with its call for prophetic theology and action.[8]

A pivotal event that shook and shaped our being and work was the brutal murder by a group of young White people of Stephen Lawrence, aged eighteen, on 22 April 1993, in a street near his home in London. Stephen's mother and father, Doreen and Neville, committed themselves to a struggle for truth, justice, and change centred on Stephen. Their persistence led to the public inquiry into Stephen Lawrence's Murder, led by Sir William Macpherson, in 1998. The Macpherson Report made seventy recommendations for change, including changes in policing and education, and acknowledged "institutional racism" in policing.

The Macpherson Report did not underline the endemic and deep-set racism that results in murder, but Doreen Lawrence has been relentless in her pursuit of justice and change in tackling racism. She addressed the Methodist Conference in 2000, saying again that the time of justice and change had come.

In my mind, a key task ahead was the development of Black leadership and Black Theology. In 1993, with support from the Black Methodist Ministers Group, I organized the first International Black Theology Conference to be held in the UK, and hosted it in Carver Street Wesleyan Methodist Church where I was minister with pastoral charge. The need to work internationally was clearly important. Participants came from the UK, the USA, and South Africa and included Anthony Reddie, Robert Beckford, Jacquelyn Grant, Randall Bailey, and Itumeleng Mosala.

We laid the foundations for the development of British Black Theology, which has been led subsequently with distinction by Methodist layman and Local Preacher, Professor Anthony Reddie, now an established academic and writer based in Oxford. Anthony has written around one hundred scholarly essays, articles, and books. His sustained, scholarly, groundbreaking research and writing has been an outstanding contribution to the challenges of achieving racial justice.

Anthony has diligently worked with the training of preachers and pastors, lay and ordained, in the areas of race, class, and diversity. His training style is that of participative education, including action, reflection, art, and drama. In his latest work he has written an incisive analysis and critique of the development of racial justice training in the Methodist Church over the last thirty years.[9] He critiques racism awareness training and points toward addressing the deconstruction of the norm of whiteness. Anthony's work cannot be ignored by anyone exploring racism awareness, racial justice, and whiteness.

Youth Leadership

The first Methodist Connexional Conference of Young Black Methodists was held from 2 to 4 November 1990, to encourage and develop the leadership skills of young Black and Asian Methodists, supporting them to positively contribute to the life of the church. In 1998, the Racial Justice Office established the Black Methodist Youth Conference. In 2005 this became the Association of Black Methodist Youth, and later merged with the Methodist Youth Conference. Up to the year 2021, four young Black and Asian Methodist leaders have held the role of Methodist Youth President: Tamara Wray (2014), Jasmine Yeboah (2018), Thelma Commey (2019), and Daud Irfan (2021). Prior to this, Chidi Onyeforo was Chair of the Methodist Youth Executive (2007).

Asian Leadership and Theology

Within all this work, attempts have also been made over the last few years by me, Israel Selvanayagam, and Mukti Barton to gather Asian theologians in Britain. This has been important alongside the progress of Black Theology in Britain, which has grown since the first International Conference on the subject in 1993.

The first International Conference on Asian Theology in Britain was held in April 2018, marking twenty-five years since the first Black Theology Conference. The focus was on the contributions of Asian female theologians of Indian, Pakistani, Sri Lankan, and Bangladeshi backgrounds. The Conference was organized under the general heading of *Ek Aurat* ("One Woman"), affirming the contribution and togetherness of Asian female theologians.

Racial Justice Sunday

The developments I have outlined above reflect the search and struggle for racial justice, and the attempts to ensure that this took root in the life of the church. Racial Justice Sunday is part of this strategy. There is a real desire to embed our commitment to work for racial justice in worship and prayer. The idea of Racial Justice Sunday is to ensure an annual reminder at the least, and a marker for a regular ongoing commitment. Racial Justice Sunday is a challenge to reflect theologically, in the light of Scripture, to hold up the call of God for the inclusion of all.

The idea of Racial Justice Sunday was to challenge and encourage every congregation to make racial justice part of their life, to grow in their awareness of what the issues are, and also to have available resources prepared on the whole theme of racial justice for worship and for prayer, with suggestions for sermons, written prayers, hymns, and ideas for action. The national ecumenical instrument, now Churches Together in Britain and Ireland (CTBI), took on the responsibility for Racial Justice Sunday, and for providing an annual resource pack.

Racial Justice Sunday is an important initiative, but there are other constructive ways to work and pray for and build racial justice. The response to racial justice in predominantly White areas has frequently been that "racism is not a problem here". This view suggests that racism only exists where Black people are present. The Black Lives Matter movement challenges us to move beyond this, and beyond racism awareness, to address questions around colonialism, Empire, slavery, being White, White power, and White privilege as integral to eliminating racism.

One of the key ideas upheld in a Racial Justice Sunday resource pack is that there is one race – the human race, and we are all children of God. We are all made in the image of God, whatever our ethnicity, whatever the shade or colour of our skin; with all our immense diversity we are one in Christ. Made in the image of God, we are all members of the Body of Christ. We all belong equally together.

These two themes of image of God and Body of Christ permit no discrimination on any basis. Colour and ethnicity-based discrimination is an obstacle to our highest ideals, an assault on the image of God. It mars our relationship with God and destroys our relationships with each other. As followers of Christ, we commit ourselves to uphold the dignity of all human beings and to put this into practice in our daily worship and witness. This is a central theological theme that guides us.

Anthony Reddie, in an article published in the journal *Religions*, offers an incisive and insightful analysis and reflection on racial justice work, highlighting a journey "from racism awareness to deconstructing whiteness" in the quest for racial justice.[10] Previously he wrote of the need to move beyond "apologetic rhetoric" by which churches can resist progress toward the achievement of justice. He argues that redefining "the norm" is necessary in the Methodist Church if we are to move beyond the rhetoric of apology toward a more determined and intentional mode of challenging injustice, be it on the grounds of race, gender, sexuality, or disability, and to build equity and full inclusion.[11]

Strategy: Success and Struggle

There have been countless presentations, sermons, interventions, speeches, and reflections on racial justice, in addition to actions taken for racial justice. Publications written by Black and Asian Methodists speak volumes. Considerable energy has gone into worship, prayer, and work for racial justice. But what have we achieved? We may have helped to influence and change some thought and practice in individuals and in structures. There has been some progress in terms of the promotion and development of Black leadership and Black Theology. This can be seen in the greater numbers of Black people engaged and employed in churches. Black Methodists have occupied the most senior lay and ordained roles. Black Theology publications have increased.

In 1984, the Methodist Conference meeting in Wolverhampton designated Mr Leon Murray to be appointed Vice-President of the Conference when it would meet in Birmingham in 1985. Ivan Weekes went on to be Vice-President of the Conference in 1991. Following him, Dr Daleep Mukarji (2013) and Mr Bala Gnanapragasam (2018) were also appointed to the position of Vice-President. I was appointed President of Conference 2000. Revd Sonia Hicks was elected President of Conference 2021. In 2021, Anthony Boateng was elected Vice-President designate for the Methodist Conference 2022. Revd Novette Headley was designated Chair of Birmingham District from 2022. Many Black Methodists occupy roles of superintendent presbyters and circuit stewards. The first Black Methodist to be appointed Chair of District (London) was Revd Ermal Kirby. I would like to see more Black Methodists in roles such as District Chair, and in senior Connexional roles.

There remain obstacles to the flourishing of Black leaders. Holding roles in leadership as Black people is tough and requires additional spiritual, emotional, and physical stamina, and includes constant struggle. Holding high office does not remove the feeling of being on the margins, and it can bring with it malignment from opponents. I have often found myself saying, "Let us not grow weary in doing what is right... let us work for the good of all" (Galatians 6:9, 10, NRSVA).

Our attention remains fixed on addressing racism. In a theology that insists we are all made in the image of God, and with genetics that affirm we are one human race, what is racism? Why does discrimination based on skin colour persist in people who value all the beautiful colours of God? We can strengthen our resolve to work with people of all faiths and professions to end racism and promote racial justice.

The work of racial justice remains an unfinished task that must go on without ceasing. Racial justice is a cry and call of God that demands responses at the heart of worship and prayer, theology, and preaching. Racial justice is a collaborative, congregational, "connexional" task involving us all. There are challenges in the spheres of personal, structural, and theological work. There remain obstacles of injustice and exclusion. There is much more to do. We can do better. We can be more. We can learn from and build on our history. We owe this to each other. And God beckons us on.

God calls us to build a justice-based church, where justice is served with mercy and humility, a church where all of us with all our immense diversity are honoured members in the one Body of Christ, where all are equally included at the table, with no superiors or inferiors, no centres or margins, where no one is neglected or excluded, with one goal always, to "seek first the kingdom of God and his righteousness" (Matthew 6:33, ESV UK). Everything follows from here. The pilgrimage toward our goal is stronger if we work with ecumenical and international partners, embrace each other, respect each other, give life to each other.[12]

Holy Communion is not only a foretaste of the heavenly banquet; it is also a revelation of the church and world as it is meant to be. In a world characterized by the violence of inequalities, war, bigotry, environmental degradation, and climate change, the church can reflect a model of one body symbolized in the one bread we share,[13] a sanctuary for all.[14] We can stand in solidarity with each other in our suffering humanity, not in charity but with justice, mercy, and humility, seeking the safety and fulfilment of all.

Notes

1 Ira V. Brooks, *Where Do We Go from Here? A History of 25 Years of the New Testament Church of God in the United Kingdom 1944–1969* (London: Charles Raper, 1971).

2 Heather Walton, *A Tree God Planted: Black People in British Methodism* (London: Ethnic Minorities in Methodism Working Group, Division of Social Responsibility, 1985).

3 "Community Champion: Sybil Phoenix", Windrush Foundation, windrushfoundation.com/community-champions/sybil-phoenix (last viewed 12 May 2022).

4 "Statements on Social Responsibility", Methodist Church Division of Social Responsibility, 1946–95 (Peterborough: Methodist Publishing House, 1995).

5 Dilip Hiro, *Black British, White British: A History of Race Relations in Britain* (London: Paladin, 1991); Bhikhu C. Parekh, *The Parekh Report: The Future of Multi-Ethnic Britain* (London: Runnymede Trust, Profile Books, 2000).

6 "Faithful and Equal", The Division of Social Responsibility, The Methodist Conference, 1987.

7 This definition was first coined by White US academic, Patricia Bidol-Padva, in *Developing New Perspectives on Race* (1970).

8 "The Kairos Document, Challenge to the Church: A Political Comment on the Political Crisis in South Africa", Kairos Theologians, Braamfontein, 1985.

9 See Anthony G. Reddie, "Reassessing the Inculcation of an Anti-Racist Ethic for Christian Ministry: From Racism Awareness to Deconstructing Whiteness", *Religions*, 11 (10) 497 (2020), https://www.methodist.org.uk/media/19245/anthony-reddie-article-151020.pdf (last viewed 21 April 2022).

10 Reddie, "Reassessing the Inculcation of an Anti-Racist Ethic for Christian Ministry".

11 Anthony G. Reddie, *Nobodies to Somebodies: A Practical Theology for Education and Liberation* (Peterborough: Epworth Press, 2003).

12 Inderjit Bhogal, *A Table for All: A Challenge to Church and Nation* (Penistone: Penistone Publications, 2000).

13 Gemma Tulud Cruz, *Towards a Theology of Migration: Social Justice and Religious Experience* (New York: Palgrave Macmillan, 2014).

14 Inderjit Bhogal, *Hospitality and Sanctuary for All* (London: Churches Together in Britain and Ireland, 2021).

Bibliography

Barton, M., *Scripture as Empowerment for Liberation and Justice: The Experience of Christian and Muslim Women in Bangladesh* (Centre for Comparative Studies in Religion and Gender, Department of Theology and Religious Studies, University of Bristol, 1999).

Barton, M., *Rejection, Resistance and Resurrection: Speaking Out on Racism in the Church* (London: Darton, Longman and Todd, 2005).

Bhogal, I., *A Table for All: A Challenge to Church and Nation* (Penistone: Penistone Publications, 2000).

Bhogal, I., *Hospitality and Sanctuary for All* (London: Churches Together in Britain and Ireland, 2021).

Brooks, I. V., *Where Do We Go from Here? A History of 25 Years of the New Testament Church of God in the United Kingdom 1955–1980* (London: Charles Raper, 1982).

Cruz, G. T., *Towards a Theology of Migration: Social Justice and Religious Experience* (New York Palgrave Macmillan, 2014).

Grant, J., *White Women's Christ and Black Women's Jesus: Feminist Christology and Womanist Response* (Atlanta, Georgia: Scholars Press, 1989).

Haslam, D., *Race for the Millennium: A Challenge to Church and Society* (Church House Publishing, London, 1996).

Hiro, D., *Black British, White British: A History of Race Relations in Britain* (London: Paladin, 1991).

Holden, T., *People, Churches and Multi-Racial Projects: An Account of English Methodism's Response to Plural Britain* (London: Division of Social Responsibility, Methodist Church, 1985).

Jenkins, K., *Closed Door: Christian Critique of Britain's Immigration Policy* (London: Community and Race Relations Unit, British Council of Churches, 1984).

"The Kairos Document, Challenge to the Church: A Theological Comment on the Political Crisis in South Africa", Kairos Theologians (Braamfontein, 1985).

King, M. L., Sermon. Ebenezer Baptist Church, 1967.

Murray, L., *Being Black in Britain* (London: Chester House Publications, 1995).

Phoenix, S., *Willing Hands* (Abingdon: Bible Reading Fellowship, 1984).

Reddie, A., *Nobodies to Somebodies: A Practical Theology for Education and Liberation* (Peterborough: Epworth Press, 2003).

Reddie, A. G., *Is God Colour Blind?* Insights from Black Theology for Christian Ministry (London: SPCK, 2009).

Reddie, A. G., *Black Theology.* SCM Core Text (London: SCM, 2012).

Reddie, A. G., *Theologising Brexit: A Liberationist and Postcolonial Critique* (London: Routledge, 2019).

Reddie, R. S., *Abolition! The Struggle to Abolish Slavery in the British Colonies* (Oxford: Lion, 2007).

Selvanayagam, I., *A Second Call: Ministry and Mission in a Multifaith Milieu* (Madras: Christian Literature Society, 2000).

Selvanayagam, I., *Relating to People of Other Faiths: Insights from the Bible* (Thiruvalla: Christava Sahithya Samithy – Board of Theological Textbook Programmes, 2004).

Udo, D., *We Shall Overcome: Black Men of Faith* (London: Root and Branch Consultancy, 2007).

Walton, H., *A Tree God Planted: Black People in British Methodism* (London: Ethnic Minorities in Methodism Working Group, Division of Social Responsibility, 1985).

Winder, R., *Bloody Foreigners: The Story of Immigration to Britain* (London: Little, Brown, 2004).

Reports and Articles

"Faithful and Equal", The Division of Social Responsibility, The Methodist Conference, 1987.

"Statements on Social Responsibility", Methodist Church Division of Social Responsibility, 1946–95 (Peterborough: Methodist Publishing House, 1995).

"Race to the Future", The Methodist Committee for Racial Justice, 1999.

Racial Justice Sunday Resource Packs, Methodist Church and Churches Together in Britain and Ireland.

Reddie, A. G. "Reassessing the Inculcation of an Anti-Racist Ethic for Christian Ministry: From Racism Awareness to Deconstructing Whiteness", *Religions*, 11 (10) 497 (2020).

The Parekh Report: The Future of Multi-Ethnic Britain (London: Runnymede Trust. Profile Books, 2000).

"To Overcome is to Undertake", Report of the First Connexional Conference of Young Black Methodists, 2–4 November 1990.

Chapter 3
British Baptists and Institutional Racism

WALE HUDSON-ROBERTS

In November 2007, the Baptist Union (BU) Council issued a public apology for the historic enslavement of African people, and for the racism that has been a continuing legacy of the Transatlantic Slave Trade.[1] This was an unexpected and unprecedented moment in British Baptist history, sending a positive, symbolic message to the Black Baptist community. The "apology" gave voice, even if short-lived, to the entire Black, Asian, and Minority Ethnic Baptist community. The discordant notes, long enshrined in racist practices, had for too long muted our voices.

The apology was one brief event, spanning just three days in an innocuous part of the English countryside. That Swanwick Council, however, promised hope for Black and Brown Baptists. The apology signalled the possibility of changes that were long overdue. Yet, despite this historic moment, there remains misunderstanding around "institutional racism" among British Baptists. This is not, of course, a recent development; it is something that has been consolidating over many years. At this significant moment in world and Baptist history, following the murder of George Floyd and the rapidly rising profile of the Black Lives Matter movement in 2020, this chapter is designed to energize a new and urgent debate, focused on the theme of British Baptists and institutional racism.

We begin, then, by reviewing some of the significant markers that have been laid down over the last quarter-century, associated with the Black and Brown Baptist presence in our British Baptist movement. The choice of headings in this first part of the chapter represents my own active involvement as the BU's Racial Justice Coordinator throughout this period and reflects the privileged perspective I have had as these events have unfolded.

"Daddy" Desmond Gordon Paves the Way?

When my colleague "Daddy" Desmond Gordon founded The Black and Asian Baptist Forum for Baptist Ministers, there was an uproar in some circles in the wider BU. Many were unable to grasp why we would want to congregate "in the absence" of White Baptist ministers. This was, of course, their problem, not ours. Most Black and Brown ministers greeted this gathering as a gift from God.

We met regularly, about every two months, with Daddy Desmond. It was never billed as a formal gathering. Its purpose was fellowship, and from the start, building relationships was central to its DNA. To survive as local Baptist pastors we needed to build deep and lasting friendships with each other. This would never fully protect us from the vitriolic racist language to which we were often exposed, even from worshippers in our own congregations. The strength of the forum centred on our ability to talk through the issue of racism in a safe space and with colleagues who, as they say, "got it". We did not have to explain or justify our existence to each other; we were proud ministers of colour.

With hindsight, I realize just how instrumental this forum was in my own formation, and in that of many other Black and Brown Baptist ministers. In the face of heightened racism, both individual and institutional, the forum attempted to keep young ministers like myself as safe as possible from the adverse impact of racism. For a short time every few weeks, we were able to be ourselves, away from the critical and analytical gaze of White colleagues.

Rosemarie Davidson-Gotobed Plants Seeds

By this time, overt racism appeared out of control in Baptist churches. The limited safety provided by the Black and Asian Forum, and even the challenge of the Jamaica Baptist Union (JBU) to British Baptists, was not going to be enough to resist the lethal impact of racism. In the end, one Baptist Association grasped the nettle. The appointment of Rosemarie Davidson-Gotobed as the London Baptist Association's (LBA) first ever Racial Justice Coordinator was widely applauded, especially across Black, Asian, and Minority Ethnic communities. Inevitably, the appointment would present a serious challenge to its appointee: the churches appeared awash with racism and, supposedly, it was Rosemarie's job to sort it out.

It was a gargantuan task to place on the shoulders of one person. However, Rosemarie did not disappoint. She came into the post with fresh ideas, creative and strategic thinking, strength of character, and resolute determination. Yet she was treading a lonely path and encountered a system soaked in racism and, unsurprisingly, she faced hostile resistance. Her efforts to develop cross-cultural understanding prompted a disproportionate pushback, fuelled by both White structures and White ministers.

Rosemarie's move to the USA with her family brought a regrettable end to her pioneering work, which planted seeds in the rocky ground. Those seeds continued to grow years after her departure and led to the strategic appointments among Baptists Together of Sivakumar Rajagopalan, David Shosanya, Gale Richards, Seidel Abel Boanerges, Dave Ellis, Dotha Blackwood, Winston Bygrave et al. Also, this period witnessed the appointment of a cluster of Black, Asian, and Minority Ethnic Baptist Presidents such as Fred George, Kate Coleman, Rupert Lazar, Kingsley Appiagyei, and, most recently, Yinka Oyekan. Equally, White racial justice advocates, including David Wise, Richard Kidd, Julian Gotobed, Andy Bruce, Graham Sparkes, Myra Blyth, and others, have worked assiduously with Black, Asian, and Minority Ethnic Baptists to create a BU in which we feel able to survive in the continuing racially charged environment.

Karl Henlin at the 2007 Baptist Assembly

In May 2007, at the Brighton Centre on the south coast of England, Karl Henlin, President of the JBU, made an impassioned plea to the Baptist Assembly, sponsored jointly by the BU and the BMS. On behalf of the JBU, he called again on White Baptists to apologize for the historical trafficking of Africans to Jamaica. Initially his call was rejected, but, after protracted discussions, the Racial Justice Group, ably moderated by Pat White and supported by the Faith and Unity Executive, proposed that the BU discuss the matter of an "apology" for three days during its forthcoming November Council. The proposal was backed by the BU Trustees, and the outcome was historic.

This was not the first time, and it certainly will not be the last, that Baptists Together have experienced the impact of strong leadership in the JBU. As is often the case, they had worked gently behind the scenes, adding their theological weight to racial justice matters in other parts of the Baptist world. In the UK, the question has to be asked whether an "apology" would ever have taken shape if it had not been for the tenacity of the JBU? Its clarion call for "racial justice made flesh" in the message of Karl Henlin will go down as one of the finest moments in our recent Baptist history.

The Baptist Union "Apology"?

Immediately after the council publicly acknowledged its part in the Transatlantic Slave Trade, a form of words was drafted by my colleagues Richard Kidd and Sean Winter. The resolution read:

> As a Council we have listened to one another, we have heard the pain of hurting sisters and brothers, and we have heard God speaking to us.

> In a spirit of weakness, humility and vulnerability, we acknowledge that we are only at the start of a journey, but we are agreed that this must not prevent us speaking and acting at a Kairos moment.

> Therefore, we acknowledge our share in and benefit from our nation's participation in the transatlantic slave trade.

> We acknowledge that we speak as those who have shared in and suffered from the legacy of slavery and its appalling consequences for God's world.

> We offer our apology to God and to our brothers and sisters for all that has created and still perpetuates the hurt which originated from the horror of slavery.

> We repent of the hurt we have caused, the divisions we have created, our reluctance to face up to the sin of the past, our unwillingness to

listen to the pain of our black sisters and brothers, and our silence in the face of racism and injustice today.

We commit ourselves, in a true spirit of repentance, to take what we have learned from God in the Council and to share it widely in our Baptist community and beyond, looking for gospel ways by which we can turn the words and feelings we have expressed today into concrete actions and contribute to the prophetic word of God's coming Kingdom.[2]

In no time at all, the resolution was circulating in our churches, colleges, and associations. For a while, it was the talk of the Union, leaving many Black, Asian, and Minority Ethnic Baptists stunned. Not in a million years did we expect an outcome such as this.

In 2008, as agreed by the Council, these words were taken to Jamaica personally, by Pat White, Jonathan Edwards, and myself. They were formally presented to the General Secretary of the JBU, Karl Johnson, and to his colleagues. Black Baptists could be forgiven for dreaming of the arrival of just and equitable relationships.

The Journey – A Step in the Right Direction?

The Journey was the title given to the process that began with the apology, and its aim was to help the BU address issues of racism through the lens of its new apology. From the start, two features were fundamental: this would be a process that included both listening and discernment, and in March 2011 the Racial Justice Group reported back to the BU Council on The Journey and its findings. Its recommendations included: building multicultural churches; developing the leadership skills of Black, Asian, and Minority Ethnic young people; racial justice training for ministers; multicultural events; and establishing culturally inclusive structures. These recommendations were all endorsed by the BU Council, and the Racial Justice Group was given the green light to implement them.

The Journey should have provided Baptists Together with tools to examine and scrutinize White privilege in a new way, challenging its inflated White image and signposting a new direction, one marked by equitable relationships between ethnic Baptists groupings. Although these resources opened minds and sparked theological debate (and may even have challenged the BU), they did little, if anything, to help Black and Brown Baptists survive and grow amid increasing reports of blatant racism. With hindsight, I can now see that more radical action was needed, which should have included a wide-ranging dismantling of the biased structures, alongside a restructuring of the BU through the lens of the apology. Had that happened, Black, Brown, and White Baptists together could have effected a much more substantive outcome from The Journey process. If I were able to repeat the process, I would flag up from the start the paramount importance of prophetic and empowering outcomes.

The Sam Sharpe Project

The Sam Sharpe Project is a prophetic initiative. It is rooted in a liberative theology, enabling "birth from below", and has brought a breath of new life for Black Baptists and many others.

The Sam Sharpe Partners initially included Northern Baptist College, the Heart of England Baptist Association, Regent's Park College, Baptists Together, and the Jamaican Baptist Union. Delroy Reid-Salmon and I were invited by the partners to co-ordinate the project.

There are now two programmes located within the project: the first, "Text and Story", was commissioned by the Sam Sharpe Project, and written by Gale Richards. This is a collection of study materials based on the lives of Black and Brown Baptist pioneers exploring how Bible texts have shaped their lives. The second, is the annual Sam Sharpe Lecture, which was founded by Rosemarie Davidson-Gotobed. The success of these programmes has provided a significant platform for the project.

The first in the series of annual lectures was delivered by Professor Robert Beckford on 18 October 2012. The inexorable growth of these lectures now means they garner an international following.

We now begin to explore the question that prompts the second part of this chapter. Why is it that, despite the efforts made by our anti-racist advocates and the various educational and other projects they have created, a culture of intentional change remains conspicuous by its absence from our churches, associations, and colleges? Is it, as I have suggested, bound up with our failure to address our institutional racism more generally?

To help us consider this question, I have carefully selected six headings, each designed to capture a facet of institutional racism among Baptists Together. Rather than simply declare my own opinion, my aim is to provide the tools that will enable readers to come to their own conclusions.

So What is Institutional Racism Among Baptists?

Institutional racism is a force for injustice lurking within the structures of many White-run organizations. It benefits White people and it excludes and disadvantages Black, Asian, and Minority Ethnic people. It is pernicious and subtle, and many of its beneficiaries are not even conscious of the effortless advantages it has conferred on them. Sadly, church movements such as Baptists Together are not immune from structural racism. Its indicators can be subtle and elusive, but the difficulty in locating it should never be mistaken for its absence.

There is no clearer indicator of the normally hidden existence of racism in our churches, associations, and colleges which surfaced when, as a union, we tried to formulate that clear response in 2007 to the call for an apology. The danger is that the apology will be remembered only as a historical event, a moment in history that sent a short-lived tremor across the BU of churches, associations, and colleges. Everything suggests that the apology was primarily an eloquent crafting of words, and that the quest for racial justice remains largely a utopian dream among today's Baptists.

It is this loss of momentum that now demands that we ask ourselves a difficult question: how much has institutional racism been the reason why Baptists have failed to create an anti-racist British Baptist identity following the radical stance of the apology? The following themes are designed to help us answer this question.

1 Racism is a cultural phenomenon

Institutional racism is encouraged, often unwittingly, by the culture generated in an organization like Baptists Together. This is not necessarily because the culture is irretrievably evil. It is, however, typically symptomatic of the minds and hearts of those who shape the culture – all too often White males. It is their signature that is writ large within the organization's culture. As a result, creating an anti-racist Baptist movement is a titanic struggle.

Racial justice training is key and can spark constructive conversations about dismantling institutional racism. However, real change will only become possible when White Baptists take the initiative and make conscious decisions to divest themselves of some of their power and privilege. A combination of sacrificial practice and racial justice training could begin a movement toward the creation of a culture accessible to all, and not merely some. This kind of remodelling would be a profoundly incarnational act, and be about our words becoming flesh. It would entail deep listening, discernment, and personal sacrifice. Surely, I ask, has this not always been at the heart of our Baptist movement? To live under the rule of Christ is willingly to emulate the sacrificial vulnerability of the God we have come to understand as we gather around the cross of Jesus.

2 Racism is reinforced by racialized propaganda

Propaganda easily deforms holy realities by presenting a distorted and overly embellished narrative of the truth. Historically, through diverse media, the lie has been propagated that Black, Asian, and Minority Ethnic people are not equal to their White counterparts. With this narrative of superiority, the toxicity of institutional racism has been permitted to invade the heart of Baptist culture. Such propaganda only serves to reinforce already established White superiority and, once internalized, further buttresses the lie about Black and Brown inferiority. Black and Brown people find themselves asking questions like, "Are we really what White people say we are?" "Are we not as capable as our White ministers?" "Are we not as competent and intelligent as White people?" Racialized propaganda thrives on the deep internalizing of racism and false rhetoric about the "other". Its single aim, often tragically successful, is to maintain White privilege and to keep Black people in their "rightful" place.

Its impact has certainly had lasting consequences on first-generation "British" Caribbeans; many still bemoan their rejection from Baptist churches, forcing them to find alternative places of worship, often in Pentecostal churches. Once rejection has become the norm, it does not take long for oppressed people to internalize the constant flow of dehumanizing remarks, in the churches and the marketplace, which made first-generation Caribbean people continue to feel like their enslaved antecedents. For many of them, even though they saw themselves moving from the Caribbean to the "Mother Country", they discovered that the whip remained firmly in the hands of their new White masters. Equally, racist signs on homes for rent accurately captured the environment into which they had moved. The reality was pitiful, and a constant barrage of institutional racism eventually left its mark; internalized racism is just one of its many permanent symptoms.

It was the fear of rejection by racist Baptist churches that discouraged many first-generation Baptist Caribbeans from occupying leadership roles in their new-found churches. It had nothing to do with their lack of ability or limited knowhow. It is true that many first-generation Caribbeans did not enter this country carrying much by way of degrees and diplomas, but their natural gifts of leadership and articulate participation should have been sufficient to enable them to succeed in their chosen careers. With few opportunities, and doors firmly shut in their faces, actual prospects were limited.

3 Racism is maintained by hierarchy

Racial hierarchy among Baptists ought to be regarded by Baptists as an ecclesial contradiction. "Baptists don't do hierarchy; Baptists don't do racism!" Yet the dissonance between desire and reality is reflected in the absence of Black, Asian, and Minority Ethnic regional team leaders, specialist team leaders in the Didcot offices, and Baptist college principals. Even among regional ministers and theological educators more generally, the overwhelming majority are White. Sadly, this is also reflected in the nearly all-White Baptists Together Core Leadership Team.

Historically, racial hierarchy justified the separation of Black, Brown, and White people. This shows what a divided movement we are as the leaders of our movement are almost exclusively White, and it also serves to confirm the continually recycled myth that "White is better".

A good number of White Baptists struggle with the concept of hierarchy. For centuries, Baptists have resisted this way of being. Congregations are at the very heart of who we are, and we wear the label "congregational" with understandable pride. It can be argued that congregationalism has become one-way traffic with White Baptists in our churches and within our structures, normatively central to the listening and discerning processes. Far too often Black and Brown Baptists remain at the margins, committed to the process but absent from it. Whether we like it or not, this picture speaks louder than words.

4 Racism is a White sin

Institutional racism is evil, and it is a White problem. It is Baptist sin, and Baptist people of colour, like me, live with the consequences. Too many Black Baptists feel incapable of occupying leadership positions within our structures. After all, we see and hear racialized rhetoric both inside and outside church that leaves an indelible mark. We cannot simply unshackle ourselves from centuries of indoctrination that has been drummed into our consciousness by White people. The irony should not be lost on any of us; this White problem has now become our problem. If I were to charge a White person £10 every time she or he said, "You have chip on your shoulder", or, "You are an angry Black man", I would be rich. These ill-informed comments fail to grasp a single truth: if there really is a "chip" and if it is true that we are "angry", the fact is that this has been foisted on us by White people who have forced their problem onto our shoulders and into our spirits.

A Baptist theology of covenant ought to be able to help us navigate this terrain. Baptists are committed to the Body of Christ, and this is a rich biblical concept that reminds us of the risen Body of Christ, the bread we break at the Lord's Table, and our gathered communities meeting under the rule of Christ. These are not separate meanings. They are indivisible: the risen Body of Christ becomes present for us through the breaking of bread in a particular community of believers. In the face of the "other", therefore, we have an opportunity to see another member of the Body of Christ – indeed, we are invited to see the face of Christ.

I would hope that on seeing the face of Christ in the "other", White Christians would be stopped in their tracks. They would, like all of us, recognize the particularity of their own sins, including the sin of racism, and strive to take responsibility for it. They would definitely not continue to project it onto Black, Asian, and Minority Ethnic Baptist companions. White members of the Body of Christ covenanted with Black, Asian, and Minority Ethnic sisters and brothers must be committed together to eradicating the chip and anger that has been forced onto the shoulders of those whom White people see as "other".

The evil of racism was put there by privilege. The initiative to remove it now needs to begin with privileged White Baptists before we can work effectively at this together as a single covenant community.

5 Racism is driven by White insecurity and fragility

White Baptists are usually receptive to my racial justice presentations – so long, that is, as they remain largely impersonal. The moment I name a racial problem that strikes a personal chord, White insecurity rears its head. For the best part of modern history, White people have controlled much of the world. They have systematically colonized huge swathes of the globe and ruthlessly planted their flags in pilfered soil. Enslaved people, those we now term Black, Asian, and Minority Ethnic, were soon put to work on the manor to develop the master's land.

It would be impossible to count how many times this system has been replicated by White men around the world. This "command and control" structure, devoid of compassion and integrity, has survived for a very long time. Incalculable sums of money have been generated by it, reaping substantive benefits for White communities, organizations, and churches. It is an ideology that buys, sells, and invents, and is probably the most sought-after brand in the world. It sees itself as invulnerable and invincible. There is, however, a paradox. White privilege is held from a place of considerable insecurity, and it remains inherently fragile. Whiteness is never wrong – or so it thinks. Its global economic success, some say, is evidence of this rightful supremacy.

When an Asian, African, or Caribbean Baptist leader questions White leaders, there is often pushback. Whiteness is not used to being scrutinized and questioned by "people like us", and whenever it is, the response is marked by disquiet and evident fragility. It is not at all clear how White Baptists can ever be helped to address this issue around their own insecurity and their genuine fragility. Undoubtedly, it will be necessary for Black, Asian, and Minority Ethnic people to confront it. Ideally, "Whiteness" must receive an honest reappraisal by White people, but this will never be easy. Conversations about these matters among White Baptists are always uncomfortable as White insecurity raises its head. White insecurity and fragility, however, will not ultimately be solved by people of colour acting on White people's behalf; it will need to be addressed by White Baptists for themselves.

6 Racism is also up close and personal

"You are a nigger in need of a good whipping!" I was stunned when a member of a church I was serving looked me straight in the eyes and made this reprehensible and indefensible statement. I am unable to recall the content of the sermon that preceded it, or why it evoked the primitive response it did. I do, however, recall feeling utterly sickened by the comment.

Just when I thought things could not get worse, I experienced another slice of blatant racism, and again it was up close and personal. On this occasion, I was stopped in my tracks by a worshipper from my own church. Her complaint was this: "Your hands are Black and dirty, and they should not be serving me Communion."

There is no way to respond to such ignorance. "Is this the church I was called to serve?" I asked myself. With attitudes like this, I wondered how long I could remain the pastor.

Alas, my racist experiences did not stop there. One worshipper, someone I had taken through baptismal classes, was so adamant that she must be baptized by a White deacon that she confessed that she would rather not be baptized at all than be baptized by me. I was the "wrong colour", she declared with unfaltering temerity.

Black and Brown Baptist female pastors have had an even harder time. Theirs is a double subjugation, oppressed on the grounds of both race and gender. If they are not being undermined because of their skin colour, it is their gender that takes the hit, and often it is both. It seems that every aspect of their ministerial experience is exercised under pressure, which often begins during the process of ministerial formation in one of our Baptist colleges and continues right through to receiving a call from a local Baptist church. Despite enduring a long and complicated process of formation, they continue to experience patriarchy and racism in the churches they serve. While serving, their experience of double jeopardy can be relentlessly painful. Many are forced to leave their churches, and the rapidity of departure is much quicker for Black women than for White ones.

What is the Immediate Challenge?

It is my considered opinion that our exploration of institutional racism under these six headings leads to only one possible conclusion: that institutional racism is indeed a serious issue for British Baptists, and that it has exposed issues for relationships between White and Black, Asian, and Minority Ethnic Baptists which cannot be ignored. My own view is that institutional racism is the single most important reason why Baptists Together remain deeply divided when it comes to racial justice. There might, of course, be other contributory factors, but, even if that is the case, the issue of ongoing racism cannot be left unaddressed.

There is an urgent need for further evidence of repentance, initiated by White Baptists. At the top of the list are the need to address the issue of reparations with respect to the Baptists of Jamaica, and the need to begin a systematic programme of reform that leads to a far-reaching reform of Baptists Together, beginning with the surrender of excessive White power and privilege.

Reparations and Baptists in Jamaica

The evidence now confirming the extent of the trade in African bodies that we call the Transatlantic Slave Trade is indisputable. Despite the trade's abolition in British colonies in 1807, violence continues to be meted out on Black, Asian, and Minority Ethnic bodies, and our experience of indignity has not abated. Much of today's global economy is still underwritten by the incalculable sums that were extorted by the trade in Africans, sponsored by White traders. There is wide recognition that many forms of enslavement continue all around the world, and that racism, honed on the plantations of the Americas, is still deeply imbedded in the world order. This is why reparation is an inescapable matter of justice and needs to be urgently made as a sign of repentance.

Baptists Together and the Surrender of White Power and Privilege

Just as White people never fully experience racism, so Black and Brown people never experience unconditional privilege. Our starting points are entirely different. For too long, Black and Brown people have been bound to relationships that disadvantage us and benefit White people. At root, this is about power. Racism continues to be alive and well among Baptists Together. So far, not even the powerful message reaching us through the history of Sam Sharpe shows any sign of creating change. White Baptists consistently refuse to scrutinize the implications of their Whiteness, and repeatedly avoid facing the challenge to divest themselves of privilege. For change to happen, the surrendering of their privilege must first take place.

The First Must Be Last, and the Last First!

There is only one credible way to address institutional racism in Baptists Together, and that is to tackle it head on. This will entail engaging with all the issues raised by this chapter, simultaneously and urgently. They are, in the end, all inextricably connected and can only be tackled with a coordinated strategy. Any serious Baptist responses will need to be initiated by some combination of the BU Council, the BU Trustees, the Core Leadership Team – that is, those who together form the core of our predominantly White structures. Ideally, this will be done in collaboration with the BU Racial Justice Group but, ultimately, institutional racism can only be challenged and deconstructed by those who were responsible for its creation.

As a text that could be used to front these actions, it would be hard to beat Jesus words: "The last will be first, and the first will be last" (Matthew 20:16). There is little doubt that, if only we can find the courage to tackle the poison of structural racism head on, we can open a floodgate and release real possibilities for the creation of a renewed and radical BU that reflects Black, Brown, and White Baptists united in the image of God.

Notes

1 "Faith and Society Files: The Apology for Slavery", Baptists Together, November 2007, https://www.baptist.org.uk/Publisher/File. aspx?ID=111235&view=browser (last viewed 12 May 2022).
2 "The Apology for Slavery", Baptists Together, November 2007.

Chapter 4

The Impetus for Racial Equality in the Religious Society of Friends

EDWINA PEART AND PAUL PARKER

This chapter is co-written by Edwina Peart and Paul Parker. Edwina is the Quaker's Diversity and Inclusion Coordinator, appointed in 2018. She works with the Quakers to remove barriers and actively seek wider participation to help deepen the spiritual life of the community and strengthen its witness. Paul has served since 2011 as Recording Clerk for Britain Yearly Meeting, the national organization for Quakers in England, Wales, Scotland, the Channel Islands, and the Isle of Man. He is the senior constitutional officer of the Religious Society of Friends in Britain, and the senior staff member responsible for the organization's work to support Quaker communities and promote a peaceful, just, and sustainable world. Quakers do not recognize a distinction between priesthood and laity, so all members of the Society speak from equal spiritual inspiration. Paul's contribution therefore carries no additional spiritual authority because of his position.

Part 1: Edwina Peart

It is difficult to speak of anti-racist work within the Religious Society of Friends without recognizing and contextualizing their role in abolishing slavery in the British colonies. Quakers have a public history of advocating against the Transatlantic Slave Trade, of which they are rightly proud. Widely considered to be the initiators (within the Christian tradition) of the abolition movement, they sought to highlight the true inhumanity and cruelty of this system and its complete incompatibility with the principles of their faith. They did this through faith in action.

They supplied nine of the twelve members of the influential abolition committee that began meeting in 1787, its purpose to end the trade in human beings and the system of slavery itself. For decades, Quaker merchants and businessmen provided most of the movement's financial support. The network of Quakers around the country formed the core of the local anti-slavery committees. Working within their own ranks and externally in the wider society, the intrinsic right of all human beings to liberty was promoted.

Quakers also produced the first publicity supporting abolition, championed freed Africans in telling their stories, and acted on behalf of those Africans who were still enslaved. A radical position at the time, it was in keeping with their own beliefs about equality relating to status and rank that often saw them persecuted and imprisoned. Their moral condemnation of the slave trade did not allow for the worst excesses to be smoothed over but required root and branch transformation. The outcome they worked for, and ultimately achieved as a faith group, belies a more inconsistent perspective held by individual members. Quakers both held enslaved Africans and were involved in the Transatlantic Slave Trade in various ways. This ambivalence, woven into their initial encounter with racial exploitation, survives to this day, albeit in a very different form. Friends remain actively committed to justice, peace, and equality, willingly and wholeheartedly acting to raise awareness of issues and to challenge them. Despite this, racial diversity in membership is evidently low[1] and, without data to refute or confirm this, is hard to quantify. The work is ongoing.

This chapter provides an overview of the most recent history of work on racial equality, starting with initiatives developed in the 1990s and up to May 2021. The particularly British Windrush scandal, the global focus on race via the Black Lives Matter campaign, the killing of George Floyd, and social and health inequalities highlighted by the COVID-19 pandemic, have all added impetus. I observe a step change and renewed appetite for engaging with embedded and systemic racism. As is apparent from corporate discernment on this issue by central bodies, there is once again a call to do the work needed within Quaker communities, as well as in the wider British society in which it is rooted. Radicalism may have given way to determination and tenacity, but the commitments to truth and equality remain and are increasingly guiding faith in action.

The 1990s

Advocating for racial equality is a constant thread running throughout Quaker history. Archival research[2] reveals that engagement has taken various forms, which include disputing common myths about immigration, making statements of intent on racism, and creating a fellowship group for Black Friends and their families. For the time period covered by this publication, I focus on a few examples of work to illustrate the approaches that dominate. In doing so I have drawn on the memories of Stuart Morton,[3] who provided staff support for initiatives during this period, and Marigold Bentley,[4] who shared relevant communication. It is worth noting that before I took up my post, all work in this area was supported by staff as an adjunct to their main role. As far as I am aware, my post is the first to be dedicated to equality (across the whole spectrum).

There are two related strands that seem to dominate Quaker practice. First, ecumenical work that gathers and combines the efforts of Christian denominations in highlighting and responding to racism in British society and globally, building bridges enabling dialogue. Second, an internal gaze which examines the life of Britain Yearly Meeting, ensuring the faith values expressed are acted upon. Interestingly, this is the combination that secured historical abolition success.

In 1994, following an initial gathering of Black Friends and a recognition that racism within Quakers needed to be addressed, the Association of Black Friends and their Families was launched. This was conceptualized to meet the needs of Black and Asian members as well as families who had adopted Black children. It appears to have been the first Quaker body that sought to support Black and Asian members specifically and to acknowledge that they had both particular needs and an experience that was different from that of the majority of the membership. It followed several earlier and ongoing projects that addressed race and ethnicity in ways focused on awareness raising and integration. These included a quarterly newsletter, *Quakers and Race*, which ran from 1989 to 2005 and was published by the Community Relations Committee, who also published an information pack.

There was also a report that came from a year-long fellowship on cross-cultural communication conducted in 1992–93 that included work with individual meetings. The report, which was published in 1998,[5] concluded that racism within Quakers mirrored that of wider society. Though these undertakings identified the need for change and detailed opportunities and strategies for action, they were not adopted. This was partly owing to the lack of sustained support and capacity, and failure to relate equality to the spiritual health of Quakers.

Thus, the Association of Black Friends and their Families, while considered to be "strengthening and affirming"[6] by some, did not last for very long. By 2002, it no longer appeared in the Book of Meetings. In assessing the possible reasons for this, two main factors emerge: an unwillingness to take on the roles required to support the project, and the dearth of organization-wide backing, as opposed to special interest validation. The latter also relates to how racism is defined. When a narrow definition focused on hateful words or actions is used, it is relatively easy to absolve oneself. If a comprehensive definition outlining systemic or institutional racism is applied, it becomes obvious that individuals and groups must work to extricate themselves from pervasive attitudes and beliefs, and that this is ongoing. Raising awareness and learning are important; however, these activities in and of themselves are insufficient to bring about lasting change.

The early 1990s also saw the establishment of a joint working group supported by the Quaker Social Responsibility and Education Committee and the Community Relations Committee (CRC), entitled Racism in the Life of Britain Yearly Meeting. The need for racial equality to be a stated concern, in a similar way to the peace testimony, had long been argued by members of the CRC, but it was difficult to persuade meetings of the usefulness of training resources and materials that would challenge the gap between aspirations and actions, or would suggest that changing structures required internal as well as external change. The perceived fragility of this endeavour led to high staff involvement.

Communication from this time suggests that hurt and anguish accompanied much of the effort of this group, as Quakers were angry and challenged by the suggestion that racism existed in their faith community. Newsletters were produced and an active commitment to promote diversity was sought. A video was created as part of this and as a follow-up to an information and study pack. It was showcased to a wide body and its reception was largely hostile.

This hostility is understood and explained as based on several factors. Importantly, there is an "assumed Whiteness"[7] among Quakers, an inability to imagine membership more widely than that which exists and can be seen in one's individual meeting. It is a failure to conceptualize the worldwide faith group in a truly inclusive way. It also reflected a sense that the core task, from which distraction should not be permitted, lay in promoting peace and justice outside in the world. The working group tried to raise conversations with the personnel department, seeking to question the ratio of Black staff employed within the organization as part of a holistic effort. This was also rebuffed on the grounds of professional expertise, and the effort to concentrate on racism within Quakers was eventually quelled and a wider focus on inclusion and diversity adopted.

This perspective reflects the changing language of equality and current emphasis. It masks the difficulty faced by those who laboured to bring this issue into the light and those who left dispirited. This is captured in the assessment that notes:

> Looking back, I do not think we (as White people) had developed the awareness, the experience or the skills to more clearly understand our complicity in racism and to be anti-racist. This is now changing – thanks be to God.[8]

Current work

The minute[9] that gave rise to my post comes from the Quakers' Yearly Meeting 2017 and is a recognition that racial diversity (alongside other aspects of inequality) requires continued attention within Quaker structures and practices. The following extract expresses this and unites faith and action:

> We are inspired, but we are also disquieted. How do our actions sit alongside our faith, how does our "being" move into "doing"? What is for individual activity and what will we do corporately? If we are inspired and upheld and supported in our identity and work as Quakers, is that enough? Or are we called to be more radical?[10]

The inclusion of the word "radical" encapsulates the past and, to my mind, sets an intention for the future. The post, initially intended as a year-long scoping and developing project, has been made permanent.

This affirms both the work and a commitment to the ongoing journey. In this spirit, the project has sought to continue the unity between faith and action, corporate and individual pursuits. The following examples of activities that are ongoing highlight the progress that is being made and the ground that remains to be covered.

A key endeavour built into the initial proposal is a residential gathering on diversity and inclusion jointly planned and delivered with Woodbrooke (the Quaker study centre).[11] Two have been held to date. Understanding and advocating for racial equality with a faith imperative has been an important aspect of this event. The first, entitled "Answering that of God in Everyone",[12] drew upon a favoured passage to name and critique the barriers that prevent Quakers welcoming all people equally and warmly into the faith community. The following excerpts from attendee evaluation forms give voice to their experience and capture the essence of the event:

> In the gathering we were prompted to recognise aspects of inequality and injustice in our history and currently; I realised later that the prompts were mostly reminders rather than new information. This made me wonder: do we really not know about – or do we turn a blind eye to – the impact of inequality and exclusion in our society and within the Society of Friends in particular? Do we not notice, because we are used to living within the comfort zone of our familiar lives and meetings, the ways in which systems have come to disadvantage many and to privilege a few?

Challenging and difficult conversations were held and supported with the input of leaders in the field of theology and its intersections with racial (and other aspects of) equality. They have proven fruitful in widening the discussion and facilitating learning from others, as well as recognizing the current stage of development and where advances have been made. Reflecting on the gathering and contemplating how best to take the issues forward, an attendee wrote:

> I want to examine and understand my Whiteness. I want to learn this with my community. I want to help my wider community see these questions as important and urgent. Clear eyes; humble learner; mourn, repent, change.

The second event asked, "Are you open to new light, from whatever source?"[13] The following excerpt is taken from a report written by a participant:

> There is a big conversation that needs to be had throughout the Society about a number of aspects of inclusion and diversity. And actions need to follow that conversation.

Conversations of this nature were proposed for the annual meeting of Quakers, and action might have followed. However, the pandemic intervened and plans were put on hold. My return from furlough brought a big question, one that was raised in a local meeting and sent to a central committee. It reveals historical and contemporary inequalities laid bare by the ravages of the pandemic and the global Black Lives Matter campaign. Should Quakers apologize for their role in the Transatlantic Slave Trade? This question resonates. It captures the disbelief about the extent of racism in Britain, despite the Windrush scandal, the "Hostile Environment" in the Home Office, and colonial history. It unravels the power relations of systemic racism. It grants insight into global trade relations and troubles the single heroic narrative embraced by the British, and by British Quakers. It implicates global power structures in the climate crisis we face, and the form that interventions take to stem this tide.

The appetite to engage with this question is heartening. I have raised it with youth groups, with central committees, with special interest groups, and with staff groups to sincere engagement and a real willingness to grapple with whose story is told and what truth exists in the narrative that prevails. At the time of writing, I have received many requests to facilitate sessions on this for Quaker meetings at local and regional level. This question is being asked alongside other questions that examine foundational aspects of Quakerism, such as the testimonies to truth and equality.

A group has also emerged: The Black, Brown and People of Colour Fellowship. Though in its infancy, the response is encouraging in terms of engagement and senior support. The following quote is taken from an evaluation and illustrates commonly expressed sentiments:

> Initially when I saw it on the digital noticeboard, it felt controversial, but I so enjoyed it. Recently talking about racism as the only Black person in our meeting has felt a weight and it felt good to lay it down for a few hours and still be in Quakers.

In response to asking what attendees plan to do in light of the session, the respondent continues:

> To not carry the burden of explaining racism so often; I can say no. I still have more truths to explain about what is racially offensive to me to my local meeting and I feel strengthened by hearing of others' experiences of doing this. I tend to avoid causing discomfort. In my meeting I feel that racism is seen as an issue that I face rather than an issue that everyone faces as a destroyer of equality, potential and love in wider society.

Concluding this section of the chapter, I return to the approach that produced the success of the abolition campaign. Quakers saw the need and did the work required on themselves and within the wider society of which they were a part. Separated, neither of these strands could have achieved such a profound goal. Current racism highlights the continued need for similarly integrated interventions. It is also raising consciousness of the work that remains to be done. In a memoir authored in 2020 we read:

> The Society of Friends sounds like an ideal church for a Black woman given that testimony to equality, but sadly that has not been my experience nor the experience of the few other Black people that I have met... At this particular time, for me to remain with the society it is essential that I keep uppermost in my mind a regard for the testimonies as aspirational, a work in progress, and that I also repeatedly remind myself of my own personal failings in achieving the ideals in so many other different ways.[14]

That racial equality remains aspirational is a sobering truth that I recognize. I applaud and support the corporate and individual work that is ongoing to make this a reality.

Part 2: Paul Parker

A few years ago, I came across this quotation from Harriet Tubman. Tubman was an African American woman born into slavery, who, after escaping to Pennsylvania, returned repeatedly to the site of her enslavement to rescue fellow enslaved Africans and guide them along the Underground Railroad to freedom. She said, "Quakers almost as good as colored. They call themselves friends and you can trust them every time."[15]

On first reading, the quote filled me with pride. As a member of the Religious Society of Friends, our movement's part in bringing about the abolition of the slave trade between the UK, West Africa, and the Caribbean plantations was a well-known story, one of the tales we tell our children on Sunday mornings. But on reading it again, I realized there are good reasons to feel more complicated emotions. It is all too easy for us, here in Britain, to selectively ignore aspects of the history of our movement. Before Quakers were abolitionists, some of them were slave-owners, people who not only tolerated the appalling injustices of slavery, but also participated, profiting handsomely. Once the abolition movement gathered pace, the Quaker movement threw its weight behind it, but that shadowy history and its legacy remain largely unexamined. While we can be proud of the Quakers' part in bringing that time to a close, our pride should be tempered by our recognition that our atonement for those earlier injustices is incomplete.

In any case, as a twenty-first-century White British male, I cannot lay claim to a history in which I have not played my part. I have little lived experience to bring to this, my relatively privileged life having left me seemingly untouched by racism. It wasn't me who risked my life and livelihood to accommodate and hide escaping enslaved Africans. It was not me in whom the victims of intolerable injustice placed their trust. I made no personal sacrifice, nor did I take the consequences of bold action to protect the oppressed.

So what right have I to feel proud of my part in that story?

What is more, there is that "almost" – "*almost* as good". What did Harriet Tubman mean by that? Was it that you could rely on the Quakers for safe harbour but not for companionship? Was it that you would be made welcome but would find that you could never belong? Was it that their lives and attitudes were so watermarked by their Whiteness that an escaped enslaved African would never be treated as their equal? I was a bit hurt by that *almost*, to start with. It felt ungrateful, even.

Again, on reflecting, my initial emotional response feels crass. What right have I to expect gratitude for something that merely went a little way toward rectifying the profound injustice my forebears had perpetrated? Why should I expect Harriet to want to belong, when the

Quaker community did not reach out, and arguably still has not reached out to welcome her in?

The more I think about it, the more that *almost* feels generous; magnanimous, even. We were lucky to get away with that *almost*. We have done well to be *almost as good*. But it is not an absolution. That *almost* does a lot of heavy lifting, and it is a sign of the work still to be done. And if we were to parachute Harriet Tubman into the Quaker community in twenty-first-century Britain, would we still qualify for that *almost*?

What has all this got to teach us about racial justice in our communities in Britain today? What work is still to be done?

Well, to start with, I think we have to face up to a complete failure of imagination. If you were to ask the average twenty-first-century Quaker to paint you a word-portrait of the typical Quaker, they may describe someone who is well educated, probably quite well dressed, if quirkily, socially active, quite possibly sandal-wearing. They may well be gay. But they are almost certainly not Black or Asian, or from any other group labelled Minority Ethnic in Britain. And if you were to ask them to imagine their typical Quaker meeting, it would be populated by a roomful of the same: like-minded people, with similar experiences, upbringings, and views.

Here is the failure of imagination (we might even call it prejudice). The Quaker tradition emphasizes that anybody, *anybody*, can experience divine inspiration directly in the silence of the Quaker meeting for worship. So why is it so easy, when we imagine who those *anybodies* are, for a typical Quaker like me to picture them all as White, middle-class, degree-educated, probably retired people? In short, people just like themselves.

But this is to ignore two things.

First, it is to ignore the significant number of Quakers from Black, Asian, and Minority Ethnic groups who exist today. Quakers are not all middle class, not all White, nor even all fixated on the same causes. To speak as if there is only one "right kind" of Quaker is to exclude and devalue those who don't fit the prevailing narrative about what someone has to be like to be a Quaker today. And to speak of all Quakers without acknowledging the wide diversity that already exists serves only to "other" and exclude those who do not fit the stereotype, leaving them wondering if they are not as welcome as they thought.

Second, and more important, it is a failure to imagine what a truly inclusive, fully welcoming spiritual community can be like. In a Quaker meeting – whether a meeting for worship, or the business meeting where Quakers discern "the will of God" for them on important decisions or policy positions – every voice carries. Friends gather in silence, listening for the promptings of the Spirit in their hearts, and anyone present can be moved to speak to the group. There is no hierarchy, no worldly status, no special hotline to divine inspiration – just patient, faithful waiting for divine guidance to come through the stillness. It is a remarkable thing. Together, in a meeting for worship that works well, we can sometimes catch a glimpse of the Truth.

So to enter into a Quaker meeting knowing that key people are missing, with our community less diverse than it could be – incomplete – is to miss out on important perspectives. Not everyone can see the world the same way. To reach the Truth, we need a range of perspectives and experiences. If participation in our meeting is too limited, we are then unable to see things as clearly as we should. It's a bit like going to an art gallery but not putting on our glasses to look at the pictures. They're still there, but the details are indistinct and the world is a bit blurred. Without that diverse range of perspectives and lived experiences – including people of colour, people with disabilities, people of different genders and sexualities, people of all ages and conditions – we are poorer, and worse placed to understand the work we are called to in our own community and in the world.

In one of my go-to passages in *Quaker Faith and Practice*, the Quakers' periodically updated compendium of writings and inspiration, the twentieth-century Quaker, George Gorman, wrote:

> One of the unexpected things I have learnt in my life as a Quaker is that religion is basically about relationships between people. This was an unexpected discovery, because I had been brought up to believe that religion was essentially about our relationship with God... I do not think I am alone in my certainty that it is in my relationships with people that the deepest religious truths are most vividly disclosed.[16]

If our relationships with other people are broken, or unequal, or downright missing, then we miss out on the deepest religious truths that could otherwise be available to us. What more incentive do we need to put things right? And what is the work we are called upon to do?

It turns out not to be all that straightforward. The obstacles to a diverse and welcoming community have deep roots: the language we use, the books we read, the pictures we put up, the stories we tell about ourselves – including the one about our role with slavery I started this article with – the buildings our meetings inhabit, and the opinions, spoken and unspoken, that we each hold, speak loudly about us, before you even step into the Quaker meeting. And within our faith community we are not immune to the trends, culture wars, politics, and injustices of the outside world. How could we be?

The risk is that we fail to examine the issues properly, believing ourselves "better" than that and somehow exempt from worldly considerations, when in reality all the same issues persist among us Quakers as exist in the world around us. As a faith community with a strong track record of working for social justice – on issues ranging from criminal justice to climate justice to same-sex marriage – we have a tendency to see problems in the world that need fixing and to start working on fixing them, before we see problems within our own worshipping community, which need our attention at the same time. We have both to put our own house in order and to join with others in tackling the broad systemic racial justice issues in wider society.

It also turns out that working on this is not new for Friends. It seems that the unlearning of habits, language, assumptions, and previously unexamined biases is something that each generation has to discover, and work on, anew. As described earlier, the need for this work has surfaced repeatedly in the Religious Society of Friends over the generations, and at each iteration some progress has been made. At the same time, the familiar resistance to – and, indeed, disbelief at – the idea that racism might be an issue among Quakers themselves has come to the fore repeatedly. In a faith community committed to equality and justice in so much of its outward work, we discover, again and again, that when it comes to ourselves, the beam in our own eye disqualifies us from helping to remove the mote in others (see Matthew 7:5).

Despite all this work over so many years, it still happened that a colleague of mine was asked recently (by a Black staff member), "Do Quakers really believe that Black Lives Matter, or do they just think they should matter a little bit more than they do at the moment?" Well, ouch.

Still, there are encouraging signs of progress. In 2020, the Trustees of Quakers in Britain's national organization, Britain Yearly Meeting, concluded, "Racism exists within the Religious Society of Friends in Britain and we must tackle it. This is a hard thing to admit, but recognising the problem is an important step in addressing it." Raising their concern with the Meeting for Sufferings, the standing representative council of Quakers from across Britain – named for its historic role in recording the suffering of Friends persecuted for their faith since the early days of our movement – they discovered a hitherto unspoken determination to learn, to put our own house in order, and to act on systemic racial discrimination in the world around us.

Harnessing this energy will take time, humility, and effort, but we hope to make some progress. Is it too much to imagine Quaker meetings as a place of welcome for all, regardless of skin colour, ethnic background, and heritage? Can we become a community that embraces people for the spiritual insight they bring, without judgment? Only then can we, in the words of one of our founders, George Fox:

> Be patterns, be examples in all countries, places, islands, nations, wherever you come, that your carriage and life may preach among all sorts of people, and to them; then you will come to walk cheerfully over the world, answering that of God in everyone.[17]

The key word in that passage, for me, is "answering". One of our important Quaker insights is that everyone, *everyone*, comes with that of God baked in. That divine spark is ours to answer; our response to it depends on us being open to the divine in the other. It gloriously emphasizes that there is no separation between the divine and the other – a separation that can so easily creep into our perceptions of other people, or those we perceive as different from ourselves.

Given that, how can we faithfully do anything other than welcome, embrace, and include all those who come into contact with us? Why are we allowing such human-made barriers to exclude some people from the Quaker experience?

Those Quakers who sheltered Harriet Tubman and her fellow travellers showed hospitality to strangers on the run, perhaps believing they had "entertained angels unawares" (Hebrews 13:2, ESV UK). What does that mean in our own times? And how do we shake off Harriet Tubman's "almost" to become the trusted, trusting, "Blessed Community"[18] of our wildest imaginings?

Let's do this.

Notes

1 This point was made by Tim Gee in his 2017 Gorman Lecture. "Movement-building from stillness – George Gorman Lecture 2017 by Tim Gee", YouTube, 2 October 2017, https://youtu.be/Btb4DjSdqqo (last viewed 22 April 2022).

2 The research I am referring to was conducted by Chloe Scaling for the first Diversity and Inclusion Gathering held at the Quaker study centre, Woodbrooke, in January 2019.

3 Stuart Morton joined Quaker Peace and Service (QPS) as a staff member at Friends House in August 1996 and retired in August 2011.

4 Marigold Bentley is the head of Peace Programmes and Faith Relations.

5 Lilamani Woolrych "Communicating Across Cultures", Joseph Rowntree Charitable Trust, 1998.

6 Personal communication.

7 Personal communication.

8 Personal communication.

9 A Quaker minute records the decision of a Quaker meeting.

10 Yearly Meeting 2017, minute 38.

11 Woodbrooke is an international Quaker learning and research organization, based in Britain, providing opportunities for learning, connection, and worship.

12 *Quaker Faith and Practice*, chapter 19.32, qfp.quaker.org.uk/chapter/19 (last viewed 22 April 2022).

13 *Quaker Faith and Practice*, chapter 1.02.7, qfp.quaker.org.uk/chapter/1 (last viewed 22 April 2022).

14 Rosa L. Carter, *Talking about Skin: A Memoir* (independently published, 2020).

15 "Harriet Tubman Quotes", https://quotestats.com/author/harriet-tubman-quotes/ (last viewed 12 May 2022).

16 George Gorman, *Quaker Faith and Practice*, paragraph 10.20, qfp.quaker.org.uk/passage/10-20 (last viewed 22 April 2022).

17 George Fox, *Quaker Faith and Practice*, paragraph 19.32, qfp.quaker.org.uk/passage/19-32 (last viewed 22 April 2022).

18 The phrase "Blessed Community" comes from Thomas Kelly's *A Testament of Devotion* (1941), pp. 54–55.

Chapter 5

The Catholic Church's Work for Racial Justice

RICHARD ZIPFEL

Following the Second Vatican Council, which took place in the 1960s, the Roman Catholic Community globally was becoming more aware of the gospel imperative to support the poor, to give voice to the voiceless, and to work for justice.

From 1970, the Catholic Church in England and Wales attempted to make a serious response to some of the changes that had taken place in British society since the Second World War. As a result of a long process of migration from the Commonwealth and colonies, Britain had become a multiracial, multicultural society. The three organizations described below played a central role in the Catholic Church's response to those developments.

The Catholic Commission for Racial Justice (1970–1984)

The Catholic Church's involvement in the post-war struggle for racial justice began in the early 1970s with the establishment of the Catholic Commission for Racial Justice (CCRJ). The new Commission felt it was important to reach out to different parts of the country. By the end of 1974, it had established local groups in Birmingham, Leicester, Liverpool, Manchester, and Leeds. Key issues of the time began to shape the work of the Commission, including education, criminal justice, immigration and nationality, and institutional racism.

In 1975, CCRJ launched a Report, "Where Creed and Colour Matter", a survey of admissions policy and practice in Catholic schools.

After consulting widely and reviewing the evidence, in December 1978 CCRJ published its report on "The Police and the Black Community in the Metropolitan Area". The report highlighted the existence of a serious problem between the police and the Black community. Two years later, there were serious disturbances involving the police and the Black community in Brixton, south London. These events led to the Scarman Inquiry, to which the Commission submitted evidence.

In April 1979, with support from the Commission, the bishops of England and Wales released a public statement "Concerning the Revision of British Nationality Law". The bishops argued:

Any new nationality law should state as a matter of principle that our nationality is multi-racial, thereby avoiding any potentially racialist conception of national identity which could lead to racial discrimination in the law or its interpretation.

In January 1982, the Commission published a report, "Rastafarians in Jamaica and Britain". The report suggested that "Rastafarianism should be recognized as a valid religion" and that "Rastafarians in penal institutions should be allowed the same privileges as are accorded to other religious believers."

Later in 1982, a working party on Catholic Education in a Multiracial, Multicultural Society began its work, with the Commission acting as secretariat. The working party visited seminaries, colleges of education, and schools in preparing its report; "Learning from Diversity: A Challenge for Catholic Education", which was eventually published in 1985.

In January 1983, CCRJ published a report, "Racism in British Society". The paper took its starting point from Lord Scarman's report on the Brixton disorders, which had questioned the existence of institutional racism. The Commission's paper attempted to "clarify the meaning of institutional racism and point to its existence in British society". The issue of "institutional racism" would not be fully resolved for another fifteen years, when the Macpherson Inquiry published its report on the murder of Stephen Lawrence.

During 1983–84, the Bishop's Conference went through a major restructuring. In place of CCRJ, a new advisory body to the bishops was created – the Committee for Community Relations. At the same time, a lengthy consultation led to the establishment of an independent, grassroots, Black-led, Catholic race relations organization – the Catholic Association for Racial Justice (CARJ). The new Committee and CARJ decided to work closely together.

The Committee for Community Relations (1984–2002)

It was agreed that the new Committee's work would include "race relations, urban poverty and community development".

Racism awareness training

One of the early priorities of the Committee was to help fellow Christians understand the complexities of racism. The Methodists had established the Methodist and Ecumenical Leadership Race Awareness Workshops (MELRAW), and in 1985 the Committee entered into a formal partnership with MELRAW to offer racism awareness workshops, both in the Catholic community and ecumenically. This partnership lasted from 1985 until 1997.

Education

With the publication of the Swann Report "Education for All" and the Catholic report "Learning from Diversity", both released in 1985, the new Committee decided to undertake further research into Catholic education. From 1990 to 1997, the Committee acted as secretariat to a cross-departmental working group within the Bishops' Conference on Catholic Schools and Other Faiths. In 1997, the working group published a report and guidelines on "Catholic Schools and Other Faiths".

From 1995, the Committee, in collaboration with others, organized a consultation into Catholic primary and secondary schools in poor urban areas. The report, "A Struggle for Excellence: Catholic Secondary Schools in Urban Poverty Areas", was published in 1997; and the second report, "Foundations for Excellence: Catholic Primary Schools in Urban Poverty Areas", was published in July 1999. Both reports examined in detail the specific challenges that schools in poorer areas were facing.

Continuing this collaborative research into Catholic schools, the group produced the report, "Ethnicity, Identity and Achievement in Catholic Education" in 2003. It included case studies of good practice and a survey of the experiences and views of Minority Ethnic pupils in the participating schools.

Urban poverty and community development

Following the Church of England's publication "Faith in the City" (1985), the Committee began giving more attention to urban poverty and community development alongside its continuing interest in racial justice. In 1992, the Committee published "From Charity to Empowerment: The Church's Mission Alongside Poor and Marginalized People", which included a reflection on different approaches to community development and community organizing.

Then, in 1994, the Committee initiated an Urban Poverty Round Table, which met three times a year and was open to all. Over a period of more than ten years (1994–2004), Catholics and others from different parts of the country participated.

In 1997, the Committee published a paper entitled "Acting Together for Change", which traced the history, theory, and practice of broad-based community organizing both in the USA and in the UK.

Institutional racism

In 1999, some years after the murder of Stephen Lawrence, the Macpherson Report finally addressed the issue of institutional racism. The bishops welcomed the report and encouraged Catholic organizations to review themselves in the light of it and its "useful definition of institutional racism". The Committee published guidelines and organized the review, which lasted for two years. More than sixty Catholic organizations participated, and the Committee reported on the review to the Bishops' Conference in 2001.

Northern towns

Following disturbances in Oldham, Burnley, and Bradford during the summer of 2001, the Committee circulated a briefing, "Racial

Disturbances in Oldham, Burnley, Bradford and Other Northern Towns", and over the next few years participated in an ecumenical Northern Towns Working Group brought together by the Churches Commission for Racial Justice.

Gypsies and travellers

From 2004, a Gypsy and Traveller Support Network began meeting at the Bishops' Conference. From 2006 the Network published a newsletter – *Pilgrim Catholic* – which appeared twice a year until 2011.

Transition

After 2002, the Committee for Community Relations was gradually wound down as an advisory body within the Bishops' Conference. However, some of its work continued over the next few years. Notable was the new Traveller Support Network that had begun meeting at the Bishops' Conference. By 2009, the Committee's library of books and papers had been moved to the Catholic Association for Racial Justice (CARJ), and some of the work of the Committee had been taken on by CARJ. Among other things, CARJ took over responsibility for servicing and convening an Urban Network and the Traveller Support Network.

The Catholic Association for Racial Justice (1984 – today)

The Catholic Association for Racial Justice (CARJ) had been established in September 1984. From the beginning, CARJ saw itself as a Black-led, independent organization where people of African, Caribbean, and Asian descent could find support, have a voice, and work with others for racial justice in church and society. Throughout the decades of its existence, the Chair of CARJ, the majority of the trustees, and most of the staff have been from Black, Asian, and Minority Ethnic backgrounds.

Cardinal Hume was the keynote speaker at the CARJ AGM on 27 June 1986. His talk on "Racism: The Need for Positive Action" was later published in pamphlet form and distributed widely in the Catholic community.

The First National Congress of Black Catholics, organized by CARJ, took place 13–15 July 1990 at Digby Stuart College, Roehampton. Some three hundred participants attended the weekend event. One of the regulations at the event was that only Black people could speak in formal sessions. So, those White people in attendance, including a number of bishops, had to sit in silence and listen to Black people speak from their experience of being Black in Britain.

In 1994, the Bishops' Conference agreed to participate in an annual, ecumenical Racial Justice Sunday. CARJ was asked to organize Catholic participation in the event each year and received some of the funds collected from Catholic parishes. This enabled CARJ to appoint a full-time director.

CARJ was very aware of the important role of the priest in the Catholic community. In May 1996, CARJ produced a report on "Black Vocations", which recommended further training for vocations directors, rectors of seminaries, and seminarians. About the same time, CARJ began working with the National Conference of Priests (NCP) on a series of initiatives, including the establishment of a support group for priests of African and Asian descent.

From 1999, for a number of years, CARJ worked closely with Liverpool Hope University to support its Black Science Summer School. A significant number of students who attended the Summer School went on to study for degrees in science-based subjects.

In 2001, CARJ cooperated with the Bishops' Committee for Community Relations to offer an Adult Formation Programme for Minority Ethnic Catholics in parishes. The aim of the programme was to enable those from Ethnic Minorities to take on leadership roles in their parishes

In September 2003, CARJ organized a National Racial Justice Congress. The theme was "People of Colour, People of God". The Congress took place at Southlands College, Roehampton, where Catholics and ecumenical contacts from diverse backgrounds gathered for a weekend. In the Congress Charter, delegates committed themselves to:

> analyse the structural causes of racism in Church and society... to pray and work for a conversion of hearts... to be a rock of support that victims of racism can rely upon... to create communities in which strangers are welcomed... to ensure that schools

value diversity... that seminary training includes multicultural formation... to influence Catholic organisations and networks... to challenge, support and work as partners with bishops and priests... and to work towards the eradication of racism.[1]

Following the Congress, CARJ began to reflect on the commitment that had been made to prioritize work with young people and schools. In 2006, it initiated an eighteen-month pilot project with seven schools, working regularly with small groups in each school. In early summer 2007 the project was evaluated as "positive, supportive and transforming", and two part-time workers were appointed to continue and develop the project.

During 2008, CARJ began to make plans for its twenty-fifth anniversary celebrations, which would take place in 2009.

The Past Ten Years: A Process Skewed by Brexit (2009–2019)

On 7 November 2009, CARJ marked its twenty-fifth anniversary with a celebration at Westminster Cathedral. The theme for the anniversary was "The Changing Face of Britain", and the perspective running through the celebration was largely positive:

> CARJ wishes to acknowledge and to celebrate all that has changed for the better over the past 25 years and the progress that we have all made toward becoming a truly inclusive Church in a truly inclusive society.[2]

Ten years later, in 2019, CARJ was striking a different note, reminding us of the complex challenges we still face:

> The BREXIT Referendum has highlighted some of the serious divisions in our society. These divisions are set against the threat of terrorism, migration to and from the UK, a widening gap between rich and poor, discrimination, disadvantage and hate crime. In the face of this complex local and global challenge, we in CARJ are seeking a strategy which offers equality and community to the diverse groups who need support.[3]

CARJ argued that "these contrasting perspectives are both true – they represent two sides of UK society and a ten year process of evolution skewed by BREXIT".

Schools and young people

In 2006, CARJ started to develop a project with schools and young people. Over the years, a team of associates were appointed to work on behalf of CARJ with primary and secondary schools.

On 19 May 2011, CARJ held a Conference on "Identity, Achievement and Active Citizenship through Catholic Education" at Farm Street Jesuit Church in London. The Conference reflected on the experience of Cristo Rey Schools in the USA and other examples globally of initiatives in Catholic education to support young people from diverse ethnic and social backgrounds.

In June 2014, CARJ produced a report, "Stepping Stones to a More Equal Society", which reviewed a variety of educational initiatives designed to support schools, families, and young people in marginalized communities. This was followed by two Stepping Stones seminars in London (2014) and Leeds (2015).

In 2012, CARJ received funding to establish a satellite young people's project in Liverpool. The Liverpool project commenced on 1 April 2013 to work with young people in a variety of contexts, such as the Belvidere Homeless Shelter, St Vincent's School for the Blind, a Sports Leaders Award in two schools, a gospel choir in two inner-city primary schools, and an African animals project in five schools. The project expanded and continues today.

On 10–12 July 2014, CARJ organized a Young People's Congress on World Citizenship in Liverpool. Young people from Catholic secondary schools gathered at Liverpool Hope University. The Congress was a rich experience for all concerned, and a key moment in the event was the testimony of a young Traveller who spoke of her long struggle to overcome prejudice and discrimination.

Gypsies, Roma, and Travellers

Since 2009, the CARJ Traveller Support Network has been meeting three or four times a year to discuss issues relating to Gypsy, Roma, and

Traveller (GRT) communities and to provide opportunities for mutual support among those involved in a ministry to Travellers. The Network is made up of priests, lay people, academics, and representatives of other organizations.

A Rome pilgrimage for Travellers took place from 22 to 27 October 2015, when more than eight thousand Travellers from all over the world gathered in Rome. A number of members of the Network attended with their diocesan groups, and the event included visits to holy places, Sunday Mass, and a Papal Audience. Pope Francis called for better treatment of Travelling People and an acceptance of customs and lifestyles different from our own.

In 2016, Fr Dan Mason was appointed National Chaplain to GRT communities. He has been a very important support to others working in this area and a regular member of the CARJ Network.

CARJ is also represented at the ecumenical Churches Network for Gypsies, Travellers and Roma (CNGTR), which meets every few months and gives us contact with people working in this area in other churches.

Poverty and inequality

The CARJ Urban Network, which grew out of the earlier Round Table, includes 125 participants from across England and Wales. The Network meets two or three times a year to discuss key issues such as housing, health, employment, and criminal justice. A note of the meeting goes to the entire Network and we stay in touch as issues arise. The Urban Network has for years been a place where colleagues with similar concerns can meet face to face and discuss serious issues in some depth.

Caste discrimination in the UK

In 2009–10, CARJ began working with Voice of Dalit International (VODI) to support victims of caste discrimination and to address issues of caste discrimination in the UK. In 2013, the Christian Network Against Caste Discrimination (CNACD) was formed. CNACD organized a non-residential conference on Christian Responsibility to Dalits and Caste Discrimination, on 18 and 19 February 2014, at St George's Cathedral, Southwark. The Network held another Conference on 2–3 May 2017, at which Cardinal Turkson was the keynote speaker.

Leadership training

Over a period of five years, CARJ worked in partnership with VODI and Maryvale Institute, Birmingham, to develop a training programme in "Leadership for Social Change". Participants were drawn from the UK and India. The workshops aimed to prepare participants to work more thoughtfully and effectively for social change – especially in those movements defined or inspired by issues of race, caste, religion, and class.

Public policy

Over the years, important issues have been discussed publicly, and these discussions have influenced public policy. Sometimes these issues take many years to be resolved. CARJ has tried to stay in touch with these issues, and where appropriate they have made submissions to government inquiries and consultations, such as the following:

- In July 2015, Dame Louise Casey was asked to look into the situation of isolated and deprived communities. CARJ made a submission to the Review.
- In January 2016, Rt Hon David Lammy MP was asked to lead a Review of the Criminal Justice System in England and Wales and to investigate evidence of possible racial bias. CARJ and Caritas Social Action Network (CSAN) made a joint submission to the Review.
- In September 2016, the Government published the "Education Green Paper: Schools that Work for Everyone". CARJ submitted a response to the consultation.
- In 2016, the Women and Equalities Committee initiated an Inquiry into inequalities experienced by Gypsy, Roma, and Traveller communities. Caritas Social Action Network (CSAN) joined CARJ in making a submission to the Inquiry.
- In 2018, the Government published its "Integrated Communities Strategy Green Paper", and CARJ made a submission to the Consultation.
- In 2018, Professor Tendayi Achiume, the United Nations Special Rapporteur on contemporary forms of racism, made an official visit to the UK. CARJ submitted a paper in preparation for her visit, during which CARJ was invited with others to participate in a round table session.

Brexit

The Brexit Referendum and the ensuing process of leaving the EU has changed UK society, polarizing communities, families, and political parties and surfacing underlying tensions. During years of debate, before and after the Referendum, the UK became more divided and saw increased incidents of hate crime, anti-Semitism, Islamophobia, the Windrush scandal, and terrorist attacks in London and Manchester.

CARJ sees it as an important part of its mission to identify and support vulnerable groups. The publication of the Government's Race Disparity Audit was helpful in spelling out the complexities of racial disparities in UK society and identifying vulnerable groups.

In October 2019, CARJ held a national conference on "Belonging: A Challenge for the Church in a Diverse Society". The conference was an opportunity for Catholics from across England and Wales to share ideas and experience on how we can help new and marginalized groups feel they truly belong in UK society. Representatives from fifteen dioceses, various CARJ networks, and other Catholic organizations attended.

On 2 November 2019, the AGM marked CARJ's thirty-fifth anniversary by exploring the theme, "Looking Back Reflectively in Order to Move Forward in Hope".

A Wider Perspective

The work for racial justice, briefly described above, is only a partial picture, which should be seen in a wider context. The prejudice, discrimination, and disadvantage suffered by ethnic minorities is linked to the suffering of other groups that are marginalized by poverty, culture, language, religion, or geography. The struggle for racial justice is part of a wider struggle – namely the effort to create a more just, more equal, more cooperative society for all.

A fuller picture of the Catholic community's involvement in work for racial justice might include many other individuals, groups, and organizations at national, regional, and local level. One might even suggest that wherever the Word is spoken and heard, a seed is planted for a more just, more equal, more cooperative society.

Notes

With permission from CARJ, this chapter draws on two earlier publications: "The Catholic Church and Race Relations in England & Wales 1970–2008" (CARJ, 6 January 2009) and "A History of the Past Ten Years" (CARJ, 1 May 2019). It also draws on the experience of the author who has been personally involved in this history from 1978 until today.

1 National Racial Justice Congress Charter, 2003.
2 CARJ 25th anniversary pamphlet, 2009.
3 Notice of CARJ AGM, 3 November 2018.

Chapter 6

The Journey Toward Racial Justice in the United Reformed Church

SANDRA ACKROYD

Introduction

My name is Sandra Ackroyd and I am a member of the United Reformed Church (URC). I have been an advocate and activist for racial justice and intercultural relations for more than thirty years. I have worked within the URC, ecumenically, and beyond, as a volunteer. This work has included many different aspects: awareness raising, educational, training, pastoral, projects, producing material with others for worship, and action, including challenging unjust practices discovered in the URC. The groups of people I have engaged with are church adult groups, youth groups, church committees, conferences, special events, and theological colleges. I have always worked as part of an ethnically diverse group of facilitators. Also, I have contributed to many of the training and educational resource materials referred to in this chapter. I feel blessed to have worked with so many people, in Britain and in other countries, who share the same commitment of working toward creating a just church and just a world.

Experiences that were local and personal, pre-1995

The year 1985 is my earliest memory of having to face the reality of racism and racial injustice in the community of Tottenham, north London, where I lived at the time. This was when the Broadwater Farm (housing estate) disturbances erupted. At the time, our sons were eleven and eight and our foster daughter was sixteen. That Sunday night on 6

October 1985, being within the police cordon, we telephoned people we knew on the estate, including a few church worshippers belonging to High Cross URC in Tottenham, to ask them to come to our house for the night. However, that was not possible as the police were stationed at every entrance/exit of the estate, so no one could leave or enter.

On the Saturday two weeks after the disturbances, I was invited to address the Thames North Synod meeting of the URC, to reflect on what had happened. I discussed the causes and the potential outcomes of the riot, including the racism of some police officers in their behaviour toward young Black people in particular. I helped to raise challenges that lay before us as churches and as a society.

For several years following, there was a lot of activity involving the police, the community, and churches in Tottenham. The borough deans and church ministers in Haringey became active in establishing Haringey's Peace Alliance, which later spread to other London boroughs. In May 2001, the Peace Alliance began to recruit a team of chaplains to work with the police. This team was composed mainly of Black church leaders from a diversity of churches. The minister of High Cross URC, Revd Francis Ackroyd, along with other church ministers, played a key part in these processes in Haringey.

During the period following the 1985 disturbances, the subject of racism and racial justice was a major topic for discussion and prayer in the local churches, including High Cross URC, which also worked with many young people. The discussions were not intellectual exercises; they were raw and painful. During the next few years, the debate about racism and racial justice in the URC moved from the local to the wider URC.

Developments in the URC

In the Thames North Synod in the 1990s it was becoming more obvious that awareness of the needs of "urban" churches, most of which were multi-ethnic and multicultural, needed attention. What became known as the Urban Churches Support Group was set up, with part-time workers who engaged with urban churches across the Southern and Thames North Synods. I was one of these workers (1998–2011). During the 1980s, we established Cause for Celebration, an annual event that subsequently led to the initiation of a survey to determine the situation of Black leadership in our churches. The survey recognized that the denomination needed to recruit a worker to help the churches and denomination to be able to face the challenges of racism in society and in church life. Plans needed to be put in place; a resolution was formulated and taken to a Thames North Synod meeting. This was passed and subsequently sent to the URC General Assembly, where the resolution was carried with a large majority.

Our first worker was Revd Dr Marjorie Lewis from the United Church in Jamaica and the Cayman Islands. Our second worker was Dr Katalina Tahaafe-Williams, from the Uniting Church of Australia; the third was Revd Dr Michael Jagessar, a URC minister. During the last few years of Michael's ministry, the job of Secretary for Racial Justice and Intercultural Ministry was changed to include Global Ministries, and Commitment for Life.

One initiative that had some very positive outcomes was a youth exchange programme, which was a landmark for some young people in the URC. This initiative was formed between the URC and the United Church in Jamaica and the Cayman Islands. Discussion took place between youth ministers in Jamaica, me as a Youth Leadership Training Officer (YLTO) in the URC, and officers of the Council for World Mission. The initiative was thought to be relevant for many reasons, especially because there were growing numbers of young people of Caribbean heritage belonging to British churches and youth activities run by the URC. This programme took place in three phases: 1988–89, 1991–92, and 1995–96. The latter two events included young people from the Congregational and Presbyterian Churches of Guyana as well.

For the last two programmes, the URC was part of the team led by Wallie Warmington (YLTO of West Midlands Synod) and me (YLTO of the Thames North Synod). Two of the young participants later trained for URC ministry, and a third one qualified as a Christian Youth Worker. All the URC young people who were involved over the years were invited to churches to lead worship and share their experiences of the exchange. Written reports were made and circulated among the churches across the Synods.

In the preparation for these programmes, we believed that sessions on race awareness and diversity issues were extremely important for young people from Britain to engage with, before going to the Caribbean. Also, all three programmes included a few young Black people from URC churches. Many friendships were made between the young people across Jamaica, Guyana, and the UK.

Sadly, the finance to fund such programmes was not available beyond the mid-1990s. It was hoped that other such programmes between the URC and churches in other countries would evolve.

Benefits of Working Ecumenically in Racial Justice Initiatives from 1995 to 2012

With the URC being an ecumenical Church comprising the three denominations – Congregational, Presbyterian, and Churches of Christ – it seemed natural to engage in several racial justice initiatives ecumenically. Also, we have a number of united churches, together with Methodists, Baptists, and Anglicans. In the URC, in some of our Synods were Local Ecumenical Projects (LEPs). The URC had developed a commitment to Racial Justice Sunday, which I will expand on later.

My ecumenical experience included developing work with race awareness training and working with local churches and groups of churches. We ran short courses for training the trainer, enabling facilitators to work with church groups in race awareness. We also produced resource materials ecumenically. For example, "Strangers No More", "Workers for the Harvest" (URC/Methodist), "We Belong" (URC/Baptist), "Let Justice Flow" (URC/Christian Aid), and "Challenging Racism" (A Youth Work Pack URC/Evangelical Christians for Racial Justice). There were others, such as a children's resource called "Just Now Stories".

The benefits of working together in small ecumenical groups were numerous. In selecting worship material together, we learnt more about the aspects of worship that are precious to different traditions, and how we were able to take on board the differences with which we may have been unfamiliar. Each tradition was able to bring resources such as hymns, meditations, and prayers to the table. Biblical reflection was also creative: in terms of education, we were able to learn a lot about how the different denominations approached racism in communities and churches. Some denominations had been involved in initiating projects and programmes relating to different issues, such as asylum, sanctuary, and refugee work. Others have run courses and training sessions for church groups, to improve awareness and good practice.

We grew spiritually because of growing insights into each other's spirituality. I was privileged to work with Revd Arlington Trotman, the Secretary for the Churches Commission for Racial Justice (CCRJ) from 1998 to 2006. (Revd David Haslam was the former head, but he had moved on by the time I became involved in this initiative.) Being an active part of CCRJ meant we interconnected with other racial justice initiatives. Also, we were able to build working relationships with the racial justice officers from the other church denominations who were engaged with training programmes in churches. When Churches Together in Britain and Ireland (CTBI) decided to bring CCRJ to a close, we lost its worker and much of the ecumenical work came to a standstill.

Around the same time as this was happening, we saw the demise of denominational racial justice officers, or saw them take on a different workload that would include equalities in general, racial justice and intercultural ministry being just one of several.

These decisions saw the ending of much ecumenical working together because the ecumenical structures, as well as denominational structures, were removed or changed. Volunteers alone were not able to resource and continue to develop work on racial justice issues. The kind of ecumenical work involving the production of material for Racial Justice Sunday and other publications seems to have gone into a backwater. Without the structure of CCRJ being in place, it has been more difficult for many churches to know how to access material.

Racial Justice Sunday

As referred to earlier, each year the churches set aside a special Sunday, normally in September but more recently in February, when it was hoped that they would focus on particular issues relating to racial justice, including biblical reflection, worship, practical activities, information for discussion, and suggested action. Most of our sources were British based, but we also included insights and resources from other countries, including songs. This group was fluid from year to year, and included a few people who participated each year. This group was well supported by CTBI, particularly through the CCRJ worker. In the URC, the initiative to address this nature of work came from the grassroots.

The seeds were sown in the previously mentioned event, Cause for Celebration, involving the Thames North and Southern Synods. In working with the aforementioned Revd Arlington Trotman, who was then CCRJ Secretary, I really appreciated the strong pastoral care element that he developed with families, as part of his role, especially Black families who had lost children to gun and knife crime, as well as a few whose children had died in police custody. Arlington provided much pastoral care and support to these families in their loss. (It is important to note that young people have died through aggressive handling by police over the years. Other high-profile cases have taken place that predate George Floyd in the USA, also involving suffocation.)

I have a poignant memory of two occasions when services were held, bringing together so many suffering families for worship and fellowship. My strongest memory was of the service in Southwark Cathedral, London, organized by Arlington; the worship was truly powerful, and engaging with families afterwards was very moving, humbling, and thought provoking.

Examples of Racial Justice Sunday Materials

Racial Justice Sunday invariably has a theme, and in 1996 the theme was "We Belong to One Another", and this continued to be the main theme for several years afterwards. The topic was drawn from Romans 12:9–13, and the material was centred on the importance of loving one another as sisters and brothers, and on having a profound respect for each other. The act of penitence in the worship that year was:

Lord, forgive us for the silence that
Condones injustice
Withholds forgiveness
Disguises anger
Prolongs quarrels
Breeds misunderstandings
Shows contempt
Permits ignorance
Kills love
Expresses indifference

Increases fear
Makes barriers.
Lord, have mercy.

In 2001, the Racial Justice Sunday material highlighted the plight of refugees and asylum seekers in Britain and abroad. That year's title was "Reflection: The Church, Refugees, and Asylum Seekers" and stated that both in the Bible and in people's experiences, God often comes as a voice or a stranger. Examples in the Bible include Abraham and Elijah (Genesis 18; 1 Kings 17), and on the road to Emmaus when, after his resurrection, Jesus appeared to his disciples as a stranger (Luke 24:13–35). The resource explored the definitions of refugee and asylum seeker and why and how people become refugees. The reasons include war, political persecution, environmental disaster, rape, and genocide. In addition, the resource contained stories from people who shared what it felt like for them as asylum seekers in the United Kingdom and Northern Ireland, which included experiences of trauma, nightmares, and so on. The publication also revealed that the official welcome which asylum seekers receive in Britain is often based on disbelief, detention, dispersal, and discrimination. And it noted that many churches and other groups were doing beneficial work with asylum seekers at a local level, with many more opportunities opening up. The worship material that year included a poem/meditation on justice:

A Prayer for Justice

Bring liberation in
Root out the sin
Of prejudice and power
Plant seed, grow flowers

Destroy unjust structures
Cause dissent and disruption
Until people, put down,
Can wear a gold crown

Till they claim their place
In the human race

Sitting round the table
Not the Tower of Babel

Sharing Pentecost grace
Reflecting God's face
In all the diversity
Discovering divinity
(Sandra Ackroyd)

In 2009, the Racial Justice Sunday theme was "One Race, the Human Race" and included a question Jesus asked his disciples (Mark 8:29): "Who do you say I am?" as a strapline. In this material there were articles on what it means to be a stranger and what it may mean to be a foreigner. One writer suggested that a stranger was a "person in a place or company that he/she did not belong to and felt like a stranger". The resource suggested that a "foreigner was a person who was born in a foreign country or speaks a foreign language". Equally, they may feel that "they do not belong to a place due to the colour of their skin or the way they speak". The resource noted that such a person is made to feel like an outsider when people stare at them, or receive constant reminders that, "You're not from here," which can create difficulties for them in gaining their footing.

The resource pointed to Jesus' words, "Who do you say I am?" (Mark 8:29), and says that they become clearer as we practise the Gospel stories, not as bystanders, but like Jesus: responding to the hurts, hopes, fears, and confusion of the people standing in front of him. It also highlighted that on another occasion Jesus said, "Whatever you did for one of the least of these brothers and sisters of mine, you did for me" (Matthew 25:40), which may indicate that Jesus' question, "Who do you say I am?" cannot be answered apart from the question "Who is my neighbour?" (Luke 10:29). The resource argued that these lead to a question asked of our churches: "How can the church embody grace in a multicultural, diverse, and complex world?" It recognized that churches are called upon not just to soothe and comfort those already present, but also to invite and welcome all who would never think of wanting to be there, because they believe that they are not welcome as they are.

In 2015, Inderjit Bhogal (Leeds Church Institute, in partnership with CTBI) developed some material, "Hospitality and Sanctuary for all: I was a stranger and you welcomed me" (based on Matthew 25:35). Here we learn that God is revealed in the Bible as a companion, accompanying people in all their journeys and as someone who is present with them in all contexts. It is in their journeying that people encounter God, and particularly in the context of hospitality to the stranger (Genesis 18:2). The writer of this material goes on to raise awareness and suggestions for positive action – there is a very long list of how to consider working toward making our city, town, village, church, school, university, club, or place of work a "sanctuary" committed to building cultures of welcome and hospitality, especially for those in greatest need and danger. We are encouraged to do what we can to end hatred and hostility and to build harmonious and hospitable communities where all are welcomed, valued, and belong equally.

Since the end of CCRJ, a few individual denominations have produced some material online, which can be accessed by other churches for Racial Justice Sunday, for example, material produced by the Catholic Association for Racial Justice (CARJ). Also, during 2017 the URC provided some Racial Justice Sunday material, which was put together by a group of people drawn from the Advocates for Global and Intercultural Ministries team. The theme was "Choosing a Side", and the sub-themes included "Choose life" and "Way of Faithfulness". The resources invited us to internalize and inhabit a new way of being and living. They spoke of the difficulty in giving one's heart and being entirely orientated to goodness, love, and doing justice. In the Beatitudes (Matthew 5:3–12), Jesus offers a more radical ethic, commenting on the poor in Spirit, those who mourn, and the pure in heart, that they are all blessed, although not necessarily paragons of virtue; what is important is the inward orientation of the heart.

Further Development of Racial Justice Work in the URC: 2000–2020

The URC has developed different programmes at various times in its work to address the challenges of racial justice. These programmes were invariably introduced by the URC Racial Justice Secretaries, following feedback from people working on racial justice issues on the ground. The first of such programmes was "The Multicultural Ministry Toolkit", a training resource for growing multicultural churches. This resource focused on the importance of welcome and hospitality being at the centre of all we do. It also explored the centrality of worship, liturgy, theology, spirituality, and the Bible to our exploration of racism and overcoming of prejudice. The toolkit argued that supportive and positive leadership is essential throughout and reminded us that we live, work, and worship across different age groups, and so intergenerational relations need to be worked on. It also explored rites of passage in relation to ideas and practices of different ethnic groups around birth, baptism, marriage, and death, and so on. In 2005, the URC acted prophetically and proclaimed itself to be a "multicultural church". It heard God's call to be a community where all are welcome and the gifts of all cultures valued. As a denomination, we realized that it is only by encouraging each other in all our diversity that we will appreciate the full richness of the Christ who comes to each of us in our own cultures.

This toolkit, which was compiled by Katalina Tahaafe-Williams, offered all of us the opportunity to learn more of God's extraordinary love and grace as we learnt to accept the Christ in each other. A few years later, Michael Jagessar, who was then the Racial Justice Secretary, introduced the second programme, which was known as "Multicultural Church, Intercultural Habit" and which was launched at the URC General Assembly in 2008. This movement and process was promoting a way of being and living, drawing from the belief in the abundant generosity of God made real through Jesus Christ. The purpose was to model a habit of generous lives as we try to fulfil the following:

- Being open to, trusting in, and being joyful at the leading of God's Spirit;
- Committing ourselves to deepening our discerning and rereading of our biblical and spiritual basis of intercultural life together;
- Affirming new and different experiences, recognizing a variety of expressions of the one faith;
- Journeying beyond our cultural comfort zones and boundaries;
- Seeking to become an enlarged, inclusive, welcoming, and justice-seeking community;
- Engaging in the transformation of heart, mind, structure, and policy; trying to redress power balances, challenging systemic injustice, generally cultivating diverse leadership, and seeking participation of all;

- Working intentionally toward mutuality in giving and sharing, for all of us are in need. All must be ready to be mutually inconvenienced for the sake of the other and the gospel;
- Committing ourselves to the constant habit of self-examination, lifelong learning, and reflection through ongoing education, training, monitoring, and evaluation of our intercultural engagement.

Groups of people in churches tried and tested these principles through storytelling and discussion points, including grappling with some of the barriers and blockages that people in churches, sometimes without realizing it, use to prevent the church and individual Christians from implementing the points in the charter. For example, some groups focused on joy, highlighting the fact that joyless faces and voices are unlikely to attract and embrace others, particularly newcomers.

Some found the idea of rereading the Bible and looking at our theological basis in the context of our intercultural life together to be very exciting, especially when we can discover new insights that we had never thought of before. It was recognized that it was not possible for a whole group of people to look at inclusivity in the same way. However, justice seeking had to be a priority. There were different perspectives about justice, and some areas of justice seemed to conflict with others. This provided the space to explore such issues by listening to one another, which is a very important activity if we are to move forward as a church in relation to justice and inclusivity.

Then the power imbalance became a talking point as people discussed how to welcome people into leadership roles and how to encourage them to use their gifts and skills in the life of the church and the community. It was felt that leaders who liked to hang on to their power needed to be helped to deal with their insecurities. Those with power need to have the humility to hand it on to others, and to support and trust new people. We felt that the church had lost the art of personal invitation and preferred to issue general invitations in church notices or via group emails. Comments were made that Jesus never stuck notices on a tree to invite people to do things. Neither did he stand on the side of Lake Galilee announcing information and offering invitations to disciples and potential disciples. Jesus invited people by name to come and follow him to help build the work of God's kingdom. We remember, for example, the story of Zacchaeus, when Jesus called him to come down from the tree and said he would go and have tea with him, which resulted in Zacchaeus becoming a follower of Jesus and changing his behaviour toward his fellow human beings (Luke 19:1–10).

Another issue relating to reflections on the main points of the "Multicultural Church, Intercultural Habit Charter" is that of considering the idea of all being mutually inconvenienced for the sake of the other and the gospel (see earlier bullet point). During the discussion we revisited the issues of comfort zones. In order to come out from our comfort zones we need to reset our mindsets and attempt to get into the shoes of others, to see things from other points of view, thus enabling us to reflect at a deeper and wider level.

We need to acknowledge that change in our faith journeys and in church life is inevitable, and presents new opportunities for us to grow. We can also grow by committing to habits of self-examination, learning, education, and evaluation, with storytelling becoming an essential aspect. Through self-examination, it is possible to converse and be able to engage with others with humility. We must be careful not to repeat things we have heard without thinking them through and checking them out. It is also important for us to look on the other side, even if we thoroughly disagree and would not take it on. Jesus challenged people's inability to change, and encouraged them to see things differently for the sake of the gospel at all levels (personal, church, community, society, global, and so on). We need to do the same.

Following our tradition of producing training and educational materials, the URC initiated a new resource in 2016, called "Diversity Awareness Conversation". This included conversations on identity, diversity, and difference, uncovering the 3 Ps – power, prejudice, and privilege – challenging and changing cultural practices, working within structures, and policies and practices.

In March 2020, Karen Campbell, who had been a URC-linked Community Worker, became the URC's fourth Secretary for Intercultural Relations. She came into office at the beginning of the COVID-19 outbreak and the first lockdown. However, during that difficult year, the URC (some URC-initiated and others in partnership with other justice bodies) was able to introduce seminars and webinars, through Zoom, featuring issues and situations relating to Black Lives Matter and the legacies of transatlantic slavery. Also, at the Mission Council Committee of the URC in November 2020, a resolution was passed, committing the URC to a journey toward becoming an anti-racist church. The General Assembly of the URC's Task Group for Affirmative Action is endorsing the report that is challenging the Church to take positive action towards being an anti-racist church in terms of recruitment and representation.

Moving Forward

There has been acknowledgement of some progress made through the years, and the value of race awareness education that has taken place. However, it has been recognized that these initiatives in themselves were not enough, hence the need for the November 2020 resolution which challenged the church to look forward, opening up new possibilities of working together in different ways. We as a denomination need to examine the cultural practices by which we shape our organization, such as looking at our committees, our networks, and other decision-making bodies. Do they enable inclusion, or do they exclude different groups of people by the way they do things?

The "Legacies of Transatlantic Slavery Task Group" is working toward the URC making a Confession and Apology, both within and beyond the URC, including global partners in Africa and the Caribbean. The URC is also committed to making reparations that are working toward practical actions to address the negative impacts of the legacies of Transatlantic Slavery on Black communities in the UK, Caribbean and Africa. The Methodist Church has been journeying with the URC in reflecting on these challenges.

One resource that has proved invaluable is that of a network of people, known as Racial Justice Advocates. Advocates were recruited and appointed in synods across the URC at about the same time as we appointed our first Racial Justice Secretary. They have supported and explored racial justice issues in the communities and synods they serve. Currently, we need to strengthen and develop this network, which can support the work of anti-racism. These advocates also give support to those who are challenging injustices in society and churches, and promote good practice in following guidelines for presentations in our churches – considering language and visual images used, inclusion of people in photos, leadership, and so on. It is not enough to tick boxes and think we have achieved equal opportunities and inclusion. Are people feeling valued and enabled to make their contribution? It is not sufficient just to be around the table. They need to be able to be heard and valued for who they are and what they can offer.

The resolution discussion included that it is insufficient to affirm that all lives matter (stating the obvious), when Black lives particularly have been treated as if they do not matter. The resolution also draws attention to the need for examination and change in relation to our church structures and policies, our leadership at all levels, our processes and practices, our theologies, and our relationships. Furthermore, if we are serious about being an anti-racist church, we need to understand the significances of White privilege, the issue of the use of power, and the need for power sharing. It will require most of us to leave our comfort zones and open our hearts and minds to bring about new ways of being, for the sake of God's kingdom in his world today.

Chapter 7

Black Majority Churches and Racial Justice in Britain

MARK STURGE

This chapter is a personal reflection on the engagement of Black Majority Churches (BMCs) in Britain and their efforts over the last twenty-five years to address the racism that is still evident in British churches and society.

The Context of Racial Justice Sunday

Racial Justice Sunday was a late addition to the life of BMCs from the Caribbean diaspora. These churches had been in existence for forty-five years, since after the Second World War when migrants arrived in Britain en masse and by invitation of the British government, on the HMT *Empire Windrush* in 1948, and other similar vessels.[1] They were also an early companion to churches from the African diaspora in the late 1990s. From their inception, churches emerging from Africa and the Caribbean had to grapple with the issue of race. Their genesis was a combination of a call to mission and the need to belong to and identify with their community, which provided a home away from home. They were a counterpoint to experiences of living in a racialized society that espoused the loquacious and derogatory sentiments of "No Blacks, No Irish, No Dogs". As we have come to realize, but might never accept, the churches reflected, and still do to this day, the same cultures and behaviours as the rest of society.

Black Christian leaders were in no doubt that their existence as separate entities, with visual homogeneity – yet multicultural, multi-ethnic congregations, with a dominant culture – and alternative ways of worship, were two sides of a coin. On the one side, they represented a failure of the "established" or host congregations to adequately welcome, integrate, or make room for them; and on the other side, they were responding to God's mission of rescue and care for the migrating flocks. Migrants' response to the rejection was either to abandon Christianity or to use their agency to embrace more fully the communities of Black-led mission. Notwithstanding, some members of the community had better experiences and remained part of the "historic" denominations.

Most African and Caribbean leaders saw race as a political matter and wanted to keep politics out of their pulpit. However, their very existence meant the issue of race was never absent from their minds. The place to deal with race, and its consequences, was through prayer, intercession, and intervention when it was in their gift to act. Nevertheless, seminal works like Ira V. Brooks' *Where Do We Go from Here?* (1982) and *Another Gentleman to the Ministry* (1986); Philip Mohabir's *Building Bridges* (1988) and *Pioneers or Settlers* (1991); Revd Io Smith's *An Ebony Cross* (1989); Revd Phyllis Thompson's *Here to Stay* (1990); Bishop Dr Selwyn Arnold's *From Scepticism to Hope* (1992); Joel Edwards' *Let's Praise Him Again!* (1992) and, later, Overseer Oliver Lyseight's *Forward March* (1995), among others, all bear witness to the earlier convictions and wrestling with racism and discrimination within BMCs.[2]

Alongside these articulations were the establishing of institutions, with varying success. Archbishop David Douglas initiated The International Ministerial Council of Great Britain (1968), Oliver Lyseight co-founded The Afro-West Indian United Council of Churches (1976), The Centre for Black and White Christian Partnership was led by Bishop Patrick Kalilombe (1978), Father Olu Abiola formed The Council of African and Caribbean Council of Churches (1979), Revd Carmel Jones established The New Assembly of Churches and the Pentecostal Credit Union – the largest Black-owned credit union (1980); Revd Philip Mohabir established the West Indian Evangelical Alliance, later the African and Caribbean Evangelical Alliance (ACEA) in 1984; Bishop Esme Beswick started the Joint Council for Anglo Caribbean Churches, now the Joint Council of Churches for All Nations (1985).

Dr Joel Edwards, former General Secretary of ACEA and later General Director of the Evangelical Alliance, stated:

> Black Churches *and their institutions*, came into being to fulfil spiritual, social and cultural needs which would have otherwise have gone unmet – and the African and Caribbean church in the

UK is an indication of God's ability to meet a people's need through their ministry to themselves.[3]

However, Bishop Wilfred Wood, the Bishop of Croydon and the first Black Bishop in the Church of England, suggests, "Unquestionably it was the lack of genuine Christian love and fellowship on behalf of the host community which was the decisive factor in promoting burgeoning growth of black congregations."[4] On 25 October 2020, Revd Canon Jonathan Boardman of St Paul's Church, Clapham, London, issued an apology to Revd Carmel Jones who, as a seventeen-year-old, was told not to come back to the church. Although it has taken sixty-five years, it depicts the legacy and long tail of racism in the church.[5]

Race: An Uneasy Alliance

By the time I arrived as General Director of ACEA in 1996, the uneasiness with racism was well established. The murder of Stephen Lawrence in 1993 had put the issue of race back on the agenda, and responses from BMCs were limited. Over the years, there had been a fair amount of criticism and condemnation of the racism within and by the "historical" denominations. This same dissent and restlessness were also now present and directed toward BMCs, owing to their deafening silence in the public arena. Progressive and courageous leaders in the "historical" denominations publicly displayed their contrition, with repentance, at every opportunity. Racial justice coordinators undertook the uphill struggle to educate their leaders, and to improve the recruitment and progression of Minority Ethnic adherents to leadership and ministry.

My predecessor, Revd Ronald Nathan, had a much better grasp of the issues than I, and spoke prophetically to the community and disaffected members of BMCs, who felt that the church should have a bigger role to play on the issue. Yet, very early on, I was made acutely aware by senior church leaders that they were uncomfortable with the politicized and public stance ACEA had taken. They did not appreciate being in the firing line and being asked to account for their response, or lack of, to the issue of race.

Individually and privately, leaders had personal and shared convictions and transformative stories to tell. Bishop Delroy Powell,

Presiding Bishop of the New Testament Assembly, recalled the history of the denomination. His father, the late Bishop Melvin L. Powell, co-founded the denomination with Bishop Donald Bernard. It was at the New Testament Church of God's National Assembly in Tennessee, USA, where there was a rope on the floor that divided the Black leaders from the Whites ones, that his father decided, "If they cannot cross the rope then they would not cross the door again."

BMCs also emerged from mixed parenthood and oversight. The likes of Calvary Church of God in Christ, the African Methodist Episcopal Church, and the Ransom African Methodist Episcopal Zion Church were affiliated to African American denominations, while the New Testament Church of God, the Church of God of Prophecy, and the Seventh-day Adventists, who were by far the largest denominations, were overseen internationally by White-led denominations in the United States.

Churches from the African diaspora already had an African distinctiveness and separateness from the "historical" denominations in their home countries. Collectively, their heritage and churchmanship were either within the "historical" denominations or from distinctively African traditions and roots. The timing of their arrival meant that they did not have a long history of discrimination in Britain. Their primary challenge was the immigration status of their congregants. Yet there was a huge disconnect between the race dimension of immigration policies, the usurping of the law, and the right to remain in Britain, and their prayers. Racism, it seemed, was a Caribbean problem, largely owing to its history, socio-economic, and education status. Only much later was it acknowledged, by the leaders, that the African diaspora benefited from the sacrifices and pain of the Caribbean diaspora.

The Assemblies of God and Elim Pentecostal denominations, with a large segment of BMCs, also avoided the task of holding up a mirror on the issue of race. Their national leadership have over the years remained exclusively White. Unwittingly, they rely on the same arguments as the "historical" denominations: Black candidates not putting themselves forward; lack of experience; not seeing colour; it is not race but calling and gifts; and experience or language. All this when these same members are in leadership positions in the corporate sectors, are the most faithful givers, and often more gifted than their White counterparts. There is an ethos of culture management to retain a quintessentially English identity. I recall being asked by my White pastor, "What are you doing in an organization like ACEA?" Equally, Black leaders wanted a condition for my appointment at ACEA: to attend an African or Caribbean BMC.

This mixed heritage, the presence of mixed ethnicities, however small, and the dogged, if not misguided, belief that the White community and Christians per se will trample BMCs' doors, is a denial and abrogation of what has happened over the past twenty-five years where White flight has resulted in mixed congregations becoming Black. This misplaced hope and avoidance of racial discourse has made integration less likely, and impeded churches from speaking out with one voice on racial justice. Instead, the desire to attract White members to churches has resulted in "whitening" and "mis-advertising" their identities. Moreover, it leaves unchallenged anachronistic belief systems and worship practices that deify "Whiteness" and denigrate "Blackness" in iconography, hymnology, liturgy, and society at large.

There is another fundamental reason for this uneasiness. The *raison d'être* for both African and Caribbean leaders and congregations is mission. Their primary concern is soteriology (the doctrine of salvation) and eschatological hope (the last days and the return of Christ). These theological emphases rightly speak to the context of the lived experiences of their communities, including racism. They are concerned about the lives and lifestyles of their communities. They also place the churches' mission firmly in the realm of "rescue" and "escape" – rescue from sin and all its ills, and escape from the judgment and wrath of God. They also locate human existence in this world as temporary. These beliefs and tropes are reinforced with songs such as, "This World Is Not My Home; I'm Just a Passing Through".[6] The racial, economic, social injustice, and other suffering will pass – "We'll Soon Be Done With Troubles and Trials".[7] The names of churches not only speak to their fetishes and theological emphases, but also their ambition and scope as international churches.

Unity and its Fallacies

There is very little resistance and concern when it comes to unity and reconciliation. Unity has a sound theological premise (John 17:23; 1 Corinthians 1:10; 2 Corinthians 13:11; Galatians 3:28; Ephesians 4:11–13, for example). It is an essential part of what it means to be Christians and the church. Acknowledging and forgetting the past and creating a new co-existence is often the subliminal message. Ecumenically, The Centre for Black and White Christian Partnership was at the forefront, while among evangelicals, ACEA and the Evangelical Alliance were at the heart of this drive. The multiple efforts to promote unity in the Body of Christ, between Black and White Christians, churches, and institutions have been endless. Sad to say, they have all had a short shelf life.

To my mind, the cost of unity is too high. First, it is assumed that unity brings leaders, their congregations, and denominations together. In their seasons, events like Accord, Prayer for Christian Unity, and Missions to London, have brought Black and White Christians together to acknowledge our differences, hurts, hopes, and dreams. Unity, it seems, has been expressed as events and moments rather than movements with purpose and transformational outcomes (change that lasts).

The first place for transformation must be the church. However, to avoid navel gazing and introspection, the temptation is always to look outwards. Little acknowledgement is given to the fact that when we talk about unity, we avoid using the words "race" and "racial justice". It is not recognized that unity is a fast-forward button concerned about the future and the accompanying optics. Unity is escapism, isolating Christians from the realities of their communities and daily lives. Unity is where truth is moderated and sacrificed for its own sake and at the expense of godly transformation of the world we inhabit. During Joel Edwards' leadership, the Evangelical Alliance's strapline was, "All Uniting to Change Society". It should not surprise us that this disappeared at the end of his tenure. The inbuilt assumption and demand that we must also be changed and transformed was traded for "Making Jesus Known".

In my book, *Look What the Lord has Done! An Exploration of Black Christian Faith in Britain*, I define racism as an "inbred attitude based on assumptions, prejudices and stereotypes that are applied wholesale to an entire people group, which thereby disadvantages, excludes, and negatively discriminates against them". Further, I point out that "it is an attitude rather than an act because it is intrinsic to a culture's tradition, social arrangements, policies, processes, education and faith, as well as its development as a society".[8] It is this towering height that unity must overcome. Not only is it a tall order, but it also seems out of reach for the church to create a new reality that reflects God's ambition for all of his creation.

Understandably, there will be outliers and circumstances where individual congregations can attest to successfully integrating their communities. However, overall, it remains Black Christians and communities who make themselves vulnerable and join White majority congregations. It remains BMCs whose recognition is synonymous to "postcarding" – having their pictures taken by public figures soliciting support for their pet projects or securing votes for impending elections. While this is never acceptable, and even if it suffices, Black and White leaders need to acknowledge what their relationships are. If it is not unity, it is merely "postcarding" and therefore falls far short of the biblical and theological requirement for unity.

BMCs and Racial Justice Sunday

It is regrettable that BMCs have not embraced Racial Justice Sunday (RJS) in Britain. As is often the case, participation is determined by the origin of an initiative and who takes the lead to galvanize support. RJS was established by the Methodist Church as a result of the racially motivated killing of Stephen Lawrence in London in April 1993. In essence, RJS asked Christians to "Remember, Reflect and Respond" to racism in church and society by:

- Remembering the importance of racial justice;
- Reflecting on human diversity and thanking God for it;
- Responding by working to end injustice, racism, and ignorance through prayer and action.

BMCs simply did not engage with RJS and its methodology of linking church with society, and this was a lost opportunity. As an alternative to RJS, many developed Community Sundays and welcomed civic and community leaders. It might be unfair to suggest that this alternative was a deliberate "instead of"; however, it does represent where their focus and energies have resided. Some only focused on the challenge posed to the church and decided that as they naturally did not experience racism in their worshipping community, this was not an issue for them and they singularly failed to engage. Many "historical" churches in monocultural areas (with all White congregations) adopted a similar approach, which argues that no Black, Asian, or Minority Ethnic worshippers means they do not have a problem.

BMCs and Windrush Sunday

One of the many successes I had at ACEA was the institution of Windrush Sunday on 22 June 1998. It marked the fiftieth anniversary of the arrival HMT *Empire Windrush* with around 490 migrants from many Caribbean countries. It was a seminal moment for the Black Christian community as it signalled the birth of BMCs, who were now the most cohesive representation of African and Caribbean communities in Britain. There was to be a wider national awareness and it seemed unthinkable that the BMCs should not be reflected and acknowledged in the commemorations and celebrations. According to Angela Sarkis, then Chief Executive of the Church of England's Church Urban Fund and Vice President of ACEA, "The Black church is the success story of the arrival of the Windrush. Therefore, the church should not be an appendix to the celebration, but at the very heart of the celebration."[9]

I made the case that Windrush Sunday was for the rainbow spectrum of Christian churches in the UK, and we needed to thank God for:

- The birth and contributions of BMCs in the UK;
- The faithfulness of the early pioneers, who struggled and overcame, despite the difficult situations and injustices they faced in the early years;
- The vitality and "fresh rush of wind of the Spirit", which the pioneers brought to Britain and which remains one of the hallmarks of the BMCs today.

The BMCs' achievements included being an economic force, the level of educational achievement and employment of their members, their community and social responsibility contributions, strong faith and strengthened culture in communities, and their contribution to building the infrastructure of British society, as well as revamping and revitalizing derelict church buildings as vibrant places of worship. To aid the Windrush Sunday celebration, we secured the copyright and republished

Forty Winters On as *Many Winters On*[10] which, pictorially and in their own words, told the stories of arrivals. Dr R. David Muir wrote a brief history of the BMCs, which I published in-house as a booklet titled *A Mighty Long Way*, and we produced a pack encouraging churches to make this a significant day.

Alongside the quest for unity and reconciliation between Black and White majority churches was the festering challenge of acceptance and embrace between the African and Caribbean churches. Building these bridges was an urgent task to strengthen the voice, leverage capacity, and capabilities of the community as a collective. As a focal point, I organized a conference titled "We Belong Together: A Plea for Unity, Understanding, and Reconciliation Among African, Caribbean, and the Wider BMCs". There, we reflected on the histories, contributions, and futures of the various segments of BMCs. I presented a paper, "Joseph: A Paradigm for Black Christian Faith in Britain". Analogies were drawn of Joseph being sold into slavery with Caribbean churches, who then arrived in Egypt (UK) and made way for his brothers (African diaspora). The opportunity for reconciliation presented itself to secure the mutual flourishing of the family. It was a sombre, difficult, and liberating conversation which required the intervention of prayer before communicating with communion. I have written candidly about the issues.[11] This work of reconciliation is not complete and should continue to be encouraged.

Even then, both the African and Caribbean churches failed to grasp the significance of Windrush. It has taken many more years, including the Windrush scandal in 2017, which identified the divisive and discriminatory "Hostile Environment" created by the British Government, and the Home Office in particular, for the church to revisit and understand the politicization of race and migration and the disregard for the Windrush generations.[12] Instead, we continue to leave these responsibilities to organizations like the Joint Council for the Welfare of Immigrants, without supporting them morally or financially.

The hoped-for diminishing of racial tensions and challenges has not materialized and has been exacerbated in recent years. There has been no let-up in the disproportionate numbers of Black people stopped and searched by the police,[13] and racial discrimination, professional stagnation, and under-recruitment continue apace.

BMCs and Political Engagement

Political engagement is evolving much more slowly in BMCs than anticipated or desired. At the forefront of our engagement today is the National Church Leaders Forum, which provides a voice for BMCs. Co-chaired by Pastor Ade Omooba and Dr R. David Muir, it has been in existence since 2011.

At the general election in 2015, the forum published the first BMC Manifesto. The momentum for change is within its custody. However, our communities consistently point out that BMCs have not emulated their US counterparts in terms of the struggle for racial justice in society. Black churches in the US were at the forefront of the modern-day US Civil Rights Movement which saw leading church figures such as Revd Dr Martin Luther King Jr, Revd Jesse Jackson, Revd Ralph Abernathy, Revd James Lawson, and Revd Adam Clayton Powell, to name a few, at the helm of campaigns. The contention is, why has the UK not produced comparative leaders, despite them being the success story within Britain's Black communities and its most "dynamic, cohesive representation of Britain's Black community"?[14]

The growth of BMCs has not gone unnoticed by Britain's politicians, who invariably beat a track to BMCs in the run-up to any local and/or national elections. Indeed, any gathering that brings Black Christians together has garnered political attention. An early example of this occurred at ACEA's Faith in the Future: Millennium Celebrations in 2000, at which both the then Prime Minister, Tony Blair, and the leader of the Opposition, William Hague, were in attendance. Equally, the Redeemed Christian Church of God's biannual Festival of Life at the Docklands in east London, regularly attracts tens of thousands of attendees and is always an entry in many politicians' diaries.

After Labour came to power in May 1997, the then Home Secretary, Jack Straw, prioritized engagement with faith communities. It meant that a number of BMC leaders were invited to 10 Downing Street for meetings to discuss how the government could better address the aspirations and concerns of Britain's Black (Christian) communities. There is little doubt that these invitations to the corridors of power were indicative of the clout, maturity, sophistication, and sheer potency of the BMCs. Within less than two generations, BMCs went from being marginal voices within the church to being feted by those in the highest office.

While politicians are keen to engage with BMCs, there is a still a dearth of real strategy and objective setting in terms of this engagement. A good example has been the political visits to church-related events, which invariably involve politicians being given the pulpit to uncritically promote their agenda.[15] They are rarely questioned by anyone about their policies, particularly how they will positively impact Black communities.[16] For a politician, the "money shot" is usually a photograph of a BMC's prayer team laying hands on them during prayer. The outcomes for BMCs are "postcarding" and planning permission for their premises, or parking issues with the local council.

Unlike community-based campaigning groups such as Citizens UK, who appoint spokespeople to take forward their focused agenda when meeting with local and national politicians, BMC leaders are often guilty of jockeying with their peers for the ear of ministers or civil servants to obtain support and/or financial backing for discrete pieces of work. Inevitably, if politicians subsequently fail to make good on their promises, they are not held to account.

Yet, there is hope. Pastor Nims Obunge, Senior Pastor of Freedom's Ark, was an independent candidate for Mayor of London in the May 2021 elections, and co-chairs the Legatum Institute's Commission on Racial Equality, which was launched in December 2020. And there are a number of serving MPs who have a BMC background.

Black Christians and Racism

A distinction needs to be made between the corporate actions of denomination and churches, and Black Christians. BMCs have been incubators of many of the leading advocates and racial justice practitioners. Many of their congregations were at the heart of change in their professions: Dr Leroy Logan MBE of the Black Police Association; Denise Milani, Director, Business Change and Diversity at the Metropolitan Police; Dr R. David Muir; and Pastor Abraham Lawrence represented the BMC voice on the Stephen Lawrence Inquiry. Equally, Revd Ronald Nathan was a consistent voice to the Black community, and similarly, the theologian, academic, writer, and broadcaster Professor Robert Beckford has for a long time been prophetically cajoling BMCs to develop a theology and a way of thinking that better addresses the conditions of Black British (Christians) in contemporary society.

Gospel musicians and choirs have often not been fully acknowledged for the role they play and the contributions they make in bridging the divide between Black and White Christians, across both the wider communities and the sacred/secular divide. Often their songs and music speak to the challenge and values that Christ sees in us. The presence of The Kingdom Choir at the wedding of The Duke and Duchess of Sussex went global. However, London Community Gospel Choir and IDMC, among others, have been on the road worldwide for decades.

BMCs, Education, and Social Justice

While BMCs have been less vocal about racial justice, they have been more active in responding to the lack of educational attainment of Black pupils. Consistently, Black students, especially boys, have not been achieving the prerequisite five GCSEs at age sixteen. Bernard Coard is a Grenadian-born academic, whose treatise, *How the West Indian Child is Made Educationally Sub-normal in the British School System* (1971), lambasted the then education system for its myriad inadequacies. He inspired a range of academics, including those in BMCs.[17]

Grenadian-born, Oxford-educated academic Professor Augustine (Gus) John, Bajan-born Bishop Wilfred Wood (now Sir Wilfred), and Dr Keith Davidson were among the pioneers who responded to the issue with alternative provision of Supplementary/Saturday Schools, establishing the first school in Shepherd's Bush in the late 1960s.[18] This movement has since become commonplace in Black communities up and down the country, and one of the best-known supplementary schools was established by Revd Hewie Andrew, a Methodist minister and community activist based in Brixton, south London. His charitable school, Queen Mother Mary Moore, which was established in the early 1990s and based at a Methodist Church in Clapham, southwest London, worked to raise the attainment levels and aspirations of young Black students.

Dr Davidson became the Head of John Loughborough, a Seventh-day Adventist Secondary School in Tottenham, north London, that catered for a large Black student cohort. After the school closed, Dr Davidson led the Seventh-day Adventist education department and wrote extensively about the importance of BMCs engaging in the educational sector.

While evidence suggests that individual BMCs are doing an excellent job academically, less has been done for those not attending their churches. Once again, ACEA entered the fray; it launched its Faith in the Future: Millennium Conference with a call for churches to enter the education sector and consider using their premises as "church" schools during the week. It subsequently organized the Making the Grade education conference on 17 April 2000 for those working with Black pupils, and later established an Education Forum Network which supported Black teachers and educationists.

One standout BMC educational initiative has been the Church of God of Prophecy's National Black Boys Can which was established with the aim of raising the aspirations and attainment of pupils from socially and economically disadvantaged backgrounds in the UK. It also "aims to address the specific needs of Black boys and seeks to break the vicious cycle of underachievement, unemployment, crime and imprisonment".[19]

A regret must be that BMCs have not made more of the Government's Academies/Free Schools Act of 2010, which encouraged faith groups to establish their own schools.[20] BMCs have excellent infrastructure (facilities) and community assets (congregations that include qualified teachers and the requisite knowledge capacity) to ideally take advantage of this legislation. Despite this, very few have done so.

Serious (Youth) Violence

Issues linked to serious violence and crime within Black communities can be traced to the 1980s and 1990s and were connected to Jamaican "Yardie" (drug) gangs.[21] In response, the Metropolitan Police established Operation Trident in 1998 to "tackle gun crime and homicides in London's Afro-Caribbean communities following a series of shootings in the London Boroughs of Lambeth and Brent".[22] At the time, such violence was described as "Black on Black", which supposedly characterized the ethnicity of both the perpetrators and victims.[23]

With the advent of a new millennium, it was noticeable that the average ages of both victims and perpetrators became younger, the weapons of choice were knives and stabbing implements, as opposed to guns, and that it was now wholly a local phenomenon. BMCs, with their penchant for law and order, saw those involved as being sinners or wicked. Paradoxically, the children of their members were becoming involved too. Those who found themselves incarcerated were left to their own devices or seen as opportunities for prison ministries and BMC prison chaplains.

The two watershed moments were the knife-related killing of Damilola Taylor in November 2000 and the shooting of Birmingham teenagers Charlene Ellis, 18, and Letisha Shakespeare, 17, outside a hair salon in the city, as they were leaving a party on 2 January 2003. Damilola and his mother attended The Everlasting Arms Ministries (then Mountain of Fire and Miracles) on Old Kent Road, southeast London, which was led by Pastor Olukayode Owolabi. I created the order of service and arranged the broadcast for the high-profile service. Paul Boateng, the then Home Office Minister and Minister for Youth, attended on behalf of the Government and challenged people to "Speak! Speak! Speak!"

The Birmingham girls, who were caught in the crossfire of a drive-by shooting, were described as "innocent victims"[24] and had connections to BMCs. These killings highlighted that everyone is vulnerable if senseless violence prevails in our communities.

The Peace Alliance, which Revd Nims Obunge established in 2001 to tackle knife crime, works with "the Church, the Home Office... the Metropolitan Police and the Borough Council, as well as local MPs, and community leaders, to promote peace" in London and its environs.[25] In Birmingham, local pastor and activist Revd Dr Carver Anderson established Bringing Hope, a Birmingham-based charity that works in prisons and the community with those involved in serious violence and crime.[26] Revd Les Isaac OBE, founder of Ascension Trust which works to empower marginalized communities, also created the pioneering Street Pastors initiative, which is now an international programme.[27] Bishop Dr Joe Aldred, who hails from the Church of God of Prophecy but whose main work has emanated from the academic and ecumenical movement, produced the ground-breaking report, "Who is my neighbour?" This Churches Together in England report explored social disorder linked to young people, gangs and knives.[28]

In April 2019, the Synergy Network organized Churches Standing Together – Day of Prayer and Action in Trafalgar Square, central London.[29] It was an acknowledgement that the churches' silence and inaction on serious youth violence is a tragedy. Prior to the COVID-19 pandemic, clergy across the denominations were presiding over funerals of young Black boys, including those with connections to the church. Yet churches have buildings that could be opened from 3 p.m. to 6 p.m., the time when many of these incidents take place. Moreover, churches are awash with volunteers who could work with these young people as mentors and advisors. These are some of the issues that Revd Ron Nathan and I sought to address at ACEA.

George Floyd and Black Lives Matter

The killing of George Floyd in May 2020 and the re-emergence of the Black Lives Matter protests proved to be a catalyst for BMCs to engage with racial justice. Our senior leaders, bishops and pastors, who had hitherto been silent, found a voice to speak powerfully about all aspects of racism and the importance of bringing change in church and society.[30] These voices took their places alongside those church leaders in the historic denominations, including the Archbishop of Canterbury, Rt Revd Dr Justin Welby, head of the Anglican communion,[31] and Cardinal Vincent Nichols, head of the Catholic Church in Britain.[32] BMCs could not avoid this moment. The conscience of humanity was aroused with righteous indignation; young people were angry and demanded a response from their leaders. They took to the streets protesting that "Black Lives Matter" and insisted the system is not broke; rather, it was built this way.

While racism and racial justice are now clearly on the BMCs' agenda, the litmus test will be what happens when the issue is no longer part of society's zeitgeist or when the changes they call for take time to occur. Time alone will tell.

Notes

1 See Mike Phillips and Trevor Phillips, *Windrush: The Irresistible Rise of Multi-Racial Britain* (London: HarperCollins, 1999).

2 See bibliography for publication details of these works.

3 Joel Edwards, "The British Afro-Caribbean Community", in Martyn Eden (ed.), *Britain on the Brink: Major Trends in Society Today* (Crossway Books, 1993), p. 4.

4 Selwyn. E. Arnold, *From Scepticism to Hope, One Black-led Church's Response to Social Responsibility* (Cambridge: Grove Books, 1992), p. 7.

5 "Church apologises publicly to Windrush Generation member", Keep the Faith, 20 February 2021 keepthefaith.co.uk/2020/10/29/church-apologises-publicly-to-windrush-generation-member (last viewed 25 April 2022).

6 A. P. Carter (attributed) (1891–1960), "This World Is Not My Home", public domain.

7 Cleavant Derricks (1909–77), "We'll Soon Be Done with Troubles and Trials".

8 Mark Sturge, *Look What the Lord Has Done! An Exploration of Black Christian Faith in Britain* (Milton Keynes: Scripture Union, 2005), pp. 146–47.

9 From Windrush Sunday promotional literature, ACEA, 1998.

10 *Forty Winters On, The Voice Newspaper/South London Press*, 1988. Updated and reprinted by ACEA in 1998 as *May Winters On*.

11 Mark Sturge, *Look What the Lord Has Done!*

12 "Destitution, Discrimination, Distrust: The Web of the Hostile Environment", Joint Public Issues Team: Churches Working for Peace & Justice, June 2018, www.jointpublicissues.org.uk/wp-content/uploads/2018/06/Destitution-Discrimination-Distrust.-The-web-of-the-hostile-environment.pdf (last viewed 25 April 2022).

13 Black people are nine times more likely to be stopped and searched by the police than White people. See Vikram Dodd, "Black people nine times more likely to face stop and search than white people", *The Guardian*, 27 October 2020, www.theguardian.com/uk-news/2020/oct/27/black-people-nine-times-more-likely-to-face-stop-and-search-than-white-people (last viewed 25 April 2022).

14 Sturge, *Look What the Lord Has Done!*, pp. 109–10.

15 Will Worley, "Theresa May 'worships' with pastor who campaigned against gay equality and same-sex marriage", *Independent*, 30 May 2017, www.independent.co.uk/news/uk/politics/theresa-may-worshipping-pastor-agu-irukwu-campaigned-against-gay-equality-jesus-house-a7763996.html (last viewed 25 April 2022).

16 See "Blair's appeal to black churches", BBC News, 3 April 2006, news.bbc.co.uk/1/hi/uk_politics/4873242.stm (last viewed 25 April 2022). On 2 April 2006, the then Labour Prime Minister, Tony Blair, visited Ruach Ministries Church in Brixton, southwest London, where he spoke about

the importance of BMCs and the way they should do more to encourage Black Christians to vote.

17 Bernard Coard, *How the West Indian Child is Made Educationally Sub-normal in the British School System*, 5th Edition (independently published, 2021).

18 See Wilfred Wood, *Keep the Faith, Baby! A Bishop Speaks on Faith, Evangelism, Race Relations and Community* (London: The Bible Reading Fellowship, 1994).

19 See "Black Boys Can", Faith-based Regeneration Network, www.fbrn. org.uk/project%20profiles/black-boys-can (last viewed 25 April 2022).

20 "Policy paper: 2010 to 2015 government policy: academies and free schools", Department for Education, updated 8 May 2015, www.gov.uk/ government/publications/2010-to-2015-government-policy-academies-and-free-schools/2010-to-2015-government-policy-academies-and-free-schools#issue (last viewed 25 April 2022).

21 Geoff Small, *Ruthless: The Global Rise of the Yardies* (London: Warner Books, 1995).

22 See: https://www.bbc.co.uk/news/uk-england-london-21773275

23 Karim Murji, "It's Not a Black Thing", *CJM*, No 47 spring 202, www.crimeandjustice.org.uk/sites/crimeandjustice.org.uk/ files/09627250208553378.pdf (last viewed 25 April 2022).

24 See Peter Wilson, "Letisha Shakespeare and Charlene Ellis shootings: 10 years on", BBC News, 2 January 2013, www.bbc.co.uk/news/ uk-england-birmingham-20861868 (last viewed 25 April 2022).

25 "About Us", The Peace Alliance, thepeacealliance.org.uk/about-us (last viewed 25 April 2022).

26 "About Us", Bringing Hope, www.bringinghope.co.uk/about.html (last viewed 25 April 2022).

27 "Mission & Core Values", Ascension Trust, www.ascensiontrust.org.uk/ about-us/mission-core-values (last viewed 25 April 2022).

28 https://cte.org.uk/app/uploads/2021/08/Who_is_my_neighbour_ report_-_final_copy_in_PDF-2.pdf

29 See the website: wearesynergy.org.uk (last viewed 25 April 2022).

30 Harriet Sherwood, "UK institutions need more black people, says Pentecostal church leader" *The Guardian*, 10 June 2020, www. theguardian.com/world/2020/jun/10/uk-institutions-need-more-black-people-says-pentecostal-church-leader (last viewed 25 April 2022).

31 "Archbishop of Canterbury says Church must "set its house in order"

over racism", *The Telegraph*, 10 June 2020, www.telegraph.co.uk/news/2020/06/10/archbishop-canterbury-says-church-must-set-house-order-racism (last viewed 25 April 2022).

32 Madoc Cairns, "Racial equality is 'crucial' says cardinal", *The Tablet*, 16 June 2020, www.thetablet.co.uk/news/13055/racial-equality-is-crucial-says-cardinal (last viewed 25 April 2022).

Bibliography

Arnold, Selwyn. E., *From Scepticism to Hope: One Black-led Church's Response to Social Responsibility* (Cambridge: Grove Books, 1992).

Brooks, Ira V., *Where Do We Go from Here? A History of 25 years of the New Testament Church of God in the United Kingdom 1955–1980* (London: Charles Raper, 1982).

Brooks, Ira V., *Another Gentleman to the Ministry* (Birmingham, Compeer Press, 1989).

Edwards, Joel, *Let's Praise Him Again!* (Eastbourne: Kingsway, 1992).

Edwards, Joel, "The British Afro-Caribbean Community", in Britain on the Brink: *Major Trends in Society Today*, edited by Martyn Eden (Crossway Books, 1993).

Lyseight, Oliver, *Forward March* (G. S. Garwood, 1995).

Mohabir, Philip, *Building Bridges: A Dramatic Personal Story of Reconciliation and Evangelism* (London: Hodder & Stoughton, 1988).

Mohabir, Philip, *Pioneers or Settlers* (Milton Keynes: Scripture Union, 1991).

Phillips, Mike and Trevor, *Windrush: The Irresistible Rise of Multi-Racial Britain* (London: HarperCollins, 1999).

Smith, Io, *An Ebony Cross: Being a Black Christian in Britain Today* (London: HarperCollins/STL, 1989).

Sturge, Mark, *Look What the Lord Has Done! An Exploration of Black Christian Faith in Britain* (Milton Keynes: Scripture Union, 2005).

Thompson, Phyllis, *Here to Stay: A Collection of Stories by Women* (Oxford: Lion, 1990).

Chapter 8

Racial Justice: An Ecumenical Journey

ARLINGTON W. TROTMAN

Away with the noise of your songs!
　　I will not listen to the music of your harps.
But let justice roll on like a river,
　　righteousness like a never-failing stream!
(Amos 5:23–24, NIV)

"Take a look at this!" she called out excitedly from another room. Hurrying by, Marcelle, then my wife, placed the news publication on my lap. She had for twenty-four years known my deep passion and prudent yearning for racial equity in Britain. Fortuitously – or divinely determined, depending on your perspective – she had come across an advertisement for the role of Secretary of the Churches' Commission for Racial Justice (CCRJ), one of seven departments within the UK ecumenical body, the Council of Churches for Britain and Ireland (CCBI).[1] No lack of conviction as to my interest or potential was conveyed, given that my first eleven-year pastoral stint had days prior naturally ended.

I briefly, if nonchalantly, screened the advert and, with an altogether contrary reaction, immediately set *The Voice*, Britain's leading Black newspaper, aside. "Not often, or indeed ever, have I noticed a White mainstream church organization advertising in a largely Black newspaper in Britain," I muttered to myself, perhaps feeling bereft of the personal experience of combing the advertising columns.

With haste, I continued my travel preparations to pay my final respects to my best friend and colleague, the Reverend Ernie Teague, who had recently died, at the age of forty, in Toronto, Canada. A young preacher, sculpted in the Wesleyan tradition, a former collegiate of King's

College London, well known for his distinctive and deep modular tones, had passed after a year-long battle with leukaemia. We had shared wide interests, not least frequent theological and pastoral care debates on justice issues in our quests for the ideal (or basically, to win the moment).

Ernie's memoriam befitted his deep devotion to God and church, and by this left an indelible mark on all mourners, not least through one of his poems, the privilege of delivering which, his widow Ruth bestowed on me. As I reflect in this chapter on CCBI's Churches' Commission for Racial Justice (CCRJ), this incredible journey undeniably commenced with a profound sense of "the call," a subject Ernie and I had often mused on at length.

Embracing the Call

"You know that ad you showed me few weeks ago: do we still have the paper?" I quizzed unashamedly, given my prior, almost dismissive, response.

After the affirming phone call, what seemed like years later – it was actually only a few days – we sat overwhelmed, with fits of extraordinary excitement and calm contemplation as the challenge before me began to sink in. We were shocked: they had chosen us! The rest, as they say, reflects a journey, unimaginable, unending, facilitated through the UK ecumenical architecture. I readily embraced the opportunity of fulfilling a new dimension of the divine call, to serve, as Secretary, the churches and the community in the quest for racial justice.

It is necessary in this chapter to appreciate the two interlocking strands in call and character. In this I attempt to register my particularity in the context of British ecumenism, and my untapped capacity for the pursuit of racial justice. Acceding to the task, I naturally foresaw the critical importance of leadership. In practical terms, the Commission Secretary to CCBI's Churches' Commission for Racial Justice – the organization founded under the Swanwick Declaration of 1987[2] to deliver its coordinating work – world be defined by multiple recognizable skills and a confident, if understated, creativity. Foresight elicited my particular urge to "do it!" In this new reality, the ideal was embedded in the chance to see hate change to love, to challenge church to love more deeply, and to confound the status quo. It meant the demonstration of radical *agape*, the unbelievable power to love, in and against enmity, that is, emptying self and systems and embracing transcending goodwill.

Moreover, character and the role in this journey – with more than denominations, confessions, councils, and associated bodies, with established international ecumenical associations such as the World Council of Churches (WCC), the Conference of European Churches (CEC), and Churches' Commission for Migrants in Europe (CCME), plus secular community organizations – would be fundamental. It would ensure CCRJ continued to seek a more just and equitable church and society. To a degree, a profound sense prevailed that this role would elicit skills and temperament in many spheres: enabling, representing, suffering – new, probably, but only in scope and intensity – wrestling, educating, coordinating, influencing, guiding, admonishing, creating, and, of course, loving others as yourself (Matthew 25:31–46; Mark 12:30–31). Utterly convinced, I was under no illusion that learning and relearning in such august company would be paramount from commencement.

It was 1 September 1998 when one of the most challenging, yet wholly welcomed, chapters of my journey began. Not only was this segment rooted in the call, but also my readiness was nurtured by an educational and leadership-oriented first pastorate at Wesleyan Holiness Church (Wesleyan Christian Centre (WCC)), Harrow Green, East London. Interestingly, a devoted and loyal member of WCC, Pauline Wilkinson, soon remarked, "God saw your faithfulness in handling small things; now he's given you larger responsibilities." This clear confidence-builder merged with four events that were central to the response and enhanced my determination to connect.

First, while leading a young adults' Bible study, five years earlier in 1993 at London's Forest Gate, at a home where several young adults were assembled, the news being broadcast in the background distracted me: it was being stated that a young black man, Stephen Lawrence, "was murdered tonight in southeast London".[3] An immediate sad mood, not least mine, closed the study. Yet again my sense was ablaze: "You have to do something." I harboured a visceral conviction, an absorbing motivation following another fatal consequence of hate.

Second, while completing undergraduate divinity studies in Boston, USA, twelve years earlier, 1986–87, I came across the book, *Let the Trumpet Sound*, Stephen B. Oates' biography of Dr Martin Luther King

Jr,[4] in a bookshop in Cambridge, Massachusetts. As I settled in with it, grit, desire, and resolve rolled off its pages and shaped their inescapably persuasive impact. I noticed Dr King's uncompromising confrontation with the perpetrators of racial violence and relentless injustice; yet he maintained a loving, caring, and efficient disposition toward the "enemy", simultaneously respecting the tenets of his faith. As I approached ordination in 1987, my anticipation of pastoral life was gripping and shone brightly, but consuming from this cup of righteousness served only to reinforce my bourgeoning pledge.

Third, I had arrived in England, aged twenty, one of the last immigrants invited by the British government to work on the Underground, in the last group of what we now refer to as the Windrush generation. Almost immediately I was made aware of my obvious ethnic heritage. This new, radical consciousness of my "Blackness" thus thrusted upon me, I was astounded, if naive. For when the minister of the church I attended that first Sunday on arrival in the UK approached me, I could not have predicted his attitude – except, perhaps, to offer a warm welcome!

He strode down the aisle toward me at the very rear of the nave, and immediately quizzed, "Who invited you?" His eyes betrayed nothing a welcome would radiate.

"No one," I replied. "I am living close by and wanted to worship with you today," with the due respect I had been taught as a child growing up in Barbados.

With obvious haste, the young cleric led me out to the adjacent street and gestured toward a location and said, "There you'll find the church you want," clearly imploring me not to return!

Well, I said thank you and left. I soon learnt that such experiences were typical for Black people in Britain. "What do I do now?" I wondered.

I proceeded to play cricket every Sunday for two years, but remained troubled throughout!

Fourth, eighteen months later, an uncle arrived at my new workplace in Croydon, most surprisingly. "Hi, Arley, are you OK?"

"Yes," I replied, with some concern, though happy to see him.

"I just got a message from home; your father died this morning."

What a gut-wrenching blow! Disbelief and grief engulfed me.

I returned to Barbados for my father's funeral (he was fifty-two). The visit, however, scorched another indelible impression in my mind. At around 2 p.m. one day, when the Bajan temperature is at its perishing peak, I was out driving and noticed about eight black elders (likely aged seventy-plus) bent double, manually tilling a sugar cane field at Graeme Hall plantation. I stopped immediately, such was my sense of injustice.

I had seen similar images before and was untroubled, but now I was horrified and felt the blunting pain of oppression. Why? A young White man, mounted on horseback some 8–10 metres away from the labourers, had his rifle aimed at them as they manually dug the ground. In my developing race-conscious mind, he was slave-driving my "elders" with a brutal threat. It was unconscionable! I left the scene with the compelling refrain: "I have to do something." That refrain would define much of my life and work ever since.

For me, this was not merely another job. I would need to be ready and efficient, the best I ever could be in any situation. Years followed while chasing O and A Level education, undergraduate theology, pastoral, and divinity studies, furthered by postgraduate research in systematic (philosophical) theology, seeking sustainable responses to racial hatred. The problem demanded it.

The Problem

Given such comprehensive rejection and derision of Black and Brown people, one might dismissively ask, "Why do anything?" Apart from his personal quest, the force of logic and the reality of *agape* toward a just, true, and open church and society in the USA, the Baptist Civil Rights minister Dr King uncompromisingly engaged the monumental struggle for freedom, justice, and equality. He embraced a Gandhi-inspired methodology: *non-violent civil disobedience.*

How could one fight the violent, deadly ethnicity wars against Black and Brown people in Britain without negotiating away the merits of one's faith, "turning the other cheek" (see Luke 6:29)? It was an evocation, not only of a deep foreboding, but it also demanded pluck, fearlessness, and a thick skin within the framework of redeeming goodwill.

I imagined my call (1998–2006), in essence, would inspire the wrath of God in some, evoke jealousy in a few, deepen the hatred of others, and perhaps keep others silent and suspicious. For some, however, committed action, support, and standing up would never be far away. The call would entail risks. Risk-taking was inevitable because "race" has been an economic and political construct for more than four hundred years. Our work as a Commission, therefore, necessitated a pronounced political edge, in some respects. Politics, undoubtedly, drove racial injustice and shaped method.

With assurance derived from his living faith, which he regarded as "spiritual motivation", Dr King's methodical pursuit of racial justice by non-violent social and political action was hugely impactful. "Darkness," he said, "cannot drive out darkness, only light can do that. Hate cannot drive out hate, only love can do that."[5] Who or what might quell the fear, change the narrative, heal the wounds of widespread intergenerational transmission of racial injustice, both subtle and overt? A culture of such magnitude also characterizes much of Britain's present reality.

As I contemplated the task ahead, I understood that the striking symbolism of non-violent civil disobedience in the USA would mean a commitment to further suffering induced by ridicule, a variety of injustices, and possibly even death, all implicit in non-violence. Dr King was imprisoned more than thirty times across his thirteen-year struggle. But that sacrifice is indeed the nature of a living faith, a call that is intrinsic to Christian mission.

The Mission

Some twenty-two persons met in South Wales for the weekend and welcomed me to my first regular meeting of the CCBI's CCRJ. Commissioners' reports, updates, and lively discussions throughout the weekend conveyed thoughtful and resolute individuals representing their churches' racial justice briefs. With particular care and informed guidance, the Reverend Prebendary Theo Samuel, CCRJ's moderator helped to deepen my grasp and improve my appreciation of the degree to which collective engagement could deliver the remit. Mission involved collaboration. This was different!

Theo, of South Asian descent, tall, greying a little, and exhibiting a distinguished aura with a distinctly Anglo-Asian drawl, gave the impression that he would never scoff at high tea served in the finest china. His measured insights were matched only by his boundless yet reflective passion for racial justice. Completely conversant with the issues, Theo's stint ended three years later.

Theo Samuel (now deceased) was succeeded by the Right Reverend Roger Sainsbury, Bishop of Barking, and later the Reverend Myra Blyth of the Baptist Union of Great Britain. It was a privilege, as the first Black person to have held the role, to have had the wisdom, dedication, and guidance of the three moderators and the Vice Moderator, Patricia (Pat) White, a Baptist racial justice advocate.

Administered by the newly installed General Secretary, Dr David Goodbourn (now deceased), who succeeded the Reverend John Reardon, Churches Together in Britain and Ireland (CTBI) – the newly named governing body of the four nations ecumenical instruments (1999) – comprised Churches Together in England (CTE), Churches together in Wales, (Cytûn), Irish Council of Churches (ICC), Action for Churches Together in Scotland (ACTS), and representatives of Black Majority Churches. Duty-bound to invest resources in anti-racism, the nature and breadth of coverage appeared also subject to three other disciplines.

First, it was inevitable that theological reflection underpinned our work, and this was evident in reports, briefings, worship, books, and other publications produced by the Churches and CCRJ. *A Tree God Planted*,[6] for example, along with *Asylum Voices*,[7] and *Redeeming the Time*,[8] in addition to the frequently stated biblical declaration that all are created in the image and likeness of God.

Second, to enable churches to respond effectively, the Commission's management and delivery of Racial Justice Sunday (RJS), for example, became a focal point in our national ecumenical effort. Initiated and observed first by the Methodist Church in Britain in September 1988, the launch of the ecumenical edition in September 1995 was momentous; it opened the programme to all churches and others to mark RJS on the second Sunday of September each year (today, RJS takes place in February, but the date can be flexible). RJS focused on prayer, reflection, campaigning action, and fundraising, and it provided the opportunity for participants to learn about each other's ethnicities, cultures, national identities, and backgrounds. Teaching materials and initiatives and sharing meals from across different ethnic and cultural spectrums sought to build and demonstrate unity in diversity and mutual respect.

Third, the power of individual congregational response to structural racism was most evident when churches hosted campaign meetings. The Methodist Church in Finsbury Park, for example, hosted prayer and campaign briefing meetings in support of its members Sheila and Rupert Sylvester, the parents of thirty-year-old Roger Sylvester, who died in police custody in 1999 after his arrest outside their home. The devastation of Roger's loss was amplified when the High Court, in 2004, overturned the earlier inquest verdict (2003) of unlawful killing on the eight officers involved in his arrest. Despite the political nature of this death, CCRJ was obliged to act, at least in a pastoral care and campaigning capacity.

It was inevitable, therefore, that CTBI/CCRJ's *modus operandi* revealed certain contrasts. On one hand, the nature of involvement in cases such as Roger Sylvester's, Stephen Lawrence's, or Ricky Reel's was deemed political, which, in some quarters, questioned the church's place in society. But transformation, healing, and anti-racism tasks conducted by a Christian organization could only justify its purpose if it faced squarely the tough political nature of racism and racial injustice, which appear intrinsic to politics and policy. On the other hand, the team's work was cut out, fielding phone-in questions about racism and injustice nationally on RJS, offering help, sharing information over a four- to six-hour period at BBC local radio studios nationwide; this seemed, on the face of it, quite apolitical. Our teams were often reminded, "Injustice anywhere is a threat to Justice everywhere."[9]

Teamwork

The management and operations of CTBI/CCRJ was impressively well resourced by CTBI membership, though questions about the ecumenical model abounded. By my arrival, the Church Representatives Meeting (CRM) had had already been exercised by these on issues across the seven commissions. Nevertheless, my role, I believed, potentially rekindled hope. The past and promise of CCRJ could and would not have been realized without the efficiency of two other executive officers (see below), and support of the administrative staff. On my arrival, New Zealander, Trudy Thorose, a committed secretary to the Commission generally and to my role specifically, added value. Margaret Pattinson, also an experienced administrator who performed admirably, succeeded Trudy a few years later. Trudy, Claire Hurley (Ecumenical Racial Justice Fund Secretary), and Margaret served the Commission with courage and efficiency, not least in their handling of some of my less-than-clear requests with patience and care.

Nigerian, James Abiodun Ozigi, Nigerian pastor of Christ the Resurrection Church in London and General Secretary of the Council for African and Caribbean Churches, frequently cracking jokes, compassionate and deeply dedicated, was CCRJ's Executive Secretary to the Ecumenical Racial Justice Fund (ERJF, 1995), the grant-making arm of the Commission. Supported by the now late Claire Hurley, James rigorously assessed all funding applications, visited applicants across the UK, and prepared applications for consideration by the Fund Committee – a group of twelve persons, moderated by the highly efficient Pat White – which oversaw the process of grant-making. Interestingly, with the Commission's help a few years prior, James[10] had won his appeal against deportation from the UK and had since regarded CTBI/CCRJ as "the voice of the voiceless". The ERJF assisted on average 120 national and local anti-racism and racial justice organizations, projects, and groups per year.

Richard Solly started working with CCRJ during the tenure of the Reverend David Haslam, my predecessor, in 1995. Focused, thoughtful, and meticulous, Richard supported campaigns for "overstayed" individuals and serviced the Education Committee as Secretary. He produced a variety of materials such as the Racial Justice Sunday (RJS) pack in consultation with colleagues from across the four nations. Richard, quirky and funny, compassionate, and hugely committed to justice, ensured local radio stations and churches nationally were available for RJS interviews. He edited *Church & Race*, CTBI/CCRJ's thrice-yearly informative periodical, and supported the Gypsy and Traveller network while assisting with the setup of the Bail Circle.

As indicated earlier, my role progressively substantiated my initial determination to pursue racial justice. Working in a pleasant atmosphere, I enjoyed representing CTBI and welcomed the detail: planning and meeting with various church and governmental personnel on immigration and anti-Black racism, servicing internal and external communications, further developing the four-nations structure, reporting, and managing staff. An important part of the role was to contribute to budgetary processes with CTBI's treasurer, a quiet but deeply reflective Narender Paul. I also shared in anti-racism campaigns and some media-engaging opportunities, enabling action, writing, and raising awareness. Yet the battle against racial injustice remained, seemingly unconquerable despite key initiatives across the anti-racism networks.

Foundational Initiatives

Bail Circle

I now turn briefly to assess key features of CTBI/CCRJ's race equality activities. We have witnessed migration crises repeatedly in recent years, with the most extreme loss of life at sea, in the air, and across land. Another sharp end has been the significant rise in detentions and deportations. The Bail Circle was established some twenty-five years ago, when CCRJ brought together individuals willing to support immigration detainees to secure their freedom, safety, and the avoidance of such outcomes. Immigration lawyers were encouraged, many successfully, to make bail applications.

In essence, twenty-seven migrants and persons seeking asylum languished for more than one year in Rochester Prison, southeast London, with little or no attention paid to their plight. Bail Circle members, often referred to as "cautioners", were generous humanitarians, volunteers, who befriended detainees, provided accommodation, and (frequently, but not expectedly) paid the bail imposed by judges.[11] This work, embedded in the delivery of humanitarian justice, became a well-established national protocol, and was used in cooperation with the charity Bail for Immigration Detainees nationwide.

Four nations

The incentive to act characterized CTBI/CCRJ's work during my tenure, increasingly at the four-nations level. Anti-discrimination work with the Scottish churches, supported by many, including Dr David Sinclair and Revd Dr Nelu Balaj (who succeeded the Church of Scotland Commissioner, Kenyan Advocate for Racial Justice and Gender Equality, Mukami McCrum) intensified as a focal point for delivery of government policy. Racial justice is thus at the heart of God's great purposes, in Scotland as indeed elsewhere through the nations.

Churches Together in Wales (Cytŭn) were connected through the work of the Reverend Aled Edwards and, later, the Revd Anthaparusha (deceased), who provided invaluable representation and support, as, for example, in his participation in the CTBI/CCRJ fact-finding tour of five southern states in the USA in 2005. Meanwhile, representation of the Irish Council of Churches was provided by Fee Ching Leong (now deceased), a Presbyterian of Malayan descent from Northern Ireland, and other Ireland-wide church representatives, including Sister Joan Roddy of the Catholic Church in Dublin, and the then Church of Ireland Bishop, the Right Reverend Dr Michael Jackson (now Archbishop of Dublin and Glendalough, Primate of Ireland). Our primary focus was the development of the All-Ireland Churches Consultative Meeting on Racism (AICCMR). This was built upon the promise of a week of meetings, convened in 2000 with equality, human rights, and Black and Minority Ethnic organizations in Northern Ireland and the Republic of Ireland. After three years the AICCMR was launched, in December 2004,[12] set up to address racial injustice and migration issues in the increasingly diverse island of Ireland.

The struggle for justice and equity across the four nations anticipated new meaning, particularly as the UK anticipated publication of the Macpherson Report (the Stephen Lawrence Inquiry report). What would this scrutiny and its findings mean for the Lawrence family, and for future police–community relations?

Stephen Lawrence

The story of Stephen Lawrence has been well documented. I reflect here only on the salient points covering the years 1998 to 2006. In summary, Stephen Lawrence was killed in a racist attack on 22 April 1993. An eighteen-year-old architectural student from Eltham, southeast London, he was heading home from a family visit with his friend Duwayne Brooks. At around 10.30 p.m., at a bus stop, a group of five White youths literally "engulfed Stephen",[13] said Sir William Macpherson, Chair of the Public Inquiry, and when they left him he was bleeding from stab wounds, and "probably died as he fell". By 1997, no one had been arrested.

After many demonstrations and campaigns across four years, when they came to power, the Labour Government immediately set up the Public Inquiry to learn lessons. The report described the police service as "institutionally racist", and urged all UK institutions to examine their processes, policies, and practices.[14] It was a watershed moment also for churches.

The Commission arranged for UK churches to gather in London on 24 February 1999 – the date the Government launched its report – to receive the Stephen Lawrence Inquiry report, having contributed to the Inquiry. The then Bishop of Oxford, the Right Reverend Richard Harries, accepted our invitation to chair the event. Some 420 persons from across the four nations attended Westminster Central Hall for a most memorable tribute to Stephen, to support his family, campaigners, and friends, and to hear speeches on the key findings of the 389-page report. The meeting welcomed Stephen's parents, Neville Lawrence and Doreen Lawrence, and Inquiry panellists, the Right Reverend Dr John Sentamu, the then Bishop of Stepney, and Dr Richard Stone. It was only in 2012 that two of the five perpetrators were charged and found guilty, after the law on double jeopardy had been changed, and they were imprisoned for life.

The Commission followed up on behalf of CTBI with two widely publicized conferences and three publications to assist CTBI members in their analysis and revisionary work:

- *A Christian Response to Racism* – The Stephen Lawrence Report;
- *Report and Action for Churches*, Part 1 (January 2001);
- *Redeeming the Time: All God's People Must Challenge Racism*, A statement of policy by Churches Together in Britain and Ireland (June 2003);
- *The Peers Project: Policing, Education, Employment, Rights, and Self-esteem* – for young people in building trust and confidence (May 2003).

Strategic collaboration

CTBI/CCRJ's coordinating activity was central to its effectiveness. Informed by experts in the field, CCRJ regularly met with the Government and NGOs,[15] including Runnymede Trust, a major race equality think tank, whose directors Sukhvinder Stubbs and (later) Michelynn LaFleche, a forthright, compassionate, and well-informed Canadian national, provided high-quality information across a range of race equality education.[16] "The Future of Multi-Ethnic Britain" – commonly referred to as The Parekh Report – argued that "Britishness" as previously understood was defunct. Britain was no longer a nation but "a community of communities".[17] Meetings with Home Secretary Jack Straw, Home Secretary David Blunkett,[18] and the Right Honourable Lord Morris (Bill Morris), the first Black person in Britain to become leader of the Transport and General Workers Union, expressed concerns about public policy. Mr Blunkett, blind from birth, was incredibly astute, and knew first-hand the impact of poverty. Importantly, he expressed concern about the issues raised, not least the call for Government to allow people seeking asylum to work while awaiting their case outcomes – though, of course, it never happened. It was not completely surprising, though, but rather deeply depressing, when the tragedy of the fifty-eight Chinese victims of smuggling became national news.[19]

Asylum and immigration

In June 2000, fifty-eight Chinese migrants were found dead in the container of a lorry at the port of Dover. It was the epitome of the spirit of humanity to act justly when, having heard the news, CTBI/CCRJ's urge to "do something" had not elicited, expectedly perhaps, a straightforward response for more safe routes. This tragedy stimulated two immediate reactions: "We must respect the humanity of the deceased," and, "What action might be taken to prevent such a tragedy recurring?"

First, we could offer a service in memoriam. Immediately I sought and struck a partnership with a London-based photographer, Jabez Lam, a Chinese national who knew well the South China region from which many of the deceased persons had originated. The memorial would mark their passing with an artistic display of generic images, one to represent each of the fifty-eight, created by Jabez, hosted at Emmanuel Evangelical Church, London. Second, the memoriam could intensify calls for a change in policy to safeguard people seeking international protection.

Black and Brown people continue to seek international protection. For many, the desperate search is founded on fear. In *Asylum Voices*,[20] sectarian religious persecution, for example, which accounted for the presence of the Taliban in Afghanistan, was the main reason quoted by Muslim asylum applicants for leaving their homes.[21] Some take great risks, believing, unwittingly perhaps, that their "agents" will guarantee their safety. CTBI/CCRJ has often stressed that, without more safe routes to safety for persons seeking international protection and effective recourse to due process, survival, well-being, and the basic right to life remain at stake. It is a challenge worthy of action.

The Challenge "To Act"

Much was achieved across the four nations, but so much more still remains to be done. It became clear, however, that the ecumenical architecture and family were anticipating, or nursing, tensions around funding and deliverables, particularly in relation to the notion of "big ecumenism". Supporting CTBI's wider portfolio and the changing needs of some of its major contributors, the CRM appeared to have found the structure a growing weight. It would lead ultimately to a reduction in the group's resources. By the summer of 2006, after much discussion about proposed changes to personnel and remit, particularly of the Commission Secretary's role, cuts in CTBI's funding meant I was unable to remain in post. The urge "to act" remained urgent, but on the substantive issue. James and Richard also took redundancy. In approximately one year, CTBI had reduced staff from thirty-four to four persons.

It is not surprising to detect an air of sadness, given the crucial importance of racial justice. We give thanks for God's mercies, and also offer deep gratitude to CTBI/CCRJ for the opportunity to serve. Yet the call to act justly for equality and freedom in multi-ethnic, multicultural Britain remains worthy of love, undimmed, and particularly in the wake of recent renewed and new voices following increased immigration tragedies and the killing of African American George Floyd in 2020. A resurgence of anti-racism work in the churches almost twenty years hence surely cannot be too late! The global witness to the truth that Black Lives Matter all points to the imperative to act.

Notes

1 The structure of CCBI comprised Anglican, Methodist, Catholic, United Reformed, Church of Scotland, Scottish Presbyterian, Church in Wales, Irish Council of Churches, Baptist Union, Council of African

and Caribbean Churches, Joint Council of Anglo Caribbean Churches, New Testament Church of God, to name a few.

2 The Swanwick Declaration was adopted by acclaim and personally signed by those present at the Hayes Conference Centre, Swanwick, on Friday 4 September 1987.

3 *News at Ten*, ITV, 22 April 1993.

4 Stephen B. Oates, *Let the Trumpet Sound: A Life of Martin Luther King Jr.* (New York: Mentor, 1982).

5 James Melvin Washington, *A Testament of Hope: The Essential Writings and Speeches of Martin Luther King Jr* (New York: HarperCollins, 1991), pp. 17, 20.

6 Heather Walton, *A Tree God Planted: Black People in British Methodism* (London: Ethnic Minorities in Methodism Working Group, Division of Social Responsibility, 1985).

7 Arlington W. Trotman, Andrew Bradstock, *Asylum Voices: The Experience of People Seeking Asylum in the UK* (London: Churches Together in Britain and Ireland, 2003).

8 *Redeeming the Time: All God's Children Must Challenge Racism* (London: Churches Together in Britain and Ireland, 2003).

9 Washington, *A Testament of Hope*, p. 17.

10 James died following a car accident while on holiday in Nigeria in the autumn of 2006.

11 Three things are needed for a detainee to get bail: 1. somewhere to stay; 2. someone to function as a "cautioner" to ensure the person will report when required; 3. Payment of a sum of money, usually, to the court.

12 The AICCMR's aim is to encourage and enable the Churches in the Republic of Ireland and Northern Ireland to acknowledge the need to tackle racial justice issues in a more systematic and holistic fashion.

13 The Stephen Lawrence Inquiry Report, an Inquiry by Sir William Macpherson of Cluny. Advised by Tom Cook, The Right Reverend Dr John Sentamu, Dr Richard Stone, presented to Parliament by the Secretary of State for the Home Department by Command of Her Majesty in February 1999 Cm 4262-I, pp. 18–19.

14 The Stephen Lawrence Inquiry Report.

15 CCRJ's decision-making role with several NGO partners included the Commission for Racial Equality (CRE, now abolished), Runnymede Trust, The 1990 Trust, Joint Council of the Welfare of Immigrants (JCWI), the Institute of Race Relations (IRR), The Monitoring Group

(TMG), the Asylum Rights Campaign (ARC), the Refugee Council, Migrant Rights Network, UK Race in Europe Network, the National Assembly Against Racism, Bail for Immigration Detainees, Operation Black Vote, National Black Police Association, The Stephen Lawrence campaign, to name a few.

16 Runnymede Trust commissioned the hugely influential Parekh Report. See Bhikhu C. Parekh, *The Parekh Report: The Future of Multi-Ethnic Britain* (London: Runnymede Trust, Profile Books, 2000).

17 Parekh, *The Parekh Report*, p. 512.

18 On this occasion, our delegation consisted of Ms Pat White (Vice Moderator, CCRJ), Revd Arlington Trotman (Commission Secretary), Dr Andrew Davey (CofE), Naboth Muchopa (Methodist), Richard Zipfel (Catholic), and the Right Honourable Lord Morris, former General Secretary of the Transport and General Workers' Union (1992 to 2003), popularly known as Bill Morris, the first Black leader of a major British trade union.

19 Nick Hopkins, Jeevan Vasagar, Paul Kelso, and Andrew Osborn, "Grim find of 58 bodies in lorry exposes smugglers' evil trade" *The Guardian*, 20 June 2000, https://www.theguardian.com/uk/2000/jun/20/immigration.immigrationandpublicservices3 (last viewed 27 April 2022).

20 Trotman and Bradstock, *Asylum Voices*.

21 Trotman and Bradstock, *Asylum Voices*, p. 6.

Chapter 9

The Church of Scotland and the Race for Justice

MANDY RALPH

What has been written makes for uncomfortable and challenging
reading that as a church we need to acknowledge and embrace.
It is all the more powerful because this speaks not just as a faith
organisation but out of personal experience. Might it be that the
Spirit is speaking to the Church?

(The Very Revd Dr Martin Fair, Church of Scotland Moderator
2020–21)

Over the last twenty-five years, racial justice and tackling racism has at
times been more of a slow wander than a quick sprint for the Church
of Scotland, both ecumenically and as a national church. Given that it
is one of the largest denominations in Scotland, in recent years it has
appeared to be slow to respond to rising racism and racial injustice.
Tackling sectarianism; the inclusion and recognition of women serving
in ministry and within local congregations; and the debates on gender,
sexuality, same-sex marriage, and civil partnership have been higher on
the agenda. That said, some of the deliverances (resolutions) passed and
reports received by the Church of Scotland General Assembly over the
last twenty years have included the following.

In 2002

Deliverance: Urge Her Majesty's Government, the other European Union
governments, and the European Commission to adopt a common action
plan covering migration, common standards for reception of asylum
seekers, and a specific programme to combat racism and xenophobia.[1]

In 2004

Deliverance: Remember with thanksgiving the overcoming of apartheid in South Africa, recommit the Church to its opposition to racism wherever it may be found. Encourage ministers and congregations to celebrate Racial Justice Sunday on the second Sunday of September, and to attend the preparation day for this on 19 June.[2]

In 2005

Deliverance: Recognize the continuing problem of racism in Scottish society and encourage church members to take every opportunity to inform themselves of the issues and to find appropriate ways to support work for racial justice, including the marking of Racial Justice Sunday. Commend to the Church interfaith dialogue and acts of solidarity that seek to overcome religious or racial intolerance.[3]

In 2011

At the 2010 General Assembly of the Church of Scotland, the then Convener of the Church and Society Council was asked about whether the Church of Scotland should have a policy with regard to racist organizations following decisions made by other denominations. As a result of this and discussions on the floor of the General Assembly, the following report was published in May 2011: "Racist Organisations".[4] The report stated:

> There is evidence that extreme racism remains present in society and that over the past decade racist movements have become better organised and gained following, on the streets as well as at the ballot box.
>
> Two British Churches – the Methodist Church and the Church of England – have responded by publicly and clearly articulating an emphatic rejection of racist politics and social movements, and have gone so far as to make statements along the lines of which it is incompatible to be a member of their Church and a member or active supporter of a racist organisation or movement.

The Church and Society Council recommends that the Church of Scotland adopts a similar policy.

The Church and Society Council brought its report, "One Scotland Many Cultures", to the Church of Scotland General Assembly.[5] The report took its name from a Scottish Government project aimed at tackling racism and discrimination in Scottish society. The Church of Scotland offered its support for the eradication of racist views, prejudice, and discrimination in Scotland, with its prayers and action for racial justice. The report and its follow-up literature for congregations stated:

> The culture of the Church itself is not homogenous. We need to ask how our culture fits in with a diverse and changing Scotland. Of central importance is how as a Church with a real focus on mission, our culture can speak to those within the Church, either as a counter-cultural witness, or as a way to reach those to whom the Church's traditional way of being is outside their comfort zone. Continuing to offer Jesus' radical hospitality must remain one of our core principles.[6]

The report focused on radical hospitality but did not go as far as actively tackling or supporting congregations to tackle racial injustice.

In 2013

Deliverance: Reject racism and religious hatred and condemn anti-Semitism and Islamophobia.[7]

In 2014

Deliverance: Note that the United Kingdom has a long tradition of being a country of sanctuary for those fleeing persecution and the words of Jesus to love our neighbour; urge the UK Government not to repeat offensive publicity campaigns such as "Go Home", either on the streets or in Home Office centres such as the one in Brand Street in Glasgow. Urge the UK government to redress those policies, such as the Azure card and refusal of permission to work, which force so many asylum seekers and their children seeking safety in the UK into severe poverty, and many into destitution, often for years.[8]

In 2017

Deliverance: Deplore the reported rise in xenophobic and racist attacks on people following the result of the EU Referendum and affirm the valuable role of citizens from other parts of Europe living in Scotland.[9]

What is unclear is whether these deliverances have had any impact over the years. Did they influence local Church of Scotland congregations and the communities they serve, both in Scotland and its English and international congregations? What impact, if any, have they had on people within these congregations who are suffering from and experiencing first-hand racial injustice?

As someone who was baptized and brought up in the Church of Scotland, volunteered as a Sunday School teacher, served as an elder, and was ordained first as an Ordained Local Minister and now as a full-time parish minister, I acknowledge that many of these deliverances over the years have bypassed me, or I have not been aware of them at a congregational level. The challenge for the Church of Scotland is to understand that agreeing well-meaning statements without further action or change is not sufficient.

My experience of church as a Black female brought up in a seaside town in the west of Scotland during the 1970s and 1980s was mixed.[10] Although there were no other Black people at my church, that was nothing unusual, as there were not that many Black, Asian, and Minority Ethnic people in my town. What did strike me even as a youngster was how everyone in the Bible was White, and so different from me, but apparently Jesus loved me anyway, so that was OK. I was never aware of anyone questioning those assumptions or why people in the Bible were portrayed as White. I also remember being very confused as a child as to why we kept sending people in Africa all our rubbish, as I was quite sure they did not want it. I wondered why could we not send them new stuff instead, and why could we not help them to help themselves.

Sometimes in our church there was an inference that I was one of these babies shipped from Africa, as I had been adopted by two White people (this was not the case – I was born in Glasgow). In the 1970s especially, people did not do political correctness. I grew up in an era where some of the images on TV, the jokes, the programmes by their nature were racist. Name-calling was the norm, as was being told to go home, back to the jungle, and being subjected to monkey chants both from people our own age and from adults.

Then society appeared to discover political correctness. Suddenly on the surface all was acceptable. Or was it? Ben Lindsay in his book, *We Need to Talk About Race*, describes this well when he talks about and illustrates the "White Supremacy Iceberg",[11] highlighting the overtly racist language at the tip and all the covert racism underneath, which will exist as long as society continues to dismiss racist views for what they are, even when they are badged as a joke. Denying privilege, not speaking up and out in the face of racial discrimination are behaviours that need to be challenged in our churches and to be taken account of in our church structures.

Years later, our biblical images still appear to be White. Discussions emerge that suggest Jesus cannot have been blond haired and blue eyed because the very nature of his origin negates that. Is this thinking accepted among our congregations? In some, yes. In some, no.

As I develop my faith and become more involved in the church, I suddenly find people who think I am a Faith Share Partner (a Church of Scotland international exchange programme) or on a visit from Malawi. I get told, "Your English is very good," and asked, "Are you cold living in Scotland?" Or, "When are you going home?" "Where are you from?" "No, really, where are you actually from, as you cannot be from Scotland?!" I find myself constantly explaining at different churches that I am Scottish, I was born here, I live here, and I am not from Malawi.

Then there was a cultural shift, first noticed after 9/11 as those in Black, Asian, and Minority Ethnic communities were suddenly deemed to be potential terrorists and became victims of increased targeted racism.[12] This escalated with the debates and divisions over Brexit, and suddenly the lid was ripped off and racism at its ugliest re-emerged within society.[13] Those who previously contained how they felt, under the guise of nationalism, went after people who did not fit the perceived mould of "Making Britain great again". Refugees and asylum seekers became targets, and social media became an easy platform for anonymous and targeted racial abuse. The air is a bit chillier, and that question surfaces again: "When are you going home?" Many no longer feel welcome in their own country, in Scotland.

Although the church spoke up and spoke out against the mistreatment of refugees and asylum seekers, it failed to recognize or represent the other Black, Asian, and Minority Ethnic individuals impacted by the rise in racism within Scotland. In predominately White congregations it has been easy to say, "It is not something that affects us." But by not talking about it, tackling it, or understanding the behaviours that contribute to and uphold racism, we continue to allow it to embed and become systemic. In a predominantly White organization, we have to ask ourselves how Black people can identify theologically, aspire to achieve leadership roles, or hope to influence the future of that organization. This is something that is reflected across our society and is not just inherent within the Church of Scotland.

So far, we have had female ministers as General Assembly Moderators and both male and female elders as Moderators. We have made inroads into the issue of women in leadership and ministerial roles within the church, but have done very little to address the disparity of Black, Asian, and Minority Ethnic people in key leadership roles within our church.

In 2020, in light of the incidents that took place in America, including the killing of George Floyd at the hands of the police and the Black Lives Matter movement both in America and here in Britain, the toppling of the Colston statue and the debates that then ensued about the legacy of statues across the UK, the church found itself no longer able to sit on the sidelines when it came to racism and racial injustice. It has begun to take a long, hard look not only at its current practices, the policies it does and does not have in place, but also at which parts of its history were linked to the Transatlantic Slave Trade and the associated wealth generated from it, and to determine where churches were built on the back of it. Many within the church asked what was being done as a faith organization to support and ensure that the lives of our Black, Asian, and Minority Ethnic members, as well as those within our communities, were being supported, their voices heard, their injustices recognized, and that they were not being excluded. At the 2020 General Assembly, the deliverance given as part of the Faith Impact Forum read:

Reaffirm that racism is a sin and declare that Black Lives Matter; instruct the Faith Impact Forum, in partnership with the Faith

Nurture Forum, Assembly Trustees, and General Trustees to report to a future Assembly on the issue of racial justice and the legacy of slavery and the Church of Scotland.

The report[14] outlined the need for the church to determine and address its historical links to the Transatlantic Slave Trade, the need to overcome systemic racism; to address privilege and power; to be a church where the majority and minority cultures are encouraged to find their true identities in Jesus Christ; and to be a church that reflects justice in strategy, policy, procedure, liturgy, theology, worship, and relationships. But even this caused some division, with cries of "All lives matter" and that the focus should not be just on one group of people. If the belief is that people are all made in God's image, then for us all to matter, we all have to be respected and treated fairly, regardless of skin colour and ethnicity.

The Church of Scotland is a wide church that includes evangelical, liberal, and conservative viewpoints, and with that come very different opinions and theological interpretations. That said, this does not negate the church from acknowledging the hurts and harms of the past; these are important in allowing the church, in faith, to move forward. It is time to get our own house in order. Yet doing so can be contentious. Reni Eddo-Lodge in her book, *Why I'm No Longer Talking to White People About Race*, talks about not being able to discuss properly the issues of race with people who do not recognize that racism exists, and are unaware of their privilege or bias.[15]

I have often heard the comment, "I don't see colour. I am not racist." My response when people say, "I don't see colour," is that they are making a choice not to see me for who I am or to respect me for who I am. The claim of not seeing colour acts as a way of opting out of acknowledging ethnicity, acknowledging their own ignorance on racism.

When you refuse to see colour, what happens? You whitewash things! You change the narrative to make it more palatable for you, rather than accepting the reality of a multicultural society. Essentially, you are diverting the conversation toward saying racial *identity* is bad, rather than racial *oppression* is bad. In order to tackle and defeat the latter, we have to acknowledge, believe, and learn from the experiences people have had based on ethnicity. Equally, the phrase, "We are all made in the image of God", which is a useful theological foundation for equality, should not be used essentially to silence the experiences of racism within our own church and among those who are supposed to believe that we are in fact equal in God's eyes.

I have heard some heartbreaking stories about the appalling way people have been treated in Scotland, and in our churches, which says we have a long way to go in tackling racism.

Apart from passing deliverances, what has the Church of Scotland done in relation to tackling racial injustice over the last twenty-five years? It was part of the work undertaken by Action of Churches Together in Scotland (ACTS), which previously employed a Racial Justice Officer, and its work was supported by an ecumenical committee – the Scottish Churches Racial Justice Group. Owing to a reduction in grant allocations, the post was made redundant in 2013 and the Scottish Churches Racial Justice Group ceased to meet.

Ecumenically, the Church of Scotland was active in terms of racial justice, but for a variety of reasons this joint working became less of a priority, which led to the view that not very much was being done nationally or institutionally in tackling racial injustice within the church. More recently, the Church of Scotland has actively supported and been part of the annual "Stand Up To Racism Scotland" rally that takes place on the Saturday nearest 21 March (International Day for the Elimination of Racial Discrimination).

In response to the issues faced by refugees and asylum seekers, the Scottish Faiths Action for Refugees (SFAR) project was established by the Church of Scotland in November 2015, in partnership with other Scottish churches and faith groups. SFAR seeks to build on work that has been undertaken by Scottish and British churches – including Churches Together in Britain and Ireland (CTBI) – in relation to refugee and asylum issues, and with partners in different faith groups and in other countries, including the Churches Commission on Migrants in Europe (CCME). The project's aims and objectives were drawn up on an ecumenical and joint faiths basis, underlining that:

> there [should be] three main strands to the work: the need for political campaigning both in Scotland/the United Kingdom and internationally; the need to work also on behalf of the hundreds of thousands in camps around the world; [and the need to] offer radical hospitality to those who arrive in Scotland.[16]

The project has published "Sanctuary in Scotland",[17] a booklet on information for faith groups on refugee issues, "Becoming Human Together",[18] produced with Christian Aid Scotland, which is a theological reflection on the theme of forced migration, and "God with Us",[19] an ecumenical anthology of worship resources on the theme of forced migration, in partnership with CTBI. SFAR has also acted as a contact point in terms of communication with journalists and civil servants, raised awareness with local churches and congregations on faith and refugee issues, and played an important role in the CCME and in CTBI's Churches' Refugee Network. It has been able to develop links with other UK faith-based groups as well as work with secular refugee partners such as the Scottish Refugee Council.

In 2018, a successful funding bid with the Scottish Refugee Council to the EU's Asylum, Migration and Integration Fund facilitated the delivery of the New Scots Integration Programme 2018–20. This is a substantial piece of work which has been the main focus of SFAR over the last two years. Significant activity has seen a programme of awareness raising in local faith groups through talks, publications, and support around the country, and the development of a pilot "New Scots Holidays" programme, where refugees from one part of Scotland were offered respite breaks in homes and communities in different parts of Scotland.

The Church of Scotland carried out a review of the SFAR partnership and outcomes in the summer of 2020 and, in consultation with partners, a new phase began in January 2021. Refugees and asylum seekers arriving in Scotland continue to need support, as outlined in the Scottish Government's "New Scots: Refugee Integration Strategy".[20] Churches and faith groups have a continuing role to play, especially in creating social connections between members of receiving communities and new Scots. Asylum seekers, who face considerable hardship and restrictions on their rights, also need community support, as well as faith groups to speak with them in their advocacy for justice, empowerment, dignity, and respect.

In 2016, the Church of Scotland put in place an Interfaith Programme Officer whose focus was on creating an interfaith strategy for the church, building relations with the faith communities, and internal education on matters that relate to or affect relations with other faith communities. This resulted in contributing to the writing groups for the centenary of the Balfour Declaration in 2017 and the report from World Mission in

2018 on global interfaith relations. There was also direct relationship building with a focus on Jewish–Church of Scotland relations. With that should come the task of raising awareness around anti-Semitism and how it functions as a form of racism.

Since 2017, the role has involved being part of a European Erasmus programme, which worked with twenty-five youth workers from five countries to train other youth workers in tackling a form of hate speech. The Scottish team focused on religious hate speech, but it also involved looking at anti-racism and other strands of equality work. By learning the ways in which interfaith relations are relevant to broader and intersecting justice causes, faith communities can learn to become allies.

In a recent restructure, the role has been used to collaborate on the Equality, Diversity, and Inclusion Implementation Plan which comes on the back of a call for more attention to be given to racial justice.

In terms of its missionary activities overseas, the Church of Scotland was seen as a White church which historically sent missionaries to bring people in other countries to Christianity. In doing this, it did not always take account of people's existing culture, often imposing its own. The Church of Scotland now has partnerships with churches across the world, many of which have their roots in the era when the Church of Scotland sent missionaries all over the world. In developing and progressing these partnerships, as part of the Faith Impact Forum, the church employs an Africa and Caribbean Secretary, an Asia Secretary, and a Middle East Secretary, each of whom gives support to these partnerships.

The original process was not just to plant churches, but also to plant schools and health centres, which then formed a mission station. Many of these mission stations still operate today and are run by the now indigenous church with which the Church of Scotland partners.

It is only in the last couple of decades that the church has moved away from the donor–recipient model and put more of an emphasis on a model of partnership, recognizing that the Church of Scotland is now a "small" church in a big world rather than a "big" church in a small world. The growth of Christianity is seen in the Global South and it is in part owing to this that the Church of Scotland now recognizes that it has a lot to learn from her partners. Unfortunately, this is not always the attitude that prevails, and some old ingrained, colonial ideas can at times still be seen.

However, the tide is changing, and there is a growing understanding that we in the Global North would do well not only to listen to our partners, but also to learn from them, and to put that learning into practice. The model of partnership that can now be seen in the Church of Scotland is one that focuses on building relationships. By focusing on individual people, we are able to build authentic relationships. Exchanges of personnel, whether it be for a short or long period, enhance the relationships and allow people at the grassroots level to interact with one another and gain a rich understanding of different cultures and ways of life. The twinning programme run through the Faith Impact Forum of the Church of Scotland enables this grassroots exchange between congregations in Scotland and across the world. The programme has seen lives changed through mutual respect and a sense of dignity.

A good example of how this is played out in civic life in Scotland is through the Scotland Malawi Partnership (SMP). The partnership was established in 2005 under then first minister, Lord McConnell, and began as an intergovernmental agreement. This partnership has evolved over the years and a sister organization, the Malawi Scotland Partnership, has been established in Malawi. It is based on love and friendship between Malawi and Scotland and is defined by being a dignified partnership. It has a number of underlying principles, which include, "Respect, trust and mutual understanding; transparency and accountability; effectiveness sustainability; reciprocity; equality and doing no harm among others."[21]

The partnership is for both individuals and organizations. The Church of Scotland is a member, as are many congregations of the Church of Scotland. They have links with Malawi and have built partnerships not just between congregations, but also between presbyteries. Yet what remains unclear is how well the true value of those partnerships is recognized and whether both are seen as equal partners with as much to give to and learn from each other.

The year 2020 saw the Church of Scotland 2020–21 Moderator, the Very Revd Dr Martin Fair, host a conversation about racism in Scotland on his YouTube discussion panel, "It's A Fair Question – What is it like to be black in Scotland?"[22] The conversation highlighted the issues that Black people face in Scotland today: those born in Scotland, those who have lived here for many years, and those who have not lived long in Scotland. The prejudices, the racism, the exclusion, the fear for personal safety at times, all highlight that as a society and as a church we still have a long way to go. It was a conversation that for many was the first realization that often Black people are not always welcomed, even in churches that profess to be inclusive and welcoming. Suddenly, people were brought face to face with the systemic racism that is embedded into the culture of the church and for the most part has gone unchallenged.

Going forward, what is the Church of Scotland doing to tackle racial injustice?

During 2019, work commenced in line with the Equality Act 2010,[23] looking at Equality, Diversity, and Inclusion (EDI) for all the protected characteristics, of which racial justice is a key strand. This must bring with it a recognition that the church must get its own house in order and achieve an understanding of what proportion of its wealth, church buildings, and other properties were built on the profits made from the Transatlantic Slave Trade. In addition to this, there is a hope to deepen our understanding of the impact and legacy of our missionary activity in Africa, the Caribbean, and other regions and countries.

There is recognition of the need to explore how diverse the Church of Scotland is, from those who are employed within the organization to those who form the leadership of the church, and from those who are represented on trustee bodies and committee memberships to those in congregations, the Guild, employed in CrossReach,[24] and other parts of social care. What about our Black, Asian, and Minority Ethnic communities in our urban and rural parishes?

Indeed, 2020 was the first time this information was gathered through congregations' annual returns, looking at parish profiles and statistics for mission[25] created from the 2011 Census,[26] to set a benchmark of where we are at, measured against where, through developing our equalities strategy and policy, we aspire to be as an organization. But in gathering this information there is a caution – Black, Asian, and Minority Ethnic is a huge category of many different ethnicities lumped together, which, if not broken down and looked at adequately, can be perceived as dividing people into "White" and "Everyone else who is not White".

The church has a social responsibility which is part of its theology and religious ideology. Even as a faith-based organization, it does need to take account of Scottish Government policy – "A Fairer Scotland for All Race Equality Action Plan".[27] The church needs to work in partnership with other Scottish charities looking at racial justice. Some dialogue has taken place with the Coalition for Racial Equality and Rights (CRER), Edinburgh Interfaith Association, and Minority Ethnic Christians Together in Scotland (MECTIS). Working together and across denominations is key to promoting and ensuring racial equality in communities across Scotland.

Research is being undertaken by the church's EDI group to investigate why it is that people coming to Scotland who are Presbyterian set up their own churches rather than attend the local one. Assumptions can be made, but if we consider ourselves to be welcoming and inclusive, why do people not attend, or choose to leave our congregations? Language and culture have a part to play, but the underlying racist attitudes, or White privilege, may also be responsible for Christian disunity.

A recent PhD study undertaken at the University of Aberdeen on new churches in Glasgow found that 110 new Christian congregations had been established in the Glasgow City Council area between 2000 and 2016, an average of seven new churches a year. Strikingly, 65 per cent of all the new congregations were from Black, Asian, and Minority Ethnic communities, with African churches (churches in Glasgow where 80 per cent or more of the congregation are from an African background) making up 79 per cent of the total Black, Asian, and Minority Ethnic church category. What this indicates is that Minority Ethnic Christians in Glasgow, and in Scotland as a whole, are creating their own new church communities. In fact, the research emphasized that new churches that have appeared in Glasgow over the last two decades are highly homogenous, having either majority African, Asian, or White Scottish memberships.[28]

Although the Church of Scotland had an important role to play in the abolition of African enslavement,[29] I would like to reiterate that the church cannot move forward without addressing its historic involvement in the Transatlantic Slave Trade and colonialism. Given its many historical church buildings, the church needs – in a time when other organizations and establishments are reflecting and reviewing their monuments, collections, and buildings – to reach out and work in partnership with these organizations who are already undertaking this work across Scotland. The church could learn from, for example, the work of the Museums and Galleries Scotland Empire, Slavery and Scotland's Museums Steering Group, set up in 2020 and chaired by Sir Geoffrey Palmer.

There is also a need to review the curriculum for initial ministry training for candidates, and training for church leaders and ministerial support staff, so we can ensure that as a church we are looking at, discussing, and raising awareness of how racism works, and how racist structures are embedded into our everyday life. As one of the established denominations in Scotland, we need to look at how we can recognize problematic behaviours and attitudes that uphold these structures. The church needs to take those first steps to facilitate and begin open and honest conversations about the role we play in racism and how privilege contributes to it.

More so now than ever, there is a need for action, not lip service or turning a blind eye to the issue of racism within our church organizations. Many will say on reading this, I am sure, "We are not racist," and, "The Church of Scotland is not racist." However, until we address fully the injustices, the stigma, and the inequality that Black, Asian, and Minority Ethnic people face daily in our Scottish communities, and until all are welcomed and all are embraced in our churches, whatever the colour of their skin, and until in faith people are fully and genuinely accepted as being made in the image of God, and not as a lesser human owing to their ethnicity, then the Church in Scotland cannot truly call itself anti-racist.

Notes

1 Reports of the General Assembly of the Church of Scotland, 2002.
2 Reports of the General Assembly of the Church of Scotland, 2004.
3 Reports of the General Assembly of the Church of Scotland, 2005.
4 "Racist Organisations", The Church of Scotland Church and Society Council, May 2011, www.churchofscotland.org.uk/__data/assets/pdf_file/0015/5910/racist_organisations_may2011.pdf (last viewed 27 April 2022).
5 "One Scotland, Many Cultures", The Church of Scotland Church and Society Council, May 2011, www.churchofscotland.org.uk/__data/assets/pdf_file/0005/5891/One_Scotland_Many_Cultures_May_2011.pdf (last viewed 27 April 2022).
6 "One Scotland, Many Cultures", Church of Scotland's Church and Society Council, May 2011.
7 Reports of the General Assembly of the Church of Scotland, 2013.
8 Reports of the General Assembly of the Church of Scotland, 2014.

9   Reports of the General Assembly of the Church of Scotland, 2017.

10 I am mindful that my experience may not be what others experienced, as I cannot speak for every Black woman in the church in Scotland.

11 Ben Lindsay, *We Need to Talk About Race: Understanding the Black Experience in White Majority Churches* (London: SPCK, 2019), pp. 11–12.

12 "Number of police recorded racially aggravated offences in Scotland from 2005/06 to 2020/21", Stastista, www.statista.com/statistics/370398/racial-offences-scotland-annual (last viewed 27 April 2022).

13 "Hate Crime in Scotland, 2019–20", Crown Office and Procurator Fiscal Service, 12 June 2020, www.copfs.gov.uk/media-site-news-from-copfs/1887-hate-crime-in-scotland-2019-20 (last viewed 27 April 2022).

14 https://churchofscotland.org.uk/__data/assets/pdf_file/0010/70111/3601-GA-Reports-to-the-General-Assembly-2020-V6.2.pdf, p.81, Accessed 26 January 2021.

15 Reni Eddo-Lodge, *Why I'm No Longer Talking to White People About Race* (London: Bloomsbury Publishing, 2017), p. xi.

16 Minute of the Church of Scotland Council of Assembly meeting, September 2015.

17 "Sanctuary in Scotland", Scottish Faiths Action for Refugees, www.sfar.org.uk/wp-content/uploads/2020/09/Sanctuary-in-Scotland-2020-FULL-FINAL-version.pdf (last viewed 27 April 2022).

18 "Becoming Human Together: A Theological Reflection on Migration", Scottish Faiths Action for Refugees, www.sfar.org.uk/wp-content/uploads/2018/05/Becoming-Human-Together.pdf (last viewed 27 April 2022).

19 "God With Us: Worship Resources on the Theme of Refugees, Migration and Sanctuary", CTBI et al, https://ctbi.org.uk/wp-content/uploads/2020/12/3507-CS-SFAR-Migration-Worship-A5-BOOKLET.pdf (last viewed 27 April 2022).

20 "New Scots: Refugee Integration Strategy 2018 to 2022", Scottish Government, 10 January 2018, www.gov.scot/publications/new-scots-refugee-integration-strategy-2018-2022 (last viewed 27 April 2022).

21 "Our Partnership Principles", Malawi Scotland Partnership, www.malawiscotlandpartnership.org/index.php/about-us/partnership-principles (last viewed 13 May 2022).

22 "It's A Fair Question – What is it like to be black in Scotland?"

YouTube, 9 July 2020, www.youtube.com/watch?v=H-13bzx2qHg&feature=emb_logo (last viewed 27 April 2022).

23 "Equality Act 2010", www.legislation.gov.uk/ukpga/2010/15/contents (last viewed 27 April 2022).

24 An organization that offers help to anyone who is in need. See www.crossreach.org.uk/care-you-can-put-your-faith-in (last viewed 27 April 2022).

25 "Statistics for Mission", The Church of Scotland, www.churchofscotland.org.uk/resources/stats-for-mission (last viewed 27 April 2022).

26 "Scotland's Census: At a glance", www.scotlandscensus.gov.uk/ethnicity-identity-language-and-religion (last viewed 27 April 2022).

27 "A Fairer Scotland for All: Race Equality Action Plan and Highlight Report 2017–2021", Scottish Government, 11 December 2017, www.gov.scot/publications/fairer-scotland-race-equality-action-plan-2017-2021-highlight-report (last viewed 27 April 2022).

28 Sheila Akomiah-Conteh, "The Changing Landscape of the Church in Scotland: New Churches in Glasgow 2000–2016" (Unpublished PhD Thesis, University of Aberdeen, 2019).

29 "Slavery and the Slave Trade", National Records of Scotland, www.nrscotland.gov.uk/research/guides/slavery-and-the-slave-trade (last viewed 27 April 2022).

Chapter 10

Wales and the Continuing Struggle for Racial Justice

ALED EDWARDS

There is a time and a season for every purpose under heaven. Unexpectedly, perhaps, now has become a good time for Wales and for the breadth of a nation's diverse churches to reflect on how well both have fared in furthering racial justice. It is apt also that a Welsh reflection, on how what has been achieved and on what is yet to be done, should be shared with the wider Christian community in Britain and Ireland. Cytûn: Churches Together in Wales, as a national ecumenical instrument, working alongside partners in Churches Together in Britain and Ireland (CTBI), can offer a solid legacy going back many decades of seeking to build a more equal and inclusive society. This reflection sets out to explore how Cytûn may be well placed to offer some transparency regarding what has yet to be achieved and to offer thoughts for the future.

The reflections offered here begin at a pivotal point with the fond but challenging memories of a warm June 2019 evening spent in the company of colleagues and friends in Cardiff Bay. That time now seems distant. In a variety of ways, that evening marked the end of an era in how churches, other faith communities, key third-sector partners, and the Welsh Government worked together in the pursuit of racial justice. We were there to recall the race riots of 1919. A year later – almost to the very day – many of those who had assembled in the Norwegian Church in Cardiff Bay to recall the events of 1919 would offer the Welsh Government a critical report on the socio-economic reasons behind the disproportionate number of COVID-19 deaths in Wales. Within a matter of months, all our lives would be changed by a pandemic. Many lives would be lost.

That evening in June 2019, we had gathered as members of the Wales Remembers Board, established by the First Minister of Wales, to facilitate the commemoration of the First World War. We were joined by a rich diversity of communities to mark the passing of a hundred years since the violent tragedy of the south Wales race riots of 1919. Four men lost their lives during the riots in Welsh ports that year and several people were injured. The way in which Wales now functions, increasingly on a social partnership basis, including a diversity of voices when key decisions are made, led to the appreciation that no commemoration of the impact of the First World War on Welsh lives would be complete without marking and exploring what had happened during that turbulent summer in the early twentieth century in ports such as Cardiff, Newport, and Barry.

The race riots we commemorated in Cardiff were not uniquely a Welsh experience. They were also experienced in English cities and towns such as Liverpool and Salford. There were protests in Glasgow and, to a different background, deadly violence was seen on the streets of a distant Chicago, USA.

The violence of that summer as experienced through a Welsh prism was stoked by economic, social, and political anxieties. Anger, on the part of White union workers and demobilized White servicemen against Black, Arab, Chinese, and other Minority Ethnic communities and businesses, erupted onto the streets in violence throughout the UK.

For a whole variety of reasons, it was deemed appropriate that the commemoration be held in the iconic Norwegian Church in Cardiff Bay. The location carried several significances. The church where Roald Dahl was baptized as a child and where his family worshipped is no longer a place of worship. It does, however, offer itself as a setting for communities to come together. The wooden church building located in the old docklands area is within walking distance of the ethnically diverse modern community of Butetown. The whole site embodies the open maritime dynamic of Wales that exported people and goods across the world. It also marks the place where Wales welcomed thousands of diverse peoples through the growing gateway that has now become the Welsh capital. A magnet for migrants from within the nation and from without. It also now provides the location of the seat of government in Wales.

That evening, historians told stories of what happened in Wales at the end of the First World War. Respected community elders shared their powerful narratives. The accounts of those from the community who remembered the storytelling of their grandparents were immensely vivid. They spoke of children arming themselves with stones and rocks as houses were being ransacked by looters and families were forced to protect themselves. Talented artistes also recited their poems and sung their songs. Preachers sought to inspire. Much appeared to be well that June night. Some may have even dared to believe that Wales had learnt a little from history and that strides had been taken over the years in the direction of building a fairer and more inclusive nation.

In terms of location and chronology, that June evening provided a useful vantage point, under the wing of the Senedd building, from which to observe a wider process at work within a nation. In many ways, looking back, that night in Cardiff Bay proved enabling and encouraging in terms of how Wales marks significant events. Some crucial elements of the story up to that point, from a shared public dynamic involving a political process and communities defined by faith, are set out here.

Working together in the quest for justice, Welsh churches have a story to tell of courage and innovation, particularly so following the establishment in 1999 of the National Assembly for Wales, known as the Senedd, or Parliament, since May 2020. Welsh churches have taken advantage of the political opportunities offered by devolution to shape public policy and to bring about change in the arenas of racial justice, immigration, and especially the care of asylum seekers and refugees. Helping to shape civic liturgies around commemorations has also played a significant part in informing public discourse and in telling a nation's stories.

While annual materials produced for Racial Justice Sunday have been immensely useful in offering a broader perspective, Wales has very much ploughed its own distinctive devolved furrow. Churches have repeatedly placed their hands on a political plough and steered it in the direction of social justice. Sometimes controversially so. Sometimes showing immense courage proclaiming a prophetic and pioneering voice in the face of racial injustices. Frequently offering diaconal hands in the service of a broken world, be that more broadly through the significant endeavours of food banks, serving the homeless, seeking to offer protection to individuals who have been trafficked, and trying to restore the lives of displaced people. Some of the key developments concerning racial justice will be set out here, but they do not reveal the whole story.

It would be useful to highlight some of the key components and events that lie behind Wales' emerging social partnership model of working. Post devolution, a core set of constitutional values has triggered and underpinned a relational dynamic. Constitutionally, sustainable development, human rights, and equal opportunities were enshrined in the legislation that brought the original National Assembly into being. They stand continually as three components of a crucial political covenant made with the people of Wales. Frequently, these underpinning values have resonated with communities characterized by race and faith and have resulted in the creation of unique partnerships and structures that have delivered tangible outcomes. To a nation's discomfort, they have also at times revealed and laid bare continuing injustices and inadequacies.

Cytûn has found itself pushing at open doors. From the outset in 1999, a distinctive social partnership dynamic began to evolve in the Welsh public space, and faith communities were from the outset included in formal consultative structures such as the Voluntary Sector Partnership Council. For the first time, in any meaningful structural way, communities of faith and bodies serving Black, Asian, and Minority Ethnic communities found themselves occupying the same structural space. They rapidly began to overlap further as Cytûn, the lead faith network at the time, was required to engage with other organizations such as the newly formed Muslim Council of Wales. Friendships forged at that time have endured and grown. The breadth of Wales' churches working alongside other faith communities began in the devolved space to achieve outcomes by moving from protest to process. Interreligious groups began to acquire new political skills and to learn together and from each other. A few early and significant events are recorded here.

During the summer of 2001, one unanticipated event, endeavouring to help asylum seekers dispersed to Wales, would trigger a long-term strategic shift in priority setting for Cytûn. Health workers at one of Cardiff's hospitals raised concerns that they were being asked to treat asylum seekers being held in the city's Victorian prison under what appeared to be remand conditions. A relational interplay from within Welsh civic society responded expeditiously, taking full advantage of the capacity of the National Assembly to hold the Home Office to account, and resulted in the removal of the asylum detainees from Cardiff Prison. The dynamic demanded both civic protest and political process. In terms of the well-being of the detainees, the prison's chaplaincy team were fully deployed.

The process triggered in 2001 began to open doors to many innovative policy initiatives around the care of asylum seekers and refugees. The dynamic moved on to churches working alongside the staff and volunteers of other third-sector organizations. In 2002, Cytûn, working with a leading refugee charity, Displaced People in Action, assisted the setting-up of the pioneering Wales Asylum Seeking and Refugee Doctors and Dentists (WARD) group with the then Minister for Health and Social Services, Jane Hutt.

A second, more substantive, policy initiative took more time to develop and commands a broader consequence. Following conversations at the Faith Communities Forum, the Welsh Government in due course launched its Nation of Sanctuary – Refugee and Asylum Seeker Plan in January 2019. The concept was originally conceived by Cytûn, having gained invaluable advice from the Revd Inderjit Bhogal from the City of Sanctuary movement. The plan seeks to ensure that refugees and asylum seekers who are dispersed to Wales are supported to rebuild their lives and make a full contribution to Welsh society.

In 2001, the decisive event that changed everything in terms of how faith communities relate formally to the National Assembly was 9/11. Discerning that our world would not be the same following the terrorist attacks on the Twin Towers in New York and on the Pentagon, the First Minister, Rhodri Morgan, sought to bring faith leaders together in Wales. Cytûn staff worked closely alongside government officials to provide a representative model for the body that is now recognized as the Welsh Government's Faith Communities Forum. Since then, the forum has provided a useful platform for communities to come together to hold vigils during times of community tension, to thrash out ideas concerning social policy, and to articulate a distinctive Welsh narrative around international events.

Over the years, the relationship has evolved and acquired a contemporary fleetness of foot in responding to difficult challenges. The co-production between Black, Asian, and Minority Ethnic communities and those defined by faith has also continued to grow. In 2019, to the backdrop of heated conversations elsewhere in Britain, Wales adopted its own relational interfaith approach to debating the development of relationships and sexuality education in schools. A question-and-answer session was held in Dar Ul-Isra Mosque, Cardiff. The Welsh Education Minister, Kirsty Williams, answered questions from the floor, and key stakeholders from different integrities offered views and highlighted concerns. Following the meeting it was resolved to set up a joint faith Black, Asian, and Minority Ethnic Involvement Group. The concerns of members of key communities continue to be highlighted.

These were some of the devolved dynamics and histories that found themselves congregated with others in a former church in June 2019, as communities came together to commemorate and learn from a difficult chapter in a nation's history. The dynamics and the histories helped to shape and inform how a difficult conversation was held. From a diverse intensity of integrities, a distinctive Welsh story, set within a broader international context, was heard. Characteristically, lessons were learnt.

The patterns of injustice seen in 1919 have prevailed since and been repeated in more modern times. The rioting of that year initially broke out in Newport on 6 June when a Black man was attacked by a White soldier because of an alleged remark he had made to a White woman. The clash rapidly escalated, with a mob of White men attacking anyone Black, Asian, or Minority Ethnic. Further clashes took place in Cardiff on 11 June involving White soldiers returning from the Great War. Four men were killed during the disturbances. and several were injured.

For good reason, a sense of injustice has lingered over the decades among the Black, Asian, and Minority Ethnic communities of south Wales. Many were arrested during the 1919 rioting, and those brought before the courts for prosecution were disproportionately from Minority Ethnic communities. There were acquittals, but a legacy of rough justice has endured.

Sometimes rough justice can adopt an intensely local face. It can even be identified with great intensity as belonging almost to a square mile. Such is the legacy of Cardiff. During the last century, Cardiff suffered two of the most notorious and horrific miscarriages of justice in modern British legal history. Both miscarriages of justice involved men from the city's Minority Ethnic communities.

In 1952, a Somali former merchant seaman by the name of Mahmood Mattan was executed by hanging, having been wrongly convicted of the murder of Lily Volpert in the Docklands area of Cardiff. His conviction was quashed many years later, in February 1998. Mattan's case, at that time, was the first to be referred to the Court of Appeal for the newly formed Criminal Cases Review Commission.

There was also the tragic case of Lynette White, whose body was found murdered in a flat above a betting shop in James Street, Butetown, on 14 February 1988. The following November, the police charged five Black and mixed-race men with her murder, even though none of the scientific evidence discovered at the crime scene could be linked to them. In 1990, three of the men were found guilty: Stephen Miller, Tony Paris, and Yusef Abdullahi, otherwise known as the Cardiff Three, were jailed for life. All three were subsequently freed in 1992. The Court of Appeal ruled that a miscarriage of justice had taken place. In 2003, the real murderer, Jeffrey Gafoor, confessed to carrying out the killing. He had killed alone.

Leaving a community's story untold has also been a repeated feature. In seeking to act justly, there is an immense power to storytelling and there are consequences to a failure to narrate some histories. For years, communities in Cardiff retained a memory of what happened in the city during the summer of 1919. Sadly, Wales as a nation neglected to remember. Plaques were not located in places where the lost lives could be remembered. Memorials were not given prominence in places where stories could be retold and adapted to a contemporary learning. Wales would have to wait until the 1980s for researchers to revisit the accounts in earnest. In due course, Welsh media outlets would bring the accounts to the nation's attention. The commemorative events held in the Norwegian Church in Cardiff Bay acquired significance. Both society and state chose to remember and to tell a story.

Sadly, history is sometimes destined to repeat itself. Also in June 2019, the Welsh Government announced that it had funded eighteen projects throughout Wales to celebrate Windrush Day on 22 June. It did so fully aware of the devastating impact that the Windrush scandal, triggered by the Westminster Government in 2017, had had on Welsh lives. The children of the Windrush generation, in the absence of documentation, which was difficult to acquire, had been denied rights in the UK. Some had been deported. Following the 1919 race riots, the British Government acted quickly to speed up deportations and would enact in due course legislation that would define some individuals from Black and Asian communities as "aliens". Clearly, remembering and learning from experiences continues to matter. Church leaders throughout Britain and Ireland chose to speak out prophetically, opposing the way in which the children of the Windrush generation had been treated.

The final reflections offered here have been garnered from the distinct way Wales has sought to respond to the spread of the COVID-19 pandemic. After twenty years, swathes of the UK's population have now become perhaps a little more aware of devolved realities, of different decisions being informed by different values from different identities. Concerning racial justice, the experiences evaluated prior to the spring of 2020 now must be observed and evaluated through a different prism. The world of reflecting on issues of faith and public policy with friends on warm and bright nights in pleasant places gave way to a harsher reality. We now contend with a new order of things and a new learning.

This final section tells something of a Welsh story. The learning from that storytelling is offered to the wider Christian community in Britain and Ireland and presented here for further reflection. Such conversations have become urgent and imperative. The pandemic has taken a sharp scalpel and prised open our perceptions of progress in furthering racial justice. It may have told us truths. The entire conversation, for expressions of government and for churches, may now have to be completely recalibrated and reassessed. A different future may now have to be crafted as churches seek to re-engage with the quest for racial justice.

Cruelty has remained the overriding hallmark of COVID-19. Globally, it has claimed millions of lives. Perversely, it has made many billionaires much richer. It has also come close to breaking the backs of national economies, frustrated businesses, and ruined individual lives. The pandemic, when it came into our midst, did not arrive as a leveller. In Wales, as elsewhere, the pandemic applied itself, in terms of its cruelty, disproportionately to some communities, especially those identified by colour and poverty. The loss has been immense and the grief considerable within Black, Asian, and Minority Ethnic and poorer communities.

The chilling nature of COVID-19 became all too real for me during the first few days of the initial Welsh lockdown in March 2020. Cardiff City Council officers and Welsh Government officials met with faith leaders around a shared intent to protect lives. Reflecting on the possibility of a significant number of excess deaths, partnerships of good will sought to ensure that end-of-life religious rituals and ceremonies would be observed. I recall leaving the meeting a little frightened but resolved. From that initial meeting, faith communities worked constantly with Welsh Government officials through newly established structures offering advice on drafting government statements and regulations. Well-attended podcasts were periodically arranged, co-chaired between Cytûn and Welsh Government, where officials and faith leaders could be questioned by members of the public.

Sadly, in terms of furthering the cause of racial justice in Wales, COVID-19 did not arrive alone. One single tragic event from the streets of Minneapolis in Minnesota in May 2020 triggered a global response. The brutal killing of George Floyd ignited a new intensity and a sense of urgency as to how Wales would respond to the damning realization, in the wake of the impact of a vicious and deadly pandemic, that the human cost of long-standing racial injustices and inequalities had once again been brought into plain sight.

It is perhaps sobering to reflect that many of us who gathered for the commemoration of the race riots in the Norwegian Church in June 2019 would a year later produce a report for the Welsh Government, under the chairmanship of Professor Emmanuel Ogbonna from Cardiff University, highlighting evidence that people from Black, Asian, and Minority Ethnic backgrounds were being disproportionally affected by COVID-19. Our report, focused on socio-economic issues, highlighted factors such as employment and income insecurity, the financial burden of immigration status, and the role of structural and systemic racism and disadvantage. Worryingly, we also highlighted the continuation of long-standing racism and disadvantage and the lack of Black, Asian, and Minority Ethnic representation within decision-making processes. Our report identified a lack of action on race equality. Many of the issues highlighted had been identified and discussed previously but had not been addressed in any systemic or sustained way. More than thirty recommendations were presented to the Welsh Government.

The process of producing the report marked a distinctive Welsh devolved approach. On discerning that the numbers of Black, Asian, and Minority Ethnic deaths were deeply worrying, the First Minister, Mark Drakeford, summoned an expert Advisory Group together under Judge Ray Singh and Dr Heather Payne. Expeditiously, one subgroup under Professor Keshav Singhal produced a workplace risk assessment tool initially for use by the health and social care workforce. Our socio-economic group ran alongside that dynamic. This highly effective co-production way of working under the most challenging of circumstances offers churches a powerful reminder of the value of adhering to the Lund Principle; the affirmation that churches should act together in all matters except those in which deep differences of conviction compel them to act separately. In response to the demands of COVID-19, Wales has tended to utilize what is already there within communities: the public sector, local authorities, and the third sector. It has now become the norm in the Welsh public square to include faith community representatives when considering equalities and racial justice issues. Partnership working rather than outsourcing key tasks to the private sector may prove to be more cost effective. It also offers greater transparency.

In September 2020, Jane Hutt, as Deputy Minister and Chief Whip, reported on progress in response to the Ogbonna Report findings. The practical nature of many of the recommendations were forged by the hands-on knowledge and experience of key stakeholders, including faith community leaders. Consequently, many of the Ministers' responses were deeply practical. It was announced, for example, that COVID-19 "Keep Wales Safe" communications had been translated into thirty-six languages to be easily accessible for diverse communities. There were also overarching initiatives indicating a significant shift in terms of how government works in Wales around racial justice. It was reported, following conversations with Lord Simon Woolley, former Chair of the British Government's Race Disparity Unit Advisory Group, that scoping was under way with a view to establishing a Race Diversity Unit for Wales. A Welsh Race Equality Action Plan was also being developed to take forward further actions on inequality.

The Ministers' response also covered the question of including Black, Asian, and Minority Ethnic voices in decision making. With a view to improving representation in public appointments, the Welsh Government is rolling out its diversity and inclusion strategy for public appointments.

The Welsh Christian community took real delight early in 2021 in the election of Daud Irfan as Methodist Youth President. The news greatly encouraged those who can remember his arrival in Cardiff with his family. His father, the Revd Irfan John, is a Synod Enabler for culturally diverse congregations with the Wales Methodist Synod. Daud Irfan, however, is an exception. It became painfully apparent to both Cytûn and colleagues in the Evangelical Alliance in Wales that the Welsh Government's Faith Communities Forum, in terms of representation, had one glaring omission: a representative from Wales' Black-led churches. It was agreed at a meeting of the Forum in January 2021 that a seat would be allocated for Wales' Black-led churches.

Reflecting earlier discussions on the significance of storytelling for communities, it was noted that a new curriculum working group had been set up to advise on and improve the teaching of themes relating to Black, Asian, and Minority Ethnic communities and experiences across the school curriculum. This work would be led by Professor Charlotte Williams.

The 2007 commemorations to mark the bicentenary of the abolition of the Transatlantic Slave Trade may now have faded a little in the memory. Working alongside the Welsh Government that year, churches in Wales worked collaboratively with others in marking the abolition of the Transatlantic Slave Trade at a high-profile "Valuing Freedom" event held in St David's Hall, Cardiff.

As informative and as valuable as all the events were, they could clearly not heal the memories associated with the Transatlantic Slave Trade. The debate around commemorating slave owners and those who benefited from their trade is ongoing and remains unresolved. One of the most vivid memories of 2020 was seeing the statue of the Bristol slave trader, Edward Colston, being pulled down and thrown into the nearby harbour. In Wales, Cardiff Council agreed in July 2020 to secure the removal of the statue of Sir Thomas Picton from the "Heroes of Wales" gallery in City Hall. It is said that he was the highest-ranking officer to lose his life during the Battle of Waterloo. It is also said that he treated his enslaved Africans abysmally, executing many during his time as Governor of Trinidad during the late 1790s and early 1800s. Picton gained notoriety in 1806 for cruelty during his governorship of Trinidad. He was put on trial in England for approving the torture of a fourteen-year-old girl, Louisa Calderon. Such Welsh connections with the Transatlantic Slave Trade are many.

It was announced in July 2020 that Gaynor Legall would lead an urgent audit of statues, streets, and building names with connections to the Transatlantic Slave Trade. Her audit, published in November 2020, highlighted that commemorations of people identified with the Transatlantic Slave Trade are often shown without any accompanying interpretation to address matters of contention. Churches may have a part in retelling the stories of former patrons. Sadly, Legall's research

161

revealed that there are alarmingly few Welsh people of Black or Asian heritage commemorated in Wales. That would be consistent with the race riot legacy.

The Black Lives Matter movement erupted in protest on seeing images of George Floyd needlessly losing his life under the knee of a police officer in Minneapolis, USA. Gasping for breath, he called out several times stating that he could no longer breathe. At a crucial point in time, his was the voice that the world refused to hear. Since then, the Black Lives Matter protests on the streets of Wales have found a new articulation for discourse. Newer conversations around racial justice, such as the innovative Privilege Café,[1] have burst on the scene, shaped at the insistences of a newer generation of voices. They are robust and have rapidly moved the discourse on from the grasp of traditional community gatekeepers to the dynamics forged by newer and younger voices. This new leadership will inevitably demand change, and rightly so. Many of the same young voices will be found in churches, mosques, and other places of worship.

From a Welsh perspective, one further event in 2020 would reshape the public discourse concerning race. In September 2020, the Home Office placed asylum seekers in a former military camp in Penally, near Tenby in rural Pembrokeshire. There had been virtually no public consultation prior to the placement, and community and key service providers were caught off guard. The housing of the asylum seekers there brought out the worst and the best in how Wales responds to challenging scenarios defined by race and immigration status.

The social media vitriol was at times vile and deeply racist. Yet public services went the extra mile, working well with third-sector stakeholders in seeking to welcome the service users. Faith communities acted at speed to establish an interfaith chaplaincy team and have frequently served as conduits between service providers. The rapidly established chaplaincy service provided spiritual care for the asylum seekers, and worked alongside the group Displaced People in Action to provide tablets to enable access to the internet. Because of COVID-19 restrictions, communicating with the asylum seekers at Penally became difficult at times.

Cytûn has constantly revisited the task of crafting a response to the quest for racial justice. It has applied a fleetness of foot to rapidly changing scenarios and the shifting needs of human inequality. A nation's history informs that dynamic. In the words of Amanda Gorman's powerful *The Hill We Climb*, recited at US President Joe Biden's Inauguration, a nation's history is more than a pride we inherit, it also contains damage and hurt that needs to be repaired.[2] Over the matter of race, much remains to be repaired, and the work continues.

Notes

1 The Privilege Café was founded by Mymuna, a Somali-Welsh resident of Butetown, and is a virtual space where voices that have been marginalized and othered for a very long time are now welcomed and included, respected and listened to.

2 Amanda Gorman, *The Hill We Climb: An Inaugural Poem* (Vintage Digital, 2021).

Chapter 11
Ireland, Churches, and Racial Justice

DAMIAN JACKSON

Introduction

The impact of Racial Justice Sunday in Ireland has, it must be said, been limited. Among the reasons for this would be that when it was established in 1995, both jurisdictions on the island were overwhelmingly White. Additionally, anti-discrimination work undertaken by the churches has been focused on addressing sectarianism. However, the racial and ethnic diversity on the island of Ireland has increased significantly since about that time onwards, leading to increasing awareness in the churches of the need to ensure that their congregations are places where all are welcome and are able to integrate into the community.

It is this focus on the need to welcome that has dominated churches' response to increasing ethnic diversity, and only in recent years has the issue of racism itself begun to be taken seriously as a real societal issue that needs to be systematically and holistically addressed in Ireland. Part of the reason for this delayed reaction is the lingering belief that we from Ireland cannot be racist. We are an island that has historically been a source of emigration, not a destination for immigration; we know from personal experience the challenges of migration and the lived experience of exclusion and discrimination and imagine that we would never inflict it on others. It could be argued that this quasi-denial is reflected in the inadequate provision for reporting racist incidents in both jurisdictions.

Having very briefly outlined state provisions for addressing racism and racist incidents in each jurisdiction, and a framework for categorizing and analysing the churches' engagement with issues of racism and integration, this chapter highlights some of the main initiatives taken by churches before seeking to assess their strengths and shortcomings. It then presents available evidence for discrimination on the basis of race within churches, and suggests some possible reasons for its continuing presence. Finally, it suggests what can be learnt for the churches in Ireland today from the work that has, and has not, been done in these various projects and initiatives, and proposes some pathways for future work. Given the constraints and scale of this piece, this analysis is necessarily brief, but is nevertheless useful.

Reporting Racist Incidents in Ireland

In the Republic of Ireland, the National Consultative Committee on Racism and Interculturalism (NCCRI), which had been established in 1998, was closed following the financial crisis in 2008. This means that there is no longer a state body in the Republic of Ireland with responsibility for collecting, analysing, and reporting on racist incidents. Civil society organizations, including the Irish Network Against Racism, recognizing the reluctance of victims to report racist incidents to the Gardaí (Police), developed a system, iReport.ie, which enables the logging of racist incidents. It has partnered with academics to produce comprehensive analysis and regular reports (published on the iReport website), which have supported advocacy work.

In Northern Ireland, the Office of the First Minister and Deputy First Minister published a Racial Equality Strategy for 2015–25, which committed to introducing "ethnic monitoring across the board", to the establishment of a Racial Equality Subgroup "to function as a strong voice within government here on issues specifically affecting minority ethnic people, migrants and race relations", and to the appointment of a Racial Equality Champion to each government department in the Northern Ireland Assembly. Current legislation is inadequate, however, according to the Equality Commission for Northern Ireland and the UN Committee on Racial Discrimination, which in August 2016 recommended in its concluding observations that the government should "ensure that the authorities of Northern Ireland act without further delay to adopt comprehensive legislation prohibiting racial discrimination in accordance with the provisions of the Convention".[1]

A judicial review of Hate Crime legislation under Judge Desmond Marrinan produced a report that was submitted to the Minister for Justice in November 2020.[2] The Police Service of Northern Ireland has responsibility for receiving reports of and maintaining statistics for racist incidents, and produces quarterly reports, but the judicial review maintains that there is significant under-reporting.[3]

Terminology

While necessarily imperfect, it is useful to have a working definition of racism for the purposes of this chapter. Racism is understood as the unfair, unjust, and unequal treatment of people on the basis of actual or perceived ethnic or national origin or background. It took its shape and form primarily in the European colonial expansion through which business and religious people from Europe, supported and authorized by their governments, subjugated, enslaved, educated, and evangelized in a way that made it appear that to be anything other than White was unfortunate.

This erroneous perception of people came to be reflected in the different ways in which educational institutions, businesses, governments, and churches structured and organized themselves and promoted and extended their causes. Racism today, like racism in the colonial period, is about the protection of social, political, economic, and religious privilege. Racism primarily benefits people who are White, and for that reason people who are White are often inclined to push back, deny their privilege, or question the continuing existence of racism.[4]

The Irish Network Against Racism (INAR) sets out the important point that:

> "Races" are... not real but are created and made real – by "racializing" people – through historical and ideological processes in society, involving the subordination of some groups over others. This means that it is not the existence of "race" which allows racism to exist, but the persistence of the political construct of Whiteness, which is at the heart of the system of racism, which continues to create and recreate "races". It racialises people.[5]

This INAR document delineates and defines four manifestations of racism which could usefully structure analysis of churches' responses and engagement:

- **Historical racism** has to do with the specific histories of domination and subordination of groups (i.e. the racialization of their relationships) in any given society.
- **Structural racism**, sometimes called societal racism, refers to the fact that society is structured in a way (including via cultural norms) that excludes substantial numbers of people from ethnic minority backgrounds from taking part equally in social institutions, or from having equal life outcomes.
- **Institutional racism** refers to forms of racism expressed in the practice of social and political institutions, to the way institutions discriminate against certain groups, whether intentionally or not, and to their failure to have in place policies that prevent discrimination or discriminatory behaviour.
- **Individual or interpersonal racism** covers the forms of racism which most people commonly understand as racism because they are the most visible forms. It covers all interactions or behaviour between individuals that are racist or have racist content. Microaggressions, racist discrimination, labelling and stereotyping, racist hate speech, and racist hate crime are examples of some types of racist incidents resulting from individual racism.

One danger to be aware of is that such frameworks, while useful in opening up awareness that racism is complex, insidious, and structural in nature, and goes beyond visible and explicit personal acts, also risk abstracting racism to a phenomenon for analysis and study rather than a source of continuous distress, exclusion, injustice, and sometimes violence in real people's lives in our streets, towns, cities, and even churches.

Another risk is that recognizing the systemic manifestations of racism can make it seem like a huge issue, and impossible for ordinary people to address, whereas when we only acknowledge the most visible, individual-level racism, the "bad apples" trope is often used to evade broader accountability. It is therefore important to sustain hope for systemic change by recognizing that structures, institutions, and their cultures are creations of people and can thus be changed through personal agency and intentional leadership. The work of identifying and naming the ways that structural and institutional racism discriminate between people of different colour is the starting point, and the work continues when we intentionally change the narratives and practices that sustain such discrimination. All of this work is done by human beings, individually and in collaboration. Therefore, though it may take time, receive opposition, and be difficult, all manifestations of racism can be tackled where there is the will.

Irish Churches' Response to Immigration

In both jurisdictions, the advent of significant immigration in the last twenty-five years has had a substantial impact on the diversity of church congregations, particularly those of smaller denominations. Many new churches have opened, both within the long-established denominations and through the introduction of new denominations to the island. These new denominations are primarily from Orthodox and Pentecostal traditions, though many independent congregations have also been established. This increased diversity, within both the churches and society as a whole, has led to various institutional responses, both denominationally and through the national ecumenical bodies.[6]

All-Ireland Churches Consultative Meeting on Racism

The most significant ecumenical initiative of the churches, in beginning the work of acknowledging and addressing racism within them, was the establishment of the All-Ireland Churches Consultative Meeting on Racism (AICCMR) in 2003. This was the fruit of meetings that had been ongoing between the Irish Council of Churches (ICC) and the Churches Commission for Racial Justice (CCRJ).

It had the following aims:

- To acknowledge the need to tackle racial justice issues in a more systematic and holistic fashion;

- To acknowledge the presence of institutional racism – whether intentional or unwitting;
- To be ready to accept the challenge of self-appraisal in order to address issues of tokenism, patronizing attitudes, and exclusive behaviour in individual organizations;
- To be willing to respond to the possible demands of such assessment by providing a genuine welcome that embraces diversity and difference and that seeks integration;
- To find ways of helping members overcome and move on from feelings of guilt, through positive action in encouraging Minority Ethnic people, communities, and churches;
- To discover and develop ways of empowering and supporting the full integration of Minority Ethnic communities into society.

The AICCMR worked for seven years, undertook research, and produced significant resources. Its major outputs included the following pieces of work.

Challenged by difference

AICCMR commissioned research by the late Dr Fee Ching Leong, which revealed shortcomings within churches in responding to the needs of Minority Ethnic people, resulting in a paper, "The Experiences, Expectations and Aspirations of Black and Minority Ethnic People in Relation to the Churches' Role in Tackling Racism".[7] This research paper fed into a major conference in November 2005: "Challenged by Difference: Threat or Enrichment", the papers from which are available online.[8] This provided an opportunity for church people to come together to listen to the experiences of people from Minority Ethnic communities and to explore the issues. Dr Leong's research found that all participant groups agreed on the need for strong and vocal church leadership in anti-racism, both at a national level through joint statements and awareness raising and at local level through preaching on racism and speaking out in response to local racist incidents.[9]

Participants also shared negative experiences of churches, with descriptions of congregation members as aloof, condescending, or patronizing, and not seeing Minority Ethnic people as distinct individuals but as a category. The participants included representatives of Traveller communities who related their very low expectations of inclusion, including by the clergy, who would not be expected to offer pastoral support or visit their halting sites. There was a desire that churches would be braver and more intentional in seeking to connect with local Minority Ethnic people, explicitly inviting them to church and inviting them to participate when they are in church, including providing opportunities to speak from the front about their lives and experiences. It was pointed out that minority ethnic leadership within White majority churches cannot emerge while there is little or no contact, interaction and consultation with Black and minority ethnic people. There was recognition that many in current leadership positions feel ill-equipped to do this, and that therefore there is a need for cultural-diversity and anti-racism training for church leaders. These findings stimulated further work, resulting in subsequent AICCMR publications seeking to address these identified needs.

Intercultural Insights

In 2008 AICCMR published "Inter-Cultural Insights: Christian Reflections on Racism, Hospitality and Identity from the Island of Ireland", edited by Scott Boldt.[10] A collection of contributions in the form of essays, theology, and poetry, it gives insight into the experiences of racism of a diverse group of people from across the island. Notably, this collection gives space for the voices of people on the receiving end of racism, including from the Traveller community, for example where Cathleen McDonagh writes on John 4:5–15 – The Woman at the Well:

I am from a rejected people. As a member of the Traveller Community neither society, nor the church knows me. And in not knowing me they fear and at times despise me. I am so tired of the rejection and ignorance. I too am much in need of the water from the well. I crave the life-giving water that is life from God... The only hope for me is to be filled with the spirit of love or I will be lost to the continuous hurt I experience as a Traveller person.[11]

What the Bible says about the stranger

Recognizing the key role of Scripture and theology in exploring the Christian response to the presence of newcomers, AICCMR also published *What the Bible Says About the Stranger: Biblical perspectives on racism, migration, asylum and cross-community issues* by Kieran O'Mahony OSA.[12] This resource contained Bible studies, questions for group reflection, and suggestions for dramatization of biblical passages.

Parish-based Integration Project

The Parish-based Integration Project (PIP) was an initiative of the Irish Inter-Church Meeting (IICM) and was largely funded by the former Office of the Minister of State for Integration. It ran between 2007 and 2010 to assist churches with the practical integration of immigrants in parishes and congregations. Resourced by the Integration Officer, Adrian Cristea, this project had several major outputs, beginning with the publication of ten "Integration Guidelines for Parishes and Congregations".

Unity in Diversity in our Churches

These guidelines were then further developed – with a theological foundation for the valuing of diversity in our church congregations, questions and suggestions for action, models of best practice, and case studies of implementation – in the 2008 publication "Unity in Diversity in Our Churches".[13]

Directory of "Migrant-led Churches and Chaplaincies"

The PIP, in collaboration with AICCMR, also developed the "Directory of Migrant-led Churches and Chaplaincies", which, for the first time, gathered a comprehensive database of what were called migrant-led churches[14] across the island.[15] The cataloguing of more than 360 newer faith communities allowed a much clearer picture of the landscape of Irish Christianity to inform the work of the inter-church bodies, and in the process developed connections between those bodies and the many newly established churches.

Affirmations on migration, diversity, and interculturalism

The PIP then developed the "Affirmations on Migration, Diversity and Interculturalism", which were adopted by the IICM and launched in 2010 in Dublin by the Minister for Integration, Mary White, and in Belfast by the Lord Mayor.[16] The affirmations have since shaped engagement on integration and asylum work by the inter-church bodies, were adopted by the AGM of the ICC in 2016, and were recalled again in the opening address to the IICM by its joint secretary, Revd Kieran McDermott, in 2019.

Summary

These two projects were the most significant interventions by the national inter-church bodies that related to issues of race and integration, and of them, the PIP was more focused on equipping church congregations to welcome and integrate newcomers rather than on racism itself. Several other projects that were initiatives of individual denominations or other inter-church groups contained elements that sought to enable dialogue and exchange, to advocate for the Government to address injustices in the asylum systems in each jurisdiction, and to foster connection with other faith communities, but few addressed racism directly.[17] There have been, however, some notable recent exceptions.

The Catholic Bishops' Conference statement, following its summer 2020 meeting, acknowledged the racism and discrimination in Irish society and the need for churches and schools to recognize and celebrate the fundamental dignity of every person.

The Church of Ireland created a resource on racial justice and equality for use in worship, "Taking the Knee", with prayers of acknowledgement and lament.[18] The Church of Ireland joint Dioceses of Dublin and Glendalough published a report of a study of cultural and ethnic diversity in its parishes which recognizes the need to shift focus from welcome (though that remains important) toward ensuring "that all aspects of life in our parishes reflect the diversity of the congregations".[19]

The Annual Conference of the Methodist Church passed a resolution calling on Methodists not just to "condemn the wicked actions of others in the present or the past, but let us examine our own hearts and attitudes".[20] Its youth ambassadors also released a statement on racism.[21] In previous years, the Methodist Conference held an annual conference on "Multi-Ethnic Churches", which sought to initiate conversations and encourage churches to be intentional about inclusion.

The Presbyterian Church in Ireland has a committee with the remit of informing its response to issues related to race and discrimination. Formerly called the Race Relations Panel, it is now the Intercultural Relations Panel and has published many resources for congregations, including in 2020 a Bible study resource on the Book of Ruth with associated videos and interviews with Minority Ethnic church members. The denomination has also established the International Meeting Point in Belfast which seeks to meet the needs of migrants and asylum seekers in the city.[22]

Analysis

The rapid increase in ethnic diversity has unsettled the Irish self-identity as a source rather than a destination for migration, which had the side-effect of engendering the conception that Irish people cannot be racist as they have been the objects of racism in destination countries. However, people from Minority Ethnic groups do experience racism and discrimination daily, in everyday life, and it is only recently that public discourse is reflecting, or admitting, this reality. The inter-church bodies have shown a consistent concern for welcome and integration in church and society over at least the past twenty years. This has been reflected in many ecumenical and denominational projects and initiatives, including those described above.

There is a clear desire in the national leadership of the churches to honour the dignity of people from Minority Ethnic groups in church life, and to work to see them honoured in our societies. However, it is apparent that most of the churches' work has focused on the *consequences* of structural racism, evident in the asylum systems and processes in both jurisdictions, rather than on racism itself. While this work continues to be important and unfortunately necessary, it is nevertheless outward-looking and so will not address issues within the churches. Exceptions include AICCMR's work on experiences of individual racism in churches and the expectations of people from Minority Ethnic groups of churches in terms of tackling racism, while Embrace NI highlighted racist incidents and ECONI's *Lion & Lamb* magazine produced articles and seminars confronting churches with the reality of racism in Northern Ireland.[23]

Similarly, the welcome- and integration-focused work of the PIP sought to equip churches to address the consequences of institutional racism, but did not directly address the need for church leadership and membership to acknowledge racism's existence in the church (both in local congregations and the national denominations) and in the hearts of churchgoers themselves – the White privilege that underpins cultural and ownership assumptions and (lack of) awareness of barriers to integration and inclusion.

"Among Our Own": The Issues in Irish Churches Today

CTBI's Churches' Refugee Network hosted a webinar in July 2020 at which Dr Ebun Joseph of University College Dublin shared that racism's biggest weapon is denial. She elaborated some principles that are now clearly needed in anti-racism today: first, to accept its existence within the church; second, that we need to "unmute ourselves" – being a bystander is no longer excusable; and finally that (White) privilege can be manifest as a lack of awareness, as the existence of a choice whether to say something or not upon witnessing explicit racism, or as an unspoken assumption of ownership.

There is anecdotal evidence from several sources of a pattern whereby recent Minority Ethnic immigrants initially join a local church from one of the long-established denominations but then leave after a time, often to join a Black Majority Church. British pastor and activist Ben Lindsay offers a similar narrative that he has repeatedly heard from his church members who have joined from other congregations. He states:

> They say, "I'm exhausted by dealing with racism and discrimination in my workplace, so why would I choose to identify with the church community that shows no more understanding of the issues I faced in my fight with work colleagues?" From their perspective, maybe attending an all-Black church would be easier.[24]

Another sign that the work of integration in Irish churches is not complete is illustrated by the observation of a minister of a Dublin church who told me that he noticed that after the service people in his congregation tended to group together along ethnic lines. He was reassured, by an elder of Nigerian origin whom he consulted on this, that the groups were linguistic rather than ethnic. While it is natural for us humans to seek out those with whom we share a common cultural and linguistic heritage, when congregations end up conversing in groups like this, it could be a sign that Minority Ethnic people do not have a sense of belonging or ownership of the space. One of the distinctive tropes in interviews I undertook for my PhD with long-standing congregation members, was that Minority Ethnic people tend to "keep to their own".[25] From the other side, Fee Ching Leong's research shows that Minority Ethnic people described church members as "aloof", "inward-looking", and "frightened of us", and that rather than getting to know them, perceptions were based on stereotype-driven assumptions.[26]

Other interviewees noted that, despite ethnic diversity in the congregation, little if any change could be observed in the way services were conducted in the culture of the church community, other than in sung worship.[27] It is perhaps telling that, of the guidelines produced by PIP, the tenth – to "Promote the participation of newcomers in leadership" – is the least realized: people from Minority Ethnic groups are under-represented in leadership positions in the longer-established churches in Ireland.

If this is so, then are churches too comfortable for the established community, tending to be merely "places of ordered calm – a safe space – where we are among our own; our enemies are outside", as the Community Relations Council noted is often the case?[28] Or, more pointedly still, a participant in a recent CTBI consultation suggested that churches are actually often places of shelter for people who are perpetuating barriers to people from Minority Ethnic communities, and that thereby we collectively become their persecutors.

Moving from Welcome to Inclusion

The pattern whereby Minority Ethnic people join an established church but then leave to join a Black Majority Church has been under-examined. My doctoral research showed that while long-standing congregation members welcomed the presence of Minority Ethnic "newcomers", especially in their musical contributions, nevertheless a sense of their "ownership" of the church remained.[29] In other words, you are welcome to come and worship with us here, but in the end, "we" decide how things are done around here. Revd Dr Sahr Yambasu, Minister of Waterford Methodist Church and President of the Methodist Church in Ireland in 2021–22, told me, "Welcome into the church is actually an invitation to consume what we do and how we do it – it is comfortable for the established community." This is the unspoken and unexamined assumption of ownership mentioned by Dr Joseph above.

My research postulated four fingerprints that are indicative of exclusionary ideology that serves to protect the interests and privilege of the established group at the expense of others. They are a conception of the status quo as natural or common-sense, categorization or essentializing of "others" as an undifferentiated group, use of emotive symbolic language when challenged, and "false altruism" whereby apparent concessions are made but do not threaten current arrangements of power.[30] It is arguable that all of these are present in Irish churches and serve to reinforce the cultural dominance of the White Irish membership.

Lindsay points out that being a place of welcome is not the same as being a place of inclusion in terms of leading and leadership, decision-making, training, and capacity building:

> There is a huge difference between churches being diverse and churches being inclusive… there is a strange colour-blind mentality within the church (seeing everything as race neutral), which can make the topic even more difficult to raise. Many Christians would argue that God does not see colour so why should we?[31]

This colour-blind racism – the idea that "we are all one human race so why can't we just get along" – hides the power dynamics at play which privilege the agency of the established, White congregation members. It's this kind of perspective that is revealed when people push back against the "Black Lives Matter" narrative with, "But all lives matter." Barriers to full inclusion need to be named and made concrete within specific contexts, for example asking, "Why, although we have had a diverse congregation for many years, has only one non-White person ever been elected to our committee/parish council?" Then practices and attitudes can be identified and named, and the work of transforming culture can begin. This enables the addressing of racism to be conceived of as possible, manageable, and achievable, bit by bit through discernible actions.

Churches in Ireland have been stronger on advocacy and provision of services than on self-examination, acknowledgement of privilege, internal naming of prejudice, and analysis of institutional barriers to equity, inclusion, and integration. The liturgical and theological practices of listening, lament, and repentance provide rich resources from our traditions to begin this journey.

Such work is not easy and often faces resistance and misunderstanding. Theologian Susanna Snyder, in her book *Asylum-Seeking, Migration and Church*, explores these dynamics, suggesting that people respond to the challenges of unexamined frameworks of understanding the world out of either an ecology of fear or an ecology of faith. She traces these responses in the Scriptures, using the accounts in Ezra and Nehemiah as an example of fearful engagement with the other, and Jesus' encounter with the Syro-Phoenician woman as an engagement rooted in faith.[32] She recognizes that fear and the reasons for it need acknowledgement, but we have an obligation to call one another out of fear and to loving encounter with the other as one who has much to offer us, confident (in faith) of our identity rooted in Christ, not in human-constructed ideas of nationality or race.

Through the ICC and IICM, the churches in Ireland are beginning a process of addressing this.[33] At a listening event in 2020, the IICM co-chairs heard about the experiences of local churches in areas where there have been protests against proposed direct provision accommodation centres for people seeking asylum, which far-right groups sought to infiltrate and exploit. The ICC/IICM Programme Officer is developing a work programme to raise awareness, equip, and encourage churches to engage and connect with one another and with organizations like the Church of Sanctuary movement who can support them in the journey to becoming places of inclusion.

However, this will not happen without intentionality. At a webinar hosted by the Churches Commission for Migrants in Europe (CCME) in November 2020, Dr Harvey Kwiyani challenged churches to *intentionally* set out first to make their membership reflect the diversity of the place where they are situated, then to make their leadership reflect the diversity of their membership.[34] Such intention is hard to imagine but can start in simple ways. One Dublin church recognized that it had progress to make in this area, so it held a meeting between the leadership and the Minority Ethnic congregation members specifically to have the opportunity to listen to their concerns and to find out "what we're doing wrong". Dr Leong's research participants recognized that leadership can be nervous, and the fear of getting it wrong often prevents action from being taken, but she encouraged them to take action nevertheless:

> We need a signal to come from church leaders because we are all the handiwork of God... We might look different, but we can't and don't want to live in isolation from others.[35]

Specifically, preaching on racism was highlighted as key, participants pointing out that:

> The pulpit [can] be an effective platform for preaching on anti-racism, for providing the theological basis for challenging racism... if churches are silent in regard to condemning, highlighting or tackling racism, then this would serve to reinforce any perception that there is a lack of leadership from the Christian churches on these issues.[36]

At the aforementioned CCME webinar, Revd Daniela Konrädi put it more forcefully:

> If we wait until we've figured out how to say it just right, we'll never get there. We have to be prepared to speak and maybe get it wrong and offend some people. But we have to speak. We have to be loud. White silence is violence.[37]

Conclusion

The churches in Ireland have a long history of work demonstrating an ongoing concern for the injustices faced by Minority Ethnic people as a result of racism and discrimination. This work has incorporated projects aiming at fostering welcome and integration of people from Minority Ethnic backgrounds within the churches, and at tackling societal, systemic racism, principally in the systems put in place for people seeking asylum and refugees. As such, it has mainly focused on the consequences of historical, structural, and institutional racism rather than examining their causes and genesis in unconscious and unexamined bias and prejudice across society (including among churchgoers).

The next challenge is to move from welcome to inclusion. American activist DeRay Mckesson, pithily states, "Diversity is about bodies; inclusion is about culture."[38] Irish churches need to go beyond welcoming bodies of colour to intentionally opening our church culture up so that it reflects the full inclusion of all the people who are physically in it, rather than being a comfortable place where we are "among our own", narrowly conceived. Our history of anti-sectarian theological and practical reconciliatory work can provide a rich tapestry of resources adaptable to the task, but will require an intentionality in the leadership, at both national and local levels, as well as at grassroots level.

Notes

1   UN Committee on the Elimination of Racial Discrimination, "Concluding Observations on the Twenty-First to Twenty-Third Periodic Reports of United Kingdom of Great Britain and Northern Ireland", August 2016, para. 8(c); Equality Commission for Northern Ireland, "Race Law Reform", www.equalityni.org/Delivering-Equality/ Addressing-inequality/Law-reform/Related-work (last viewed 28 April 2022).

2   Desmond Marrinan, "Final Report into Hate Crime Legislation in Northern Ireland Independent Review", December 2020, www. justice-ni.gov.uk/publications/hate-crime-legislation-independent-review (last viewed 28 April 2022).

3   Marrinan, "Final Report", para. 156.

4   Reni Eddo-Lodge explains, "When I talk about white privilege, I don't mean that white people have it easy, that they've never struggled, or that they've never lived in poverty. But white privilege is the fact that if you're white, your race will almost certainly positively impact your life's trajectory in some way. And you probably won't even notice it." Eddo-Lodge, *Why I'm No Longer Talking to White People About Race*, expanded edition (London: Bloomsbury Publishing, 2017), p. 87.

5   Irish Network Against Racism, "Understanding Racism: Defining

Racism in an Irish Context", Dublin, 2020, inar.ie/wp-content/uploads/2020/03/UNDERSTANDING-RACISM.pdf (last viewed 28 April 2022) p. 3.

6 The national ecumenical bodies in Ireland are the Irish Council of Churches (ICC), whose membership includes the main churches in Ireland from Protestant, Orthodox, Reformed, and Independent church traditions. Representatives from ICC meet regularly with representatives of the Roman Catholic Bishops' Conference through the Irish Inter-Church Meeting (IICM). Both ICC and IICM are, like their member churches, organized on an all-island basis, encompassing both political jurisdictions. For more information, see www.irishchurches.org/about/who-we-are (last viewed 28 April 2022).

7 Fee Ching Leong, "The Experiences, Expectations and Aspirations of Black and Minority Ethnic People in Relation to the Churches' Role in Tackling Racism", All-Ireland Churches Consultative Meeting on Racism, November 2005, irishchurches.org/cmsfiles/resources/AICCMR/AICCMR-Conference-FeeChingResearch.pdf (last viewed 28 April 2022).

8 "Challenged by Difference: Threat or Enrichment", Dromantine Retreat and Conference Centre: All-Ireland Churches Consultative Meeting on Racism, 2005, www.embraceni.org/embrace-archive/christian-voices-2005 (last viewed 28 April 2022).

9 The following groups participated in the research focus groups: Association of Refugees and Asylum Seekers in Ireland, African Refugee Network Belfast, Blanchardstown Travellers Women's Group, Clondalkin Travellers Men's Group, Comhlámh, Integrating Ireland, Irish Refugee Council, Joy in the Nation, Parish of the Travelling People, Chinese Christian Church, Belfast Islamic Centre, Multi-Cultural Resource Centre, Northern Ireland Council for Ethnic Minorities, Spiritan Refugees and Asylum Seekers Initiative.

10 Scott Boldt, "Inter-Cultural Insights: Christian Reflections on Racism, Hospitality and Identity from the Island of Ireland", AICCMR, March 2008, www.embraceni.org/wp-content/uploads/2008/09/InterCultural%20Insights%5B1%5D1.pdf (last viewed 28 April 2022).

11 Boldt, "Inter-Cultural Insights", p. 15.

12 Kieran J. O'Mahony, *What the Bible Says About the Stranger: Biblical Perspectives on Racism, Migration, Asylum and Cross-Community Issues* (Belfast: Irish Inter-Church Meeting, 2009).

13 Adrian Cristea, "Unity in Diversity in Our Churches", Irish Inter-Church Meeting, 2008, www.irishchurches.org/cmsfiles/resources/Reports/PIPmanual.pdf (last viewed 28 April 2022).

14 This term is no longer used, as a result of subsequent feedback that it is no longer appropriate as it unnecessarily categorizes churches that are now well established across the island.

15 All-Ireland Churches Consultative Meeting on Racism, "Directory of Migrant-Led Churches and Chaplaincies", All-Ireland Churches Consultative Meeting on Racism, 2009, www.irishchurches.org/cmsfiles/resources/Reports/DirectoryOfMigrantLedChurchesAndChaplaincies2009.pdf (last viewed 28 April 2022).

16 Irish Inter-Church Meeting, "Irish Churches' Affirmations on Migration, Diversity and Interculturalism", Irish Inter-Church Meeting, 2010, www.irishchurches.org/cmsfiles/resources/Reports/affirmations.pdf (last viewed 28 April 2022).

17 Significant projects include the Irish Churches' Peace Project and the Dublin City Interfaith Forum.

18 Church and Society Commission, "Taking the Knee: Prayers for Racial Justice and Equality", 28 September 2020, www.ireland.anglican.org/news/10028/taking-the-knee-prayers-for (last viewed 28 April 2022).

19 Anne Lodge, "But the Lord Looks on the Heart: Report of a 2020 Study of Cultural and Ethnic Diversity in the Parishes of the United Dioceses of Dublin & Glendalough", United Dioceses of Dublin & Glendalough, October 2020, p. 8, dublin.anglican.org/resources/diocesan-reports/cultural-and-ethnic-diversity-in (last viewed 28 April 2022).

20 Annual Conference of the Methodist Church in Ireland, "Ministerial Session – Resolution on Racism", 11 June 2020.

21 IMYCD, "Irish Methodist Youth Ambassadors Statement on #BlackLivesMatter", 8 June 2020.

22 Presbyterian Church in Ireland, "International Meeting Point", www.facebook.com/Themeetingpoint133 (last viewed 28 April 2022).

23 Evangelical Contribution on Northern Ireland, "*Lion & Lamb* Back Issues". See in particular Revd Dr Ken Newell in issue 37.

24 Ben Lindsay, *We Need to Talk About Race: Understanding the Black Experience in White Majority Churches.* (London: SPCK, 2019), p. 26.

25 Damian Jackson, "Undocumented Migrants and the Hegemonic Ideology of the System of Territorial Borders: A Critical Analysis of

Ideological Contention in Irish Christians' Moral Imagination", Trinity College, Dublin, 2013, hdl.handle.net/2262/79058 (last viewed 28 April 2022), p. 146.

26 Leong, "The Experiences, Expectations and Aspirations", p. 8.

27 Jackson, "Undocumented Migrants", p. 152.

28 Community Relations Council, "Beyond Sectarianism? The Churches and Ten Years of the Peace Process", Learning from Peace III. Belfast: Community Relations Council, 2005, p. 10.

29 Jackson, "Undocumented Migrants", pp. 150–52.

30 Jackson, "Undocumented Migrants", pp. 38–42.

31 Lindsay, *We Need to Talk about Race*, p. 21.

32 Susanna Snyder, *Asylum-Seeking, Migration and Church: Explorations in Practical, Pastoral, and Empirical Theology* (Burlington, VT: Ashgate, 2012), chapters 7–8.

33 INAR has an excellent resource entitled "Ten Things You Can Do About Racism in Ireland", which suggests the place to begin is with examination of privilege and its meaning, and unconscious prejudices, progressing to education, allyship, advocacy, and other forms of engagement. Irish Network Against Racism, "Ten Things You Can Do about Racism in Ireland", 2020, inar.ie/10-things-you-can-do-about-racism-in-ireland (last viewed 28 April 2022).

34 Harvey Kwiyani, Daniela Konrädi, Arlington Trotman, and Sarah Vecera, "Racism and Inequality in the Church: Experience and Action in Unity on Seeking Justice": Presented at the Churches Commission for Migrants in Europe, 3 November 2020, ccme.eu/index.php/areas-of-work/uniting-in-diversity (last viewed 28 April 2022).

35 Leong, "The Experiences, Expectations and Aspirations", p. 7.

36 Leong, "The Experiences, Expectations and Aspirations", p. 7.

37 Kwiyani et al., "Racism and Inequality in the Church".

38 DeRay Mckesson, "Equity vs. Equality in Tech: Which is Fair?", Black Enterprise, 30 October 2017, www.blackenterprise.com/video-deray-mckesson-equity-vs-equality-tech (last viewed 28 April 2022).

Bibliography

All-Ireland Churches Consultative Meeting on Racism,
    "Directory of Migrant-Led Churches and Chaplaincies".

All-Ireland Churches Consultative Meeting on Racism,
    2009. www.irishchurches.org/cmsfiles/resources/Reports/
    DirectoryOfMigrantLedChurchesAndChaplaincies2009.pdf.
Annual Conference of the Methodist Church in Ireland, "Ministerial
    Session – Resolution on Racism", 11 June 2020. www.irishmethodist.
    org/news/11-june-2020/ministerial-session-resolution-racism.
Boldt, Scott, "Inter-Cultural Insights: Christian Reflections on Racism,
    Hospitality and Identity from the Island of Ireland", 2008, AICCMR,
    March 2008. www.embraceni.org/wp-content/uploads/2008/09/
    InterCultural%20Insights%5B1%5D1.pdf.
"Challenged by Difference: Threat or Enrichment", Dromantine
    Retreat and Conference Centre: All-Ireland Churches Consultative
    Meeting on Racism, 2005. www.embraceni.org/embrace-archive/
    christian-voices-2005.
Church and Society Commission, "Taking the Knee: Prayers for Racial
    Justice and Equality", 28 September 2020. www.ireland.anglican.org/
    news/10028/taking-the-knee-prayers-for.
Community Relations Council, "Beyond Sectarianism? The Churches
    and Ten Years of the Peace Process". Learning from Peace III. Belfast:
    Community Relations Council, 2005.
Cristea, Adrian, "Unity in Diversity in Our Churches". Irish Inter-Church
    Meeting, 2008. www.irishchurches.org/cmsfiles/resources/Reports/
    PIPmanual.pdf.
Eddo-Lodge, Reni, *Why I'm No Longer Talking to White People About Race*.
    Expanded edition. London: Bloomsbury Publishing, 2017.
Equality Commission for Northern Ireland, "Race Law Reform".
    Equality Commission for Northern Ireland. www.equalityni.org/
    Delivering-Equality/Addressing-inequality/Law-reform/Related-work.
Evangelical Contribution on Northern Ireland, "*Lion & Lamb* Back Issues".
    Contemporary Christianity. www.contemporarychristianity.net/
    lionandlamb/lion&lamb_back.htm.
IMYCD, "Irish Methodist Youth Ambassadors Statement
    on #BlackLivesMatter", 8 June 2020. imycd.org/news/
    ambassadors-statement-blacklivesmatter/.
Irish Inter-Church Meeting, "Irish Churches' Affirmations on Migration,
    Diversity and Interculturalism". Irish Inter-Church Meeting, 2010.
    www.irishchurches.org/cmsfiles/resources/Reports/affirmations.pdf.
Irish Network Against Racism, "Ten Things You Can Do about Racism

in Ireland". Irish Network Against Racism, 2020. https://inar.
ie/10-things-you-can-do-about-racism-in-ireland/.

"Understanding Racism: Defining Racism in an Irish Context, Dublin, 2020.
inar.ie/wp-content/uploads/2020/03/UNDERSTANDING-RACISM.pdf.

Jackson, Damian, "Undocumented Migrants and the Hegemonic Ideology
of the System of Territorial Borders: A Critical Analysis of Ideological
Contention in Irish Christians' Moral Imagination". Trinity College,
Dublin, 2013. hdl.handle.net/2262/79058.

Kwiyani, Harvey, Daniela Konrädi, Arlington Trotman, and Sarah Vecera,
"Racism and Inequality in the Church: Experience and Action in
Unity on Seeking Justice": Presented at the Churches Commission
for Migrants in Europe, 3 November 2020. ccme.eu/index.php/
areas-of-work/uniting-in-diversity.

Leong, Fee Ching, "The Experiences, Expectations and Aspirations of
Black and Minority Ethnic People in Relation to the Churches' Role
in Tackling Racism". All-Ireland Churches Consultative Meeting
on Racism, November 2005. irishchurches.org/cmsfiles/resources/
AICCMR/AICCMR-Conference-FeeChingResearch.pdf.

Lindsay, Ben, *We Need to Talk about Race: Understanding the Black
Experience in White Majority Churches.* London: SPCK, 2019.

Lodge, Anne, "But the Lord Looks on the Heart: Report of a 2020 Study
of Cultural and Ethnic Diversity in the Parishes of the United Dioceses
of Dublin & Glendalough". United Dioceses of Dublin & Glendalough,
October 2020. dublin.anglican.org/resources/diocesan-reports/
cultural-and-ethnic-diversity-in.

Marrinan, Desmond, "Final Report into Hate Crime Legislation in
Northern Ireland Independent Review", December 2020. www.justice-ni.
gov.uk/publications/hate-crime-legislation-independent-review.

Mckesson, DeRay, Equity vs. Equality in Tech: Which
is Fair?, 30 October 2017. www.blackenterprise.com/
video-deray-mckesson-equity-vs-equality-tech/.

O'Mahony, Kieran J., *What the Bible Says About the Stranger: Biblical
Perspectives on Racism, Migration, Asylum and Cross-Community Issues.*
Belfast: Irish Inter-Church Meeting, 2009.

Presbyterian Church in Ireland, "International Meeting Point". www.
facebook.com/Themeetingpoint133.

Snyder, Susanna, *Asylum-Seeking, Migration and Church: Explorations in
Practical, Pastoral, and Empirical Theology.* Burlington, VT: Ashgate, 2012.

UN Committee on the Elimination of Racial Discrimination, "Concluding Observations on the Twenty-First to Twenty-Third Periodic Reports of United Kingdom of Great Britain and Northern Ireland", August 2016. tbinternet.ohchr.org/Treaties/CERD/Shared%20Documents/GBR/ CERD_C_GBR_CO_21-23_24985_E.pdf.

Chapter 12
Racial Justice within the Salvation Army in the UK

JONNY SMITH

Introduction

This chapter reflects on how the Salvation Army (United Kingdom with the Republic of Ireland) has journeyed toward racial justice over the last twenty-five years. It highlights major campaigns that have taken place, and are still happening, as well as local Salvation Army corps (churches) that have displayed incredible intercultural journeys, have embraced and welcomed all people, and seen racial diversity increase in both congregations and local leadership. This chapter celebrates the way in which Black, Asian, and Minority Ethnic people have been appointed to senior management positions. Indeed, there is much to be mentioned and celebrated when it comes to racial justice.

However, to give a true reflection of the Salvation Army's journey, this chapter also draws attention to racial injustice that has happened. It sadly highlights far too many incidents of racism and institutional racism, which go against the intentions not only of the Salvation Army but also, and more importantly, of God.

In accepting the injustices that have happened, the chapter concludes by highlighting how we are to move forward positively, seeking kingdom transformation in the communities across Britain.

Our Journey

If the church becomes welcoming – where people can feel like they are part of a larger family – then people will come.
(Mrs Mensah, Clapton Salvation Army member)

From the cross-denominational books I have read and online lectures I have attended in recent months (with speakers from different denominations), the reality is that sadly many local churches cannot claim to have been places of welcome when it comes to racism, with some living out unjust ways which at times have prevented the "whosoever" from entering through their doors. Interestingly, the Salvation Army's early members came because they had not been welcomed at other churches!

It was the ethos for the "whosoever" that started the Salvation Army, which is now an international movement, serving in 131 countries across the globe. Founded by William and Catherine Booth in 1865, the fight for justice is part of its DNA, including the fight for racial injustice. In recognizing this injustice, the Salvation Army's international positional statement on racism declares:

Racism is the belief that races have distinctive cultural characteristics determined by hereditary factors and that this endows some races with an intrinsic superiority over others. "Racism" also refers to political or social programmes built on that belief. The use of the term "race" itself is contested, but is generally used to refer to a distinct group sharing a common ethnicity, national origin, descent and/or skin colour. The Salvation Army denounces racism in all forms.

Racism is fundamentally incompatible with the Christian conviction that all people are made in the image of God and are equal in value. The Salvation Army believes that the world is enriched by a diversity of cultures and ethnicities.

The Salvation Army firmly believes that racism is contrary to God's intention for humankind, and yet we recognise that the tendency for racism is present in all people and all societies. Racial discrimination can take many expressions, including tribalism, casteism and ethnocentrism. Racism is not only the result of individual attitudes but can also be perpetuated by social structures and systems. Sometimes racism is overt and intentional, but often it is not.

While many Salvationists have acted firmly and courageously against racism, the Salvation Army acknowledges with regret, that Salvationists have sometimes shared in the sins of racism and conformed to economic, organisational and social pressures that perpetuate racism. The Salvation Army is committed to fight against racism wherever it is experienced and will speak into societies around the world wherever we encounter it.

As we pray for God's will to be done on Earth as in Heaven, the Salvation Army will work towards a world where all people are accepted, loved and valued.[1]

As a result of the events we witnessed in 2020, including the horrendous murder of George Floyd, the disproportionate amount of Black, Asian, and Minority Ethnic people who have suffered and died as a result of COVID-19, and the way that racism and institutional racism have sadly been exposed in our country, we, the Salvation Army, recognize that we have a very long way to go to bring about racial justice, both inside and outside our movement. Yet where there is God, there is hope!

Fighting for Racial Justice

Although racial injustice was exposed in 2020 arguably more than in most other years, it is important to recognize the racial justice fighters who have been speaking out for many years. Linbert Spencer, a Salvationist from Bedford who has been a fighter for racial justice for many years (including for the Salvation Army and the wider church), was asked to write a contribution to this report. It is important to recognize the role that Linbert has played with regards to Racial Justice Sunday and much more in relation to racial equality, diversity, and inclusion within and outside the church. Linbert states:

My involvement with Racial Justice Sunday came about as a result of my membership of the Archbishop of Canterbury's Commission on Urban Priority Areas, the output from which was "Faith in The City", published in 1985. I was one of our representatives on Churches Together in Britain and Ireland (CTBI) in the late 1980s, and at some point after that became a member of the Churches Commission for Racial Justice (CCRJ). Racial Justice Sunday became the CCRJ's responsibility, and a small group would work hard for many months, often starting to think about the next year's theme and resources as soon as they finished preparing the resources for the current year.

I was not personally involved on the group during the early years, but at some point I was drawn in. BBC Radio 4 used to do a live broadcast of a Racial Justice Sunday service, and in 2004 the service was broadcast from Wood Green Salvation Army; I was privileged to give the address. My final words were.

> Diversity is a biological, biblical, and theological requirement – it is God's intention for us. We mustn't strive to become or make others into clones... Your body has many parts – limbs, organs, cells – but no matter how many parts you can name, you're still one body. If one part flourishes, every other part enters into the exuberance. Let us recommit ourselves to recognizing and celebrating our diversity and acknowledging, and being exuberant about, the fact that we are part of the same body; all members of the same race – the human race.

In 2012, my last year on CCRJ, I was a member of the group responsible for preparing the resources, so I commissioned my son, Matt Spencer, to write a song to include in the resources pack. True to form, Matt did not disappoint. The sentiment, evident in the chorus below, speaks to and challenges individual congregations, mission expressions, and communities across all denominations:

> Jesus, you have prayed your people would be one;
> We have prayed to see your Kingdom come,
> Your will be done, here on Earth as it is in Heav'n.
> Jesus, help us be the answer to your prayer;
> May we be united as we share
> Every blessing you pour out on us;
> As we are one in you, Jesus.[2]

As Linbert has said, he has been involved in Racial Justice Sunday for many years. It is also important to recognize that within the Salvation Army, Linbert has devoted much time and energy to helping the Salvation Army in the UK and Republic of Ireland and internationally on the journey toward racial justice. It can be argued that, thanks to people such as Linbert, the Salvation Army has engaged in huge campaigns to help bring about racial justice within the world.

National and International Campaigns in Our Fight for Racial Justice

Since 2011, the Salvation Army, together with our partners, has supported more than 10,000 potential victims of modern slavery in England and Wales, as well as victims of human trafficking internationally. Major Kathy Betteridge, Director of Anti Trafficking and Modern Slavery, writes:

> The Salvation Army is committed to supporting victims of human trafficking and modern slavery. Our anti-trafficking and modern slavery work take place on an international scale. The Salvation Army has been protecting and supporting vulnerable people, including victims of human trafficking and modern slavery, since its inception in the 1880s. General William Booth, the Salvation Army founder, identified then how slavery still existed despite the abolition of the Transatlantic Slave Trade sixty years previously. He wrote in his book *In Darkest England and the Way Out*, "But at our own doors, from "Plymouth to Peterhead" stretches this vast continent of humanity – three million human beings who are enslaved – some of them to taskmasters as merciless as any West Indian overseer, all of them to destitution and despair."[3]

Modern slavery includes, but is not limited to, the crimes of forced labour, sexual exploitation, domestic servitude, forced criminality, and human trafficking – all offences where a person has their freedom taken away and they are kept in slavery or servitude by the use of threats, violence, abuse of power, or deception. Modern slavery and human trafficking are complex and abhorrent crimes that affect an estimated 40 million women, men, and children worldwide: one in every 184 people. They destroy lives and are taking place in the UK. Our own government estimates 10,000 to 13,000 people to be held in slave-like conditions in the UK, although some sources believe this figure is much higher.

There are many stories of people who have experienced harrowing situations and have survived; they come to us emotionally, physically, mentally, and spiritually broken. But their resilience and determination to recover is a credit to them. Here is one story, of Aleksander, who was trafficked into Britain for forced labour:

> I was sold on several times to different bosses. I was given £20 a week, and this had to pay for everything; my food, clothes, heating, and electricity. I was threatened that things would be bad for me, and my family would suffer if I tried to leave. I lived in a tiny room with five other people, everything was dirty and there was no heating. My last work was sorting through rubbish for recycling in ten-hour shifts every day.
>
> One day I found the courage to tell someone, and they took me to a police station where I made a statement. The police arranged for me to be transported to a safe house, where I have been able to recover emotionally and receive financial and medical support, get somewhere to live, and find a job. I learnt that one of my bosses was sentenced to nine months in prison.

Sadly, Aleksander's story is not unusual, and the work of the Salvation Army with our partners is ongoing and will continue. Without doubt, the Salvation Army's fight for racial and social justice is clearly seen through this incredible work.

Refugee Response

Major Nick Coke is corps officer (minister) at Raynes Park, southwest London, and the territorial Refugee Response Coordinator. Since 2015, he has played a significant role in supporting local Salvation Army corps to engage positively in responding to racial injustice facing refugees and asylum seekers. Among other matters, Nick has been a pioneer of refugee resettlement through the Community Sponsorship scheme, to date working alongside eleven Salvation Army corps to directly sponsor refugee families to come to their neighbourhoods. This began with his own corps in Raynes Park where the community and congregation came together to provide a house and a year of intensive resettlement support for a family from Syria. Nick recalls:

> I remember back in 2015 seeing on my TV screen thousands of people desperately crossing the Mediterranean into Europe and the tragic loss of life that followed. I had an overwhelming sense that I could not sit on the sidelines and that I simply had to do something. After visiting "The Jungle" in Calais and hearing first-hand the heartbreaking stories of those fleeing war and conflict, I made a commitment to take the experience back to my corps and to get everyone who would listen to work together to welcome at least one family. The response was overwhelmingly positive.

As a result, Raynes Park corps became one of the first Community Sponsors in the United Kingdom, demonstrating that communities were ready and willing to personally welcome refugees into their neighbourhoods. The corps has supported the family every step of the way, meeting them at the airport on arrival, helping them settle into their new home, and journeying alongside them as they have started a new life here.

As the corps shared its experience, others became inspired to start their own Community Sponsorship journeys, enabling refugee families to find sanctuary in towns and cities across Britain. Nick reports:

> I have been completely changed as a result of this journey. Initially I thought we were the ones who were doing the helping, but I quickly realized that this extraordinary family were helping us! It has had a profound effect on the entire church and everyone in the community who has met them. We now have a far greater grasp of what it means to welcome the stranger into our midst. They have been a wonderful gift to us.

Without doubt, this work has been a positive response to those whose lives have been turned upside down by war and conflict. As an increasing number of corps have engaged with refugees and asylum seekers and have become aware of the racial injustice that many people face. The opportunity to demonstrate genuine Christlike hospitality and welcome has provided a faithful and hopeful experience for all involved.

The Local Church

It is important to recognize that although major campaigns are making an incredible dent in racial injustice, much is happening across this territory at local level. The Salvation Army has more than 650 corps across Britain, and many would say that midweek activities held within the buildings are attended by people from a wide range of countries, with many being here as the direct result of racial injustice.

However, it is fair to say that one of the struggles many corps have is that although their midweek programme is racially diverse, often the Sunday gathering does not represent this diversity, and when it does, the leadership team does not reflect the Sunday congregation. At the 2019 Salvation Army Intercultural Mission Conference, Bishop Rose Hudson-Wilkin challenged this by saying:

> There should be a clear reflection seen within the local church! The community it is in should reflect the gathered church community, and the leadership team should then reflect the church.

In 2016, I was appointed Intercultural Mission Enabler for this territory. The term "intercultural" is an important word when it comes to tackling racial injustice; an intercultural posture implies a willingness to enter someone else's culture as much as you expect them to enter your own. In so doing, and when this happens, something new is created beyond the original intention of each group. As already mentioned, multiculturalism is definitely experienced within the walls of Salvation Army buildings each day, yet the question I want to look at is this: has the reflection vision of Bishop Hudson-Wilkin been seen, which can arguably only really happen if an intercultural desire is lived out?

Captains Tim and Charlotte Lennox were appointed to Dublin City Corps in 2016. In speaking with them recently, I discovered that an exciting local congregation is starting to be built by God, where Christians from many parts of the world are gathering within that hall and an intercultural posture is being encouraged by the officers and lived out by the congregation. Happening before their eyes is a real tangible Revelation 7 celebration, with people from many different cultural groups and backgrounds worshipping God together as one body. With many different nationalities gathering, the only people group this local congregation is struggling to gather within the walls are indigenous Irish people!

Certainly, the community reflection is being realized. The diverse community is being seen within the congregation, and the worship band and local leadership team also reflect this. Many people who have visited this local congregation come away excited by what they are seeing. It is encouraging to see and, along with other Salvation Army expressions within the Dublin area, God is moving and something beautiful is being birthed.

However, many places around Britain are not seeing this, and certainly the area where I have served all of my officership, London, has been in decline for many years. In 2016, I carried out research on the decline of the Salvation Army in the London area. This revealed that in 1942 we had 161 corps, whereas in 2016 only fifty-nine remained. Although there were various reasons for closures, one of the major ones, I believe, was the inability of these majority White British congregations to engage with an increasingly diverse community.

As a result, many large congregations saw people move away from the inner city over a period of time, and the remaining congregations seemed unable to engage and embrace diversity. Corps after corps was closed. Peckham, Brixton, Southall – three hyper-diverse communities that once had a Salvation Army presence – have now been closed for many years. If we believe that Christ is for all people and we live to bring about the kingdom, then anything short of this is an injustice. In these cases, when we have failed to create places for people from different racial groups, this is racial injustice, and it desperately needs to be put right.

A corps in London that has certainly put things right is Clapton in east London. Majors Ruth and Karl Gray were appointed there in 2004 and discovered a diverse community, yet the church simply did not reflect that community. As mentioned at the start of this chapter, welcoming was to be the key for turning around this local community church. What the Grays discovered early on was arguably that institutional racism had been implemented. Black people were being used to clear up the rubbish and make the drinks while – without an official working leadership team – there was a power group that consisted of White people. With a clear desire to see this church become a place of welcome, the Grays took on the roles of cleaning up and making the drinks. They also started to engage with the local community, starting a parent and toddler group months after arriving, and made subtle changes to Sunday worship which started to embrace and include all who entered the building. From no real leadership team, suddenly leaders emerged from within the existing congregation, and also from new people who had started to attend on Sundays. Why was this? Because people were being welcomed and embraced beyond a simple "hello", and were being included in all things that were happening within this community.

Now, this local congregation, which in 2004 had around fifteen people attending, has more than 280 people who would regard Clapton corps as their local church. Just as the church reflects the community it gathers in, so too the leadership reflects the gathered church. Sixteen people from many different backgrounds sit on the local leadership team, praying together and guiding the church as it moves forward. Not only has this fellowship seen radical transformation in every way, but it has also planted two other fellowships nearby where there had previously been Salvation Army corps which had closed: Stoke Newington in 2013 and Dalston in 2010.

"We try to be welcoming and authentic in all that we do," says Major Karl Gray. This is certainly encouraging to see and witness.

Mention has been made of the racist attitudes that were evident many years ago at the Clapton corps and the impact of this. Sadly, other unjust happenings need to be given some attention in this chapter. I was sent to this corps while training to be an officer in the summer of 2002. During that summer, I met with a Black Ghanaian man who was a Salvationist and had attended Clapton corps a few years before. However, he left as a result of racism, and also because somebody from the corps telephoned Immigration to report him, even though he was legally entitled to be in the country. Sadly, this story of blatant racism is not a one-off, and after hearing statistics that more than 10,000 international Salvationists could now live in the UK and Ireland, I wanted to try to understand more about the problem.

In 2017, Dr Naar Mfundisi-Holloway did major research, asking the question, "Why do international Salvationists choose the Pentecostal route in the UK?" Although she found few people who were willing to participate in this, enough people were brave and came forward. Clearly, there were some positive stories of hope from the territory, yet there were also sad findings of racism. Far too often, similar things were being said: people not welcomed into local places, hurtful comments made, no leadership opportunities given to Black, Asian, and Minority Ethnic people.

This report, along with an intercultural mission strategy, was presented to senior leadership in 2016–17, and although some of the content was welcomed, there was a strong sense that those listening were finding it hard to comprehend that there were racism issues within the movement here in the UK. The number one recommendation on the list was for an apology to be issued, with an understanding that to move forward, repentance was needed. Sadly, no apology was given, and also there was no comprehension that our structures, among other things, were arguably institutionally racist.

Unfortunately, this report was not the first to be produced, with several having been carried out over the years. One of these was in 2005, when a then Salvation Army officer, Captain Steve Calder (now a Baptist minister), wrote his master's dissertation on "Institutional Racism and The Salvation Army". This report provided great insight into the subject and raised deep concerns, some of which are still concerns today.

In identifying institutional racism and a lack of racial diversity among senior managers and officers, it is important to recognize that, today, change is slowly taking place, with Black, Asian, and Minority Ethnic people taking up roles in senior management. Tony Daniels, Community Services Manager, recently said, "We need to celebrate the true fact that myself and other Black people are now in senior management roles within this movement. Yes, we have a long way to go, but let's celebrate this good news."

Officership

Within Salvation Army officership, there are real concerns over the lack of racial diversity within this territory, with above 95 per cent of officers being White British. If this is going to change, then we need to hear the story of what it has been like for a Black, Asian, or Minority Ethnic person who has journeyed through Salvation Army officership. Major Marjory Parrot reflects:

If I see myself as any colour, it is Brown, although generally I forget. I was raised in a multiracial, multi-ethnic family, where colour and race were not issues. We obviously had different skin shades, but that was not seen as contributing to whether we grew up to love Jesus or to be decent people. Perhaps that, alongside the fact that subtlety is lost on me, explains why I have not felt that racism has featured much for me. Nevertheless, I can see instances where my colour has made a difference.

Before becoming an officer, I sold the [Salvation] Army papers in our local pubs. One Christmas, at a fancy-dress party in a pub, a reveller, dressed supposedly as a cannibal, wanted his photo taken with me. That photo was published in the *War Cry* [newspaper]. My corps officer was a godly man and would not have sought to offend me; indeed, I didn't even think of objecting. Still, someone, somewhere, should have thought to question the acceptability of publishing that image.

While I was a cadet, we visited a political institution, where a prominent politician decided to have his photo taken with me, which was also published. It is likely that he picked me out of our cadet group because I was the only person of colour. None of us, myself included, thought to object. It would not have even occurred to me that I had the right to do so.

When I was a young officer, the elderly father of a colleague officer asked me how they celebrated Christmas in my country. I am not sure who was more baffled – me by the question or him by the answer: "This is my country!"

Before our marriage, an officer told my fiancé (now husband) that by marrying me he would limit his chances of promotion, and, when challenged, admitted that it was because of my colour. Following our marriage, one of our soldiers said it was good to have "proper officers", it was just a shame that my husband was a lieutenant and I was Black!

That appointment was an example of headquarters not thinking things through. We were sent to a city with a large Asian population, so I should not have stuck out like a sore thumb – but I did, because we were based on a large, exceptionally White, housing estate. This followed from my previous appointment, where the sending criteria seemed to be my skin colour, as half the population were Caribbean. Had anyone asked, I could have told them that the only Caribbean part of me was whatever genes I received from my biological father.

Many years later, a civilian manager, in the presence of others, informed me that he and his wife had servants "like you", when they lived in India. It is equally true that there have been times when my skin colour has benefited my ministry, but it is just one part of me – as anyone who knows me will testify.

In speaking with other Black, Asian, and Minority Ethnic officers within this territory, real concerns are evident, which clearly point to this movement needing to do many things differently and more justly as we move forward.

Positive Steps Forward

This chapter reveals signs of hope, yet also clearly identifies real racial justice issues that need to be addressed. Following the murder of George Floyd, the disproportionate amount of Black, Asian, and Minority Ethnic people who have been impacted by COVID-19, and the uncovering of so much racial injustice within this world, our territorial leaders, Commissioners Anthony and Gill Cotterill, responded by issuing the following statement on racism:

> The Salvation Army in the United Kingdom and the Republic of Ireland today affirms that it stands in solidarity with people around the world (including our own members and employees) who experience racism, both in its blatantly ugly and its more insidious forms.
>
> Our hearts are heavy and hurting because it is increasingly obvious that Black, Asian, and other Minority Ethnic people in the UK continue to suffer institutional racism in all areas of life. Our hearts are heavy and hurting because racism infects the church – and we acknowledge and confess that this is true even in parts of Salvation Army life. We are deeply concerned by the research showing that people from Black, Asian, and other Minority Ethnic groups in the UK have suffered disproportionately from the coronavirus pandemic. We recognise this is a critical time and today we want to recommit to our journey of togetherness with people from Black, Asian, and other Minority Ethnic communities and respond with positive action.

In these days following Pentecost, and the celebration of the gift of the Holy Spirit to the world, we increasingly understand our responsibility, in the words of Jesus himself, not only "to proclaim good news to the poor" but also "to proclaim freedom for the prisoners and recovery of sight for the blind, to set the oppressed free, to proclaim the year of the Lord's favour" (Luke 4:18–19, NIV UK). The work of "recovery of sight for the blind" and setting "the oppressed free" is a priority in the fight against racism.

Consequently, the Salvation Army in the United Kingdom and Ireland will intentionally seek ways to confront and fight racism wherever it is found. We will take positive action to ensure that our culture is increasingly one in which our members, employees, service users and officers, of majority and minority ethnic origin, feel included – that is, respected, valued, trusted, safe and have a sense of belonging.[4]

I firmly believe that this statement was needed, yet, more importantly, it desperately needs to be actioned with positive steps forward. It is deeply encouraging to have seen this territory carry out major research in the summer of 2020 looking at Black, Asian, and other Minority Ethnic people's experiences as they have journeyed with the Salvation Army within this territory. Again, it needs to be recognized that there were positive experiences recorded, even while issues of racism and institutional racism were raised.

In November 2020, this report,[5] along with other research that had been carried out on culture, was presented to senior Salvation Army leadership, along with recommendations. In accepting and, more importantly, longing to see racial justice happen, a task force has been created, to attend to and action the recommendations.

In Conclusion

In reflecting on the opening paragraphs, where the Salvation Army's international positional statement on racism is identified, you will see that this territory, and indeed the wider Salvation Army, has a long journey ahead in order to make this statement a living reality. I firmly believe that as we journey forward, much cultural change is needed in order to tangibly live out racial justice. Clearly, reconciliation is needed by so many, and the real test for this and every organization as we move forward will be how much we want it. How willing are we to live out an intercultural posture, which requires us to move into other cultures outside the one we are most comfortable with?

As Catherine Booth boldly said, "There is no improving the future, without disturbing the present."[6]

The journey for the Salvation Army toward racial justice is vital and, without doubt, we will need to disturb the present if the future is to look excitingly different and more like the picture the Apostle John presents in Revelation 7. In my seventeen years on this ministry journey, I am more aware now of the hurt and pain that has been cruelly placed upon people, and the desperate need for repentance and forgiveness. Yet, I am also more optimistic that real racial justice can start to become a tangible reality within this movement, not only because it is needed and the right thing to do, but also because God directs his people toward this, and it is the God thing to do.

Notes

1 "The Salvation Army International Positional Statement: Racism", The Salvation Army, October 2017, p. 2, https://s3.amazonaws.com/cache.salvationarmy.org/7d3c015c-1af5-4211-830f-b7b0c6a65898_English+Racism+IPS.pdf (last viewed 28 April 2022).

2 Song "We are One", © Major Dr Matt Spencer from the 2012 Racial Justice Sunday resource pack.

3 General William Booth, *In Darkest England and the Way Out* (New York, London: Funk & Wagnalls, 1890), p. 23.

4 "Salvation Army in the UK and Republic of Ireland confronts racism", The Salvation Army, 4 June 2020, www.salvationarmy.org.uk/news/salvation-army-uk-and-republic-ireland-confronts-racism (last viewed 28 April 2022).

5 "Territorial Advisory Council Racial Justice and Inclusion Report", carried out between August and September 2020.

6 Catherine Booth, *Aggressive Christianity* (Philadelphia: National Publishing Association for the Promotion of Holiness, 1880), p. 57.

Chapter 13
The Seventh-day Adventist Church and Racial Justice

RICHARD DALY

Like many churches in Britain during the 1950s and 1960s, the Seventh-day Adventist Church was not immune to the challenges of racial integration owing to the influx of immigration. In 1948 the ship HMT *Empire Windrush* brought the first wave of African Caribbean settlers to Britain, thus heralding a new and significant turn in Britain's long multiracial existence. The Windrush factor occurred at a time when Britain was retreating from its role as a colonial power, rebuilding after the Second World War, and refocusing its relationship with Europe. The combination of these events meant that it was a time of profound political, economic, and sociological change for this country.

The decades of immigration that followed, which had previously amounted only to a trickle, swelled to such numbers as to arouse national concern in the 1960s. It was seen to be such an issue in the country that by 1962, the British Government had passed laws closing the door to any further large-scale immigration from the Black Commonwealth. Two common reasons normally given for this mass influx was the serious unemployment problem in some of the West Indian islands at that time, and the loss in the early 1950s of the option for West Indians to emigrate easily to America. A third reason that cannot be discounted is the undoubted success of the British in selling to the Commonwealth an irresistible vision of Britain. As a Commonwealth citizen, one's identity was British, with the belief that the "Mother Country" was the place where one was certain to find work and an opportunity to "better oneself". It was the place where the best education in the world could be had, and where careers could be successfully pursued by the capable, diligent person through hard work and study. The lure of employment, further education, and opportunities to pursue certain career objectives were the key factors.

In the case of employment, the opportunities were largely for manual, unskilled workers – jobs no longer attractive to English workers. Many of the newcomers, therefore, came with the intention of staying only for a short time to achieve a particular goal and then to return to their country of origin. However, many found that the achievement of their goals was more difficult than they had anticipated and that their stay needed to be extended. For many, such extensions led to permanent settling. Thus, by the end of the 1960s, significantly large communities from Africa, the Caribbean, and Asia had become settled and established in Britain.

It is now a matter of record the degree of disillusionment that the majority suffered. Large-scale colour prejudice was an unexpected and bitter pill. British society in the main was not ready to give the newcomers the kind of acceptance that they had been led to expect.

The Seventh-day Adventist Church in Britain could not remain isolated from these forces of change.

Brief History of the Seventh-day Adventist Church in the British Isles

The Seventh-day Adventist (SDA) Church was formally organized in 1863 in the United States of America during its first General Conference meeting held in Battle Creek, Michigan, on 21 May of that year. At the time of organization, the membership of the church stood at 3,500 members and was predominantly considered a North American sect. Today, in many ways, it is a worldwide mission church. In the half-century 1960–2010, the shift in membership from America and, to a lesser extent, Europe and Australasia to the rest of the world has been even more marked.

The overall growth since the church began has been very positive. Since then, the historical statistics continue to tell an encouraging story of church growth and geographical representation. Today, the SDA Church is very evangelical, with mission efforts worldwide, numerous publications, health institutions, and many educational facilities. It claims more than 25 million members worldwide[1] and is growing rapidly with its educational, TV, radio, and publication-based outreaches.[2]

The main tenets of Adventism would very much embrace the Nicene Creed, but would hold unique and specific areas of doctrine that would distinguish the Church from other Christian denominations. Inherent in the very name of the organization are two fundamental beliefs that spearhead its global mission and eschatology. The Seventh-day (Saturday) Sabbath being a significant doctrine is imbedded in Genesis 1–2, with God's completed work of creation in six days and resting on the seventh. Adventists believe this Seventh-day rest signified the memorial of creation and the celebration of humanity and finds its expression in the heart of the Ten Commandments with God's command to "Remember the Sabbath day by keeping it holy " (Exodus 20:8). Adventists believe this command is still relevant today and is to be kept as an expression of one's love for God rather than a means to salvation.

The Second Advent, a doctrine embraced by many Christian denominations, is one that finds its emphasis in the title of the church being a belief that Adventists deem to be a reality that can occur at any time.

Other areas of doctrine, such as the Heavenly Sanctuary, prophetic interpretations, and positions on areas such as health, family, and the millennium are compiled in the twenty-eight Fundamental Beliefs of the Seventh-day Adventist Church.[3] However, the foundation of all Seventh-day Adventist belief is the saving grace of Jesus Christ established through his death, burial, and resurrection. Salvation freely available for all is the heart of its doctrinal pillars.

As the church began to develop and expand overseas in the late nineteenth century, the call to enter Europe became a necessity. The task of forming new churches in Britain would initially become an unexpected challenge for the American pioneers who were to settle here, but through their commitment, hard work, and persistence they were able to make the breakthrough to form the beginnings of an established church.

Although it was a slow start, by the 1950s the Adventist membership within Britain had reached 6,666 – this was an average growth rate of 6.58 per cent during the previous decade.[4] This figure, however, was to increase dramatically within the next ten years owing to immigration.

Immigration and the Church

Among the immigrants to Britain were a large number of Seventh-day Adventists. They arrived with the expectation of being embraced by the church family of which they were a part. For them, this expectation grew in importance as their experience with secular society proved distressing. In the early years, while numbers were small, the welcome was largely warm and the church became, to an extent, a haven from the hostile secular environment outside. To the indigenous members, the mission field had come to visit, and that was exciting.

However, what became evident was a heartfelt degree of tension and challenge for the church to address the changes as the numbers of immigrant attendees increased. Most Caribbean people who came to Britain had attended church in the Caribbean; it was therefore natural that they would continue to do so after their arrival in Britain. It is well documented by various writers that many from the Caribbean were confronted with indifference. The treatment of the Christian churches toward them mirrored the attitude and spirit of the wider community. The writer Iain MacRobert summed up Black experiences in the churches as follows: "Christian migrants were... confronted with the same prejudice and discrimination inside the churches as they were outside."[5]

Many newcomers were expected to be returning home in a few years, so they simply tried to adjust to the new church culture and style of worship and more or less accepted a low profile in the congregations. However, a low profile is normally difficult for a Caribbean to adopt over a long period. And it is even more difficult for a fervent Adventist West Indian. As the new members became settled in the churches, the vibrant style of worship, evangelism, and fellowship to which they were accustomed could be held in check no longer, and their natural contribution to the life of worship and witness of the church produced a new experience for worshippers.

Cultural and Religious Shock

As mentioned, for many of the new arrivals, Adventism was different in Britain compared with their Caribbean background: Adventism in the Caribbean was a vibrant community of believers active in transmitting

Adventist beliefs to others in the wider community. They were accustomed to Adventism being aggressively evangelical. What they found in Britain was that the indigenous members were reserved and private.

Coming from a background where witnessing is the hallmark of Adventism, the core of the work of the church and where sharing one's faith is the primary goal and objective of the church, they felt that the true spirit of Adventism, as they had known it at home, had gone missing.[6] They did not see members prepared in large numbers to give Bible studies, nor groups holding and conducting evangelistic services, or doing door-to-door witnessing. As a result, some indigenous members, who were not yet ready to incorporate and enjoy the new worship experiences, exercised personal preference and moved to churches where the style was still that of the traditional "English". In addition, many Caribbean people, as a result of their evangelistic efforts, eventually formed new churches which became dominantly Caribbean. The make-up of the church within Britain would become a combination of one of three types of congregation: predominantly White churches, mixed, and predominately Black.

Effects of Immigration on the Adventist Church

Within Britain, racial tensions have always led to the need for re-evaluation and change. We have had, for example, legislation about race relations, a Commission for Racial Equality, and numerous official inquiries and reports, such as the Swann Report on Education, the Scarman Report, and the Macpherson Inquiry report on the Stephen Lawrence racist killing. Thus, the Windrush factor is all-pervasive and touched the Seventh-day Adventist Church in a marked way. It has impacted the church in the British Isles in five important ways.

1 Fostered a new phase of church growth

In the British Union Conference (BUC) of the Seventh-day Adventist Executive Committee in June 1980, the progress of membership growth in Britain was outlined. Membership grew at a steady rate between 1940 and 1950, from 5,915 to 6,666 members. The next decade showed a dramatic increase of more than 37 per cent, from 1951 to 1960. This increase was mostly felt in southern England, particularly in London, with static membership in Scotland and Wales and a 15 per cent loss in Ireland.[7]

In analysing the rate of growth for the Adventist church in Britain, Roswith Gerloff concluded:

From 1902 until 1925, the church in Britain grew by more than 300%. This figure drastically dropped to only 57% from 1925 to 1950, despite massive evangelistic campaigns in the twenties and thirties which attracted an attendance of thousands but did not fill the local churches. In fact, after 1945, there was even a small decline. This was unexpectedly reversed by immigration: from 1950 to 1975 the membership rose by 92.5% in 25 years.[8]

From 1953, the year when West Indians first came in greater numbers, to 1964, just after the first Immigration Act, the organization grew by more than 42 per cent. From 1964 to 1971, the year of the second Immigration Act, there was another rise of 19 per cent. The years 1971, when the new Government Bill had almost stopped immigration, to 1975 saw a slight growth of 3.3 per cent, a good percentage in comparison with other British churches.[9]

In 1950, the South England Conference of Seventh-day Adventists had a membership of 3,663 and was made up exclusively of White people. By 1980, the membership stood at 8,299 and was largely Black. The implication of such development led to further tensions around the need for greater Black church leadership and organization.

The emergence of Black SDA congregations was not deliberately designed by Caribbean members but became necessary because of the situation in which they found themselves. Between 1961 and 1965, eighteen new churches and companies were organized, all of which were African–Caribbean. Stoke Newington in north London became the first all-Black church to be organized.[10] While more churches became majority Black, the White minority either stayed or started new congregations of their own outside the London areas.

However, with the new nationals now becoming the majority, accounting for more than 60 per cent of the membership, their presence was conspicuously absent among the pastors, leaders, and other church workers. In the thirty years from 1950 to 1980, only a few Black British youth were in ministerial training. The cause of this situation naturally led to questions around Black representation within the leadership of the church. There was a growing voice in these churches urging that the church should act to include Black members as full participants at all levels of church life. Out of this developed the lay organization called the Laymen's Forum, which led within the church to deal with perceived prejudice. Founded on 23 November 1973, the purpose of the Forum was also to give leadership to the Black section of the church.[11]

The Laymen's Forum formulated a four-point campaign in which it urged the church leaders to:

- Organize more public evangelism, especially in the cities;
- Set up church schools and provide a youth centre for London;
- Provide more Black pastors for inner-city churches;
- Racially integrate the church at all levels of its administrative structure.[12]

The four points mentioned above summarized and represented the ideology of the Black Adventist community in both the Northern and Southern regions. Even though there was in general a better relationship in the Northern conference between Black and White members and pastors than in the London churches, there was a consensus that the four points presented by the Forum would further develop Adventism in Britain.

2 Developed an integrated church organization

Many Black members gave support to this programme, and although the church leadership were inclined to see the forum as "troublemakers", churches invited them to hold meetings, to which members flocked. The excitement these meetings generated by providing an outlet for open discussion led to many self-help programmes, such as summer schools and evening classes using government buildings.

This period of inner struggle came to a climax in 1978 in consultations chaired by the General Conference President. By 1978, the British church leadership were convinced that the indigenous church members were polarized around two views, and that there were only two real choices. Either, as leaders, they should work to deliver the Forum's four points and have an integrated church, or a Regional Conference administration should be set up to look after the needs of the Black membership. The view to offer a Regional Conference appeared to prevail among the BUC leaders, and a referendum was carried out to see if the membership would support such a separation on racial grounds.

The referendum on the issue of the concept of a Regional Conference versus a racially integrated church was taken through Messenger in October 1976. When the results were counted, a mere 800 favoured the Regional Conference idea. The vast majority, 4,500, voted for a racially integrated church.[13] The realities and implications of this vote so focused minds and energies that the result of the consultations with Elder Pierson (the World Church president of Seventh-day Adventists) was a proposal that has become known as the "Pierson Package". In a letter dated 15 March 1978, to ministers in the South England Conference, its recommendations included some of the following steps:

- The early employment of Black office secretaries in the Union and South England Conference offices;
- The election at each of the ensuing South England Conference (SEC) and North British Conference (NBC) sessions of one Black officer (with departmental responsibilities);
- The election, not later than the next BUC session, of a Black officer, and at least one Black departmental director for the BUC;
- The election at each of the imminent SEC and NBC sessions of one Black departmental director;
- The SEC committee, in close consultation with the BUC administration, to plan for the provision of a social evangelistic educational centre for Black youth in London.[14]

The Pierson Package placed in the hands of Black members the opportunity to be in a position of effective leadership. More importantly, it recognized the equality of members regardless of their cultural background or ethnic origin. All were responsible under the guidance of God's Holy Spirit to carry out the mission of the church together.

3 Developed a new energy for evangelism

And so, a new era in the history of the church was begun and a way opened for an explosion of evangelistic activity. The implementation of the Pierson Package meant that invitations were issued to a number of leading Black pastors from North America and the Caribbean to serve in the British Union. Foremost among these were Dr Silburn Reid and Pastors C. R. Perry, L. R. Preston, Everette Howell, D. W. McFarlane, David Hughes, Bruce Flynn, and others. These men immediately identified evangelism as the number one priority for the church. The church, at all levels, was galvanized into a commitment to this goal. This was especially pronounced when Dr Reid was elected as the first Black President of the South England Conference in 1981.

A new climate for soul-winning was created, and this continued under the leadership of Theodore McLeary, Cecil Perry, Don McFarlane, and Egerton Francis. Many evangelistic campaigns were held in tents, civic halls, or local churches. The outcome was that the membership of the church increased even faster than before. More pastors were recruited to cater for a growing church, extra congregations were formed to cope with the acceleration in membership growth, and tithes reached new records.

4 Raised the profile of the church nationally

A further impact of the Windrush factor is that African Caribbean members assisted in helping the church to become more visible to the nation. This is not purely because of skin colour, but also as a result of more profound, positive influences. In those early days, not many of the British public knew where to find an Adventist church. On locating an Adventist church in Britain, 80 per cent of them contacted the church through another Black Adventist living at the same address as themselves, 10 per cent were given the address in the Caribbean before arrival in this country, and another 10 per cent found the church after they were contacted by other Black Adventists knocking at their doors.[15]

First and foremost has been the willingness of Black Adventists to engage in house-to-house witnessing, in the distribution of leaflets and magazines, and in participating in the annual "Ingathering" programme of the church.

Second, they seized media opportunities to advance the cause of the church. The church's first Black church elder, Hymers Wilson, took part in the famous ITV television documentary *The Saturday People* screened in 1965.

Third, in the early 1970s, the noted Black community activist, Arthur Torrington, organized the interview of Dr Pitt and Pastor Dennis Uffindell on BBC Radio London to explain Adventist beliefs to the listeners. In addition, Brother Torrington, as lay activities leader for the Holloway church, placed a series of advertisements on London Transport buses, promoting evangelistic programmes in local churches.

Fourth, African Caribbean members have contributed to the development of church music in a dynamic way. In the early 1960s, The Singing Stewarts of Birmingham featured regularly on BBC Sunday afternoon religious programmes. Today, the London Adventist Chorale (Sainsbury Choir Award-winners) and the Croydon Seventh-day Adventist Gospel Choir have national and international recognition. They have not only served the church well but have also performed regularly in many of the nation's leading music festivals, including at royal and commemorative events.

5 Added new institutions to the church

Finally, the Black experience has stimulated the growth of a number of educational institutions. The Harper Bell School in Birmingham came about as a direct result of Black members in the West Midlands wanting their children to be educated by Christian teachers. The school enjoys a good reputation among primary schools in the Birmingham Education Authority and is an asset to the church in the West Midlands area.

The Theodore McLeary School in Brixton, south London, was named in honour of the pioneering work of the late Pastor McLeary, and was another educational institution resulting from the Windrush factor. The most consistent flagship for the church, however, was The John Loughborough School in Tottenham, north London. From its establishment in 1980, it attracted the attention of the media, of educationalists, and of politicians. Even since its closure in 2016, it remains a beacon of inspiration to those who attended.

Immigration in the New Millennium

The decade leading up to the year 2000 saw further immigration, this time from Africa and Eastern Europe. With the influx of members filling churches from Ghana, Zimbabwe, Poland, and Romania, to name a few countries, a new form of congregation began to develop. It could be argued that mono-ethnic churches were always in existence with the development of majority Black churches; however, the concept of purposely forming a church solely based on country of origin began to materialize.

During the late 1990s, the London Ghana Church was established – the first of its kind. This was followed by several Spanish- and Portuguese-speaking churches. These mono-ethnic churches found both support and criticism from various sectors of the church, especially when it came to the universal mission of the church to its local community. What is very clear, however, is the rapid growth of such churches as they successfully addressed all the cultural and language barriers that would exist in a mixed cultural church.

The Macpherson Report into institutional racism within the Metropolitan Police (1999), was an opportunity to take stock of our institutionalized ways of how we perceive each other within the church. Many pastoral meetings took place where the uncomfortable topic of racism was discussed, and Black and White pastors were given opportunities to talk about how it had affected them within the church. It is only through ongoing dialogue and sharing that the barriers of discrimination can be lowered, and as people are enabled to perceive their fellow church brother or sister in the same language of love that Christ would want us to engage in.

Times are changing – 9/11 brought to our attention the reality in which the Christian church needs to have a new vision in mission. The Christian church needs to break down barriers across different cultures, languages, and ethnicities in today's post-modern society. Christians must also begin to empathize and understand other cultures' beliefs and practices. This does not mean that the different Christian denominations should disregard their own distinctive beliefs, but that a relationship should be formed through dialogue with those of other cultures to promote understanding and tolerance. The Christian denominations have the human resources with which to establish such relationships through the empowerment of the Holy Spirit.

To meet the challenges facing the Adventist Church today, counselling and training skills are urgently needed for pastors and members. Developing the laity, understanding the needs of their local community, and having an understanding of social justice are areas of training that are necessary. The conduct of worship, understanding the mentality of the postmodern generation, and obtaining knowledge of other cultures are vital skills and training needed by pastors and members alike.

Adventism and Social Justice

The "broad and comprehensive" nature of the church's mission, which responds to people's "everyday pain", was one of the major themes expressed by one of the former world leaders of the Adventist Church, Pastor Jan Paulsen. He aptly sums up where our priorities as a church really ought to be despite our cultural differences:

> We would fail as a church if we became indifferent to the suffering of this world or become so "wholly" other "worldly" in our thinking that we are insensitive to the suffering of humanity and cannot be bothered. For this is the world in which we also live.[16]

It is not that the Adventist church has been active in mission in the past, but it has been particularly selective in its areas of missionary involvement, focusing on humanitarian, and educational causes, and establishing new congregations. In its involvement in these areas, the church has avoided some of the socio-economic challenges in societies that have surfaced in many parts of the country, such as declining moral and social behaviour, serious youth violence, and gun and knife crime. Addressing this situation, Paulsen makes it plain that these areas, as undesirable as they may be, or as unwilling as members may be to get involved, should also be part of the mission of the church. He acknowledges the political or cultural tensions that may exist in some of these areas, but nevertheless the church has a role to play:

> In some of these places it is very difficult to do mission for both political and cultural reasons and in those places, we move gingerly and cautiously. As a church we have deliberately avoided being drawn into the political resolution arena, or in offering public opinions on them even when politicians clearly fail to calm our uneasiness. We have held and we hold that our mission agenda has

to be accomplished in fragile and risky times as well as in stable situations. That is our role. We cannot step out of it.[17]

Challenges for the Future

If, as is widely held, the gospel is meaningful only within the ambit of one's culture, then the church in the British Isles, now largely immigrant, must learn how to make the gospel meaningful to the divergent cultures in which it finds itself. Particular attention must be paid to that culture which constitutes more than 90 per cent of the population. Members and local churches must move out of their comfort zones and worship and witness in ways that appeal not only to them, but also to the wider society. The Apostle Paul recognized that such an accommodation is often necessary if all people are to be reached with the gospel (1 Corinthians 9:19–23). Globalization is one of those words used increasingly in postmodern society. Cheap air travel, the electronic media, Hollywood, and the internet have ensured that the world is no longer an amalgam of self-contained nations or tribal groups. No organization of significance has been left untouched by these phenomena.

The British Union has not escaped its impact. Lessons used by the Voice of Prophecy Bible School are now gleaned from various sections of the globe. The Stanborough Press (the SDA's publishing house) is kept viable by the sales it makes to Africa. Globalization has also led to the Adventist Church in Britain becoming a cosmopolitan community. Its membership is currently composed of individuals from "every kindred, tongue and people", resulting in a beautifully woven human tapestry. The nature of the world today means that this reality can only deepen in the future.

The church can choose one of three directions in addressing the diversity resulting from globalization. It can ignore it altogether and behave as if it does not exist. It can seek to change it with a view to returning to an age of homogeneity. Or it can choose to celebrate this diversity as an expression of the inclusive nature of the Christian faith. The right choice is obvious.

Throughout its short history, the Adventist Church has prided itself on being at the cutting edge of matters spiritual. This has been taken for granted more than proven. While this was possibly true in the past, it is now apparent that other Christian fellowships may have stolen a march on Adventists and have left them behind in worship practices and witnessing methods. In Britain, as in some other countries, the church is awakening to the stark reality that its preoccupation with its past has rendered many of its methods and approaches and much of its vocabulary outdated. The church must get to grips with the dynamic nature of society and the imperative for it to be a church for its time.

Present truth today must retain the golden thread of the Christ who came, the Saviour who died, the Lord who is coming again, and the doctrinal verities of the church, but it must also address the ills, needs, values, and aspirations of what is now known as the postmodern society. The church must scratch where people are itching.

In light of the tremendous challenges that the church in Britain faces in the twenty-first century, there must be intentional efforts to meet those challenges. The church dare not close its eyes to its obvious needs and declare that God will put everything right. God uses his children as agents of change, and he expects leaders at every level of the organization to work prayerfully and faithfully in order to make changes where necessary. Church leaders must realize that things will never be the same again – regular, tranquil, orderly, traditional. They must come to terms with the new realities.

God has given the Seventh-day Adventist Church a wonderful message of hope and assurance. It must be declared with conviction, commitment, and clarity, that men and women in this age of elusive dreams and decadence may come to know the fulfilling life that there is in Christ for today and tomorrow.

Notes

1 "2017 Annual Statistical Report: 153rd Report of the General Conference of Seventh-day Adventists® for 2015 and 2016", Seventh-day Adventist Church, documents.adventistarchives.org/Statistics/ASR/ASR2017.pdf (last viewed 28 April 2022).

2 Anne Devereaux Jordan, *The Seventh Day Adventists: A History* (New York: Hippocrene Books, 1988).

3 General Conference Ministerial Department, *Seventh-day Adventists Believe* (California: Review and Herald Publishing, 2018).

4 "British Union Conference (1946–1950), Office of Archive, Statistics,

and Research, Seventh-day Adventist Church, www.adventiststatistics.org/view_Summary.asp?FieldInstID=5808 (last viewed 28 April 2022).

5 Iain MacRobert, "The New Black-led Pentecostal Churches in Britain", in Paul Badham (ed.), *Religion, State, and Society in Modern Britain* (Wales: Edwin Mellen Press, 1989), p. 127.

6 Dr Herbert Griffiths, "The Impact of African Caribbean Settlers on the Seventh-day Adventist Church in Britain 1952–2001", PhD thesis, University of Leeds School of Theology and Religious Studies, April 2003, p. 165.

7 M. L. Anthony, "A Survey of Church Growth Among SDAs in the United Kingdom and Eire during the period 1940–1980", report paper to the BUC Executive Committee, 1980, p. 10.

8 Roswith I. H. Gerloff, *A Plea for British Black Theologies* (Frankfurt am Main: Peter Lang, 1992), p. 284.

9 Gerloff, *A Plea for British Black Theologies*, p. 284.

10 D. Porter, *A Century of Adventism in the British Isles* (Grantham: Stanborough Press Ltd, 1974), p. 44.

11 Keith Davidson, "The Black Experience in Britain: Windrush 2000", In D. N. Marshall (ed.), *A Century of Adventism in the British Isles* (Watford: British Union Conference of SDAs, 2000), p. 23.

12 Davidson, "The Black Experience in Britain", p. 23.

13 Davidson, "The Black Experience in Britain", p. 23.

14 Davidson, "The Black Experience in Britain", p. 23.

15 Dr Herbert Griffiths, "The Impact of African Caribbean Settlers", p. 165

16 Jan Paulsen, Paper presented to world church executive committee members at Silver Spring, Maryland, USA, 7 October 2002. p. 1.

17 Paulsen, Paper presented to world church executive committee members at Silver Spring, Maryland, USA, 7 October 2002, p. 1.

Chapter 14
South Asian Christians in the UK

SIVAKUMAR RAJAGOPALAN

Introduction

In Esther 1:1 we read, "Xerxes... ruled over 127 provinces stretching from India to Cush." According to church tradition, the apostle Thomas took the gospel to India and was martyred in Chennai, Tamil Nadu. Despite these biblical roots, Christianity has not flourished among South Asians[1] (SAs), which is reflected in the number of South Asian Christians (SACs) present within the UK. Some of the reasons for this will be explored in this essay.

All immigrant communities find themselves in liminal places, and this is very much the case for SACs, who are in a tri-liminal place. On one side they have their majority "home" communities which belong to the Indic faiths of Hinduism, Buddhism, Jainism, and Sikhism, or Islam. On the second side they have the White British "Christian" majority community, and on the third the Black British and diaspora "Christian" community.[2] All three communities do not associate South Asians with Christianity, hence SACs are invisible, and this is apparent in the paucity of publications regarding them.

And yet, much could be written about SACs, so the following key areas will be addressed:

- Migration of South Asians (SAs) and South Asian Christians (SACs) to the UK;
- The presence of SACs within historic denominations and independent churches;
- The work of para-church organizations;
- SACs' experience of racism;
- SACs' engagement with racial justice;

- Reflections and suggestions;
- Perennial signs of hope.

Migration of SAs and SACs to the UK

"On 22 December 1616... an Indian youth... brought to Britain... was publicly baptised" and christened as "Peter".[3] Reverend Copland, a chaplain to the East India Company, had brought him to England "so that he could be instructed in religion and sent back as a missionary to proselytise his own people."[4] "Peter" is illustrative of two truths:

- The English sought to mould "Peter" in their own image to take the gospel back to India. In part, this mindset has contributed to the lack of fruit among SAs.
- "Peter" was brought here by an Englishman, which underlines the phrase coined by A. Sivanandan, "We are here because you were there," and accounts for why SAs came to the UK.[5]

SAs and SACs have been in the UK for several centuries, but after the Second World War their presence increased. From 1947 until 1962, the key areas from which significant numbers arrived were Indian Punjab, a region with which the British have long-standing ties, and Mirpur in Pakistan.[6] Those from Sylhet in Bangladesh primarily migrated in the early 1970s owing to civil unrest and war, and most Sri Lankan Tamils migrated during the civil war in the 1980s.[7] Those arriving from these regions worked in manufacturing, textiles, and other industries and settled in most major conurbations.[8] The other key arrival is East African Asians, who migrated in the 1960s and early 1970s owing to "policies which prioritised native Africans in the newly independent countries of Kenya, Tanzania and Uganda."[9]

After the abolition of slavery in 1834, the British transported up to 2 million Indians as indentured labourers to their colonies, where, like enslaved Africans before them, they were exploited, and their descendants migrated to the UK in the post war era.[10] From personal knowledge and information gathered from interviews with denominational contributors to this publication, in the past thirty years, SAs, particularly Indians, have migrated to work in the National Health Service (NHS), information technology (IT), and commerce.

While SACs must have been among those who have migrated to the UK, there is limited statistical information, with Revd Pradip Sudra noting that "there were a handful of Christians".[11] A regional report on older Gujarati immigrants in Birmingham, published in 2002 by the Department for International Development, records that 1 per cent were Christian.[12] Some SACs will have fled because of religious persecution, but, again, data is lacking.

The Government's post-Brexit points-based immigration system will enable high-skilled SAs and SACs from SA nations and the diaspora to migrate.[13] Despite the present Government's rhetoric, its current practice is not offering the refuge that persecuted SACs require.[14]

The Presence of SACs Within Historic Denominations and Independent Churches

For this essay, the historic denominations are Anglican, Baptist, Catholic, Methodist, and United Reformed Church (URC). The material below has been gathered by interviewing some of the contributors to this publication, ministers, and others involved in SAs/SACs ministry.

Below are some characteristics common to more than one denomination:

- SACs are very small in number. In 2010 *The Guardian* reported that 7,000 SACs, accounting for 10 per cent of SACs, worshipped in Anglican churches.[15] While some increase will have taken place through migration, conversion, and biological growth, the maximum number will be much less than 150,000.
- The historic denominations do not collect ethnicity data either for congregants or for clergy.
- Within the Anglican, URC, and Baptist churches, various SAC-language-specific churches operate alongside the main congregation. In some there is a good relationship between the two and, with active encouragement, such work has thrived to the benefit of both congregations. Within some churches, the language-specific

gatherings are not separate entities but gather to worship in their own language and to reach out to their community in culturally appropriate ways. These groupings are considered an integral part of the historic church. In others, there is just a landlord–tenant relationship between the two churches.

- Among the URC a few Urdu-speaking congregations, and among Baptists Tamil-speaking congregations and one congregation from Myanmar have joined regional and denominational networks.

Below are the notable variations between the denominations.

Anglican

The strong links with the Church of North and South India and the Church of Pakistan have contributed to migrants from these churches joining as congregants, and some serve as clergy. Some clergy arrived by virtue of joining their spouse working here, particularly in the NHS. However, they have not always either found a position or been able to adjust to White British expectations of an Anglican vicar. The number of British born SA clergy is very small. Retired Bishop Nazir Ali and Canon George Kovoor, former principal of Trinity College, Bristol, both held high office, and The Venerable Dr John Perumbalath was appointed in 2018 as Bishop of Bradwell in Essex. In May 2022, Revd Canon Arun Arora was installed as the Bishop of Kirkstall.

Catholic

From information gathered from contacts and by searching the web, there are many South Indian and other SA Catholics in the UK. Community-specific associations meet the needs of those from Kerala and of Indian and Sri Lankan Tamils.[16] In London, South Indian Catholics are in Southwark and Southall. Many SA Catholics belong to the Syro-Malabar Rite, worship in their rite, and have a bishop based in Preston. Other Syro-Malabar Catholics worship in Latin-rite churches. From the information supplied, it is clearly a complex picture.

There are likely to be several hundred individuals from SA and elsewhere serving in religious orders, and in the past there have been country-specific chaplains.

One Catholic source believes that there are fewer than six British-born Black and Asian clergy in the UK. The largest presence of SAs is within Catholic schools. I can personally attest to this as my siblings and I were sent to Catholic schools; many non-Christian SAs hold Catholic schools in high regard. Notable Catholic engagements with SAs took place in Burnley and Oldham after the riots in 2001 and in Southall, West London.

Methodist

There are some Sri Lankan and Indian congregants, but very few SA clergy. The Revd Dr Inderjit Bhogal is one of the notable SAs within Methodism, who served as President of the Methodist Conference in 2000. Equally, other prominent figures include Bala Gnanapragasam, who was Vice-President of the Methodist Conference from 2018 to 2019, and Dr Daleep Mukerji, the former head of Christian Aid.

Salvation Army

Salvationists have a strong presence within various SA nations, but migrants to the UK have felt unwelcome and have responded by:

- Not attending any Christian gathering;
- Attending other churches;
- Attending Salvationist gatherings for SAs.

These issues are being actively addressed.

United Reformed Church

Presbyterians from Pakistan have joined the church, and there are a few Urdu-speaking ministers and congregants, and one minister of Indian origin.

Baptist

SA Baptists are very few, so their presence within churches as ministers and congregants is not significant.

Scotland

According to 2011 census data, 0.4 per cent of Scottish Christian are SACs, and the majority are Catholics.[17]

Ireland (Republic and Northern)

Only in the past fifteen years have there been noteworthy numbers of SAs migrating to Ireland, with the majority serving in the health and IT sectors. SACs are present within the following churches: Syrian Orthodox, St Thomas Indian Orthodox, Church of South India, and other Indian-origin churches with their own clergy. Additionally, SACs belong to Pentecostal and independent churches.

Independent churches

Revd Sudra[18] states, "Many went to the denominational churches with which they were affiliated in the Indian subcontinent. But they often encountered a lack of genuine welcome and the sheer *foreignness* of the language and culture."[19] Consequently, many met in their own homes, finding solace by fellowshipping with each other through shared language, culture, and food, and some have grown to become worshipping communities.[20] Many are "independent of denominations", while others "have closer ties".[21] Revd Sudra, former CEO of Alliance for Asian Christians, states, "The Asian churches have dynamically moved from being mainly in one of the South Asian languages to now adopting itself with English as the next generation are better at speaking English."[22]

The South Asian Forum (SAF) of the Evangelical Alliance was formed in 2010 "to connect and support" South Asian churches and to "equip the church to confidently engage with South Asians of different faith and cultures".[23] Mr Dayalan Mahesan, SAF's current National Coordinator, estimates that the quarterly meeting of fifty SA church leaders represents just 10 per cent of SA churches. He believes there are many small house churches served by bi-vocational ministers, which are largely hidden. Some do not connect because of theology, but many others are unaware of SAF. When they do connect with SAF, however, they appreciate the chance to meet, encourage, and support one another.

An internet search reveals numerous groupings, such as the Nepali Christian Churches United Kingdom,[24] the Bengali Christian Association UK,[25] and the British Asian Christian Association,[26] to name just a few. There are likely to be other SAC groups and churches that we are unaware of.

The Work of Para-church Organizations

In the past, British missionaries travelled to different parts of South Asia to share the gospel, and now South Asians are living in Britain. However, despite such missionary endeavours, the historic denominations had little, if any, knowledge on how to evangelize these communities.

To meet this very real mission opportunity, various para-church organizations were formed, which focused on ministry to either Muslims or those of Indic faiths – Hinduism, Sikhism, Buddhism, and Jainism – and some tried to reach both. There are many such organizations, and the sensitivities in such work necessitate the need for a circumspect approach in documenting their activities. Therefore, the following few organizations are mentioned for the significant role they have played in helping to advance outreach to South Asians.

Alliance of Asian Christians (AAC)[27]

"AAC was launched in June 1990 [and] began with Mr. Raj Patel, Mr. Atul Patel" and Revd Pradip Sudra, who was appointed Executive Director in June 1992.[28] Revd Sudra states that a survey conducted in circa 1988 showed that 70 per cent of those who accepted Christ from other faiths returned "to their former faith within the first year" because of "the lack of support structures in the life of denominational churches".[29] Therefore, AAC was formed to "encourage the development of the Asian Christian community".[30] It developed leadership and built structures to enable "discipleship and nurture in culturally appropriate ways" and recognized that the SAC community is "part of the wider Church... therefore... buil[t] relationships with all parts of the Church".[31] AAC had good "links with Evangelical Alliance and Churches Together in England".[32] Furthermore, denominations sought advice from AAC when writing their mission strategies.[33] Revd Sudra believes that AAC has had numerous successes, one being that language-specific churches have transitioned to English. In 2010, AAC disbanded owing to "changing times and greater integration".[34]

South Asian Concern (SAC)

South Asian Concern had a long gestation period, from 1989 to 1991, during which time it had administered "the highly successful Christmas Cracker project; [held] relationship-building Prayer Consultations; and [ran] a series of equipping seminars across the UK".[35] Therefore, SAC "had… built a firm foundation… when, in March 1991, it became a registered charity".[36] Its key personnel were Mr Ram Gidoomal, Dr Raju Abraham, Mr Robin Thomson (now retired but still active), and Professor Prabhu Guptara.[37]

SAC engaged in a wide range of activities. In North India, it shared the gospel and brought education, community uplift, and healthcare to the last and least.[38] The South Asian Development Partnership pioneered collaboration between secular and faith-based organizations, including working with other faiths "to support emergency situations".[39]

SAC personnel ran training programmes and wrote various books to help the wider Christian community to understand South Asian cultures, faiths, and mindset, which include *Sari 'n' Chips*,[40] *Chapatis for Tea: Reaching your Hindu Neighbour: A Practical Guide*,[41] *Notes for the Journey: Following Jesus, Staying South Asian*,[42] *Engaging with Hindus: Understanding Their World; Sharing Good News*.[43, 44] Additionally, it produced some worship albums that featured Asian and Western fusion music.[45]

In February 2018, SAC handed over its "work in the UK to Interserve to concentrate on work in South Asia and the Diaspora. Interserve took up the emphasis on training and enabling churches to reach out to Hindus and Sikhs, to complement their existing emphasis on Islam."[46]

South Asian Forum (SAF) of the Evangelical Alliance (EA)

In 2007, SAC began informal conversations with the EA that led to the formation of SAF in 2010 as an "integral part of the Evangelical Alliance but with its own officers and steering group".[47] Mr Manoj Raithatha, its first National Coordinator, said, "We want to draw people – especially South Asians – to the knowledge and love of Jesus."[48] To further its aim to "equip the church to engage with South Asians of different faith and cultures", SAF produced a booklet called *Jesus Through Asian Eyes*. It answered fifteen of the most common questions that SAs, Hindus, Muslims, and Sikhs raise about or against Christianity. The booklet was recast as course to reach SAs, and is referred to as Alpha for Asians.[49] SAFs work is ably continued by Dayalan Mahesan, referred to above.

Global Connections (GC)

For almost twenty-two years, GC has been instrumental in bringing together people and networks engaged in work to share Christ with Muslims.[50] This network has been necessary for various reasons, including fostering mutual respect and understanding among those undertaking such work.

The need for "strong-minded, strong-willed... people" to pioneer work among Muslims, which is "often highly charged emotionally", can lead to difficulties within and between bodies engaging in this work.[51] Given the significant challenges but also the wonderful opportunities in this work, GC has achieved a great deal in establishing and promoting this network that supports and encourages one another.

Jewels in His Crown

Jewels in His Crown was a consortium formed in 1999 to run conferences to bring together SACs and those working among SAs to worship, receive teaching, share resources and ideas, pray, and network with others. It took place six times from July 2000 to July 2010.[52] While successful, when the residential format became difficult to sustain, a series of day partnership meetings were held in collaboration with SAF, which took complete ownership in 2014.[53]

It is to the credit of these and other organizations that they served in the area God called them to, wisely ceasing or passing on their work to others, as appropriate.

SACs' Experience of Racism

Since SACs are a subset of SAs, naturally they experienced/experience racism, both within the community and within the church.

Revd David Wise, former minister of Greenford Baptist Church, west London, states, "The whole church community facing up to the reality of racism (which was still often denied by white members) came after an Asian family in membership of the church was attacked."[54] The ubiquitous nature of such attacks even led to the common phrase, "Paki bashing".

Personally, I recall a church leader who tried to dissuade me from considering Baptist ministry and encouraged me to reach SAs. Sadly, for more than a decade it led me to distance myself from SAs and SACs for fear of being typecast.

This is not a phenomenon of the 1950 and 1960s; as recently as 2010, *The Hindu*, an Indian newspaper, carried an article entitled "Indian Christians feel unwelcome in U.K. churches". It reported:

> Indian-origin Christians who feel unwelcome in mainstream churches are forming their own small churches where they sing and pray in Hindi, Gujarati, Tamil and Punjabi to the accompaniment of "dhol" and other instruments. Ram Gidoomal, a [Christian and] prominent member of the Asian community... [said] that there were at least 200 such small churches founded by disenfranchised Christians across Britain as a response to feelings of rejection.[55]

Additionally, one interviewee confirmed the experience of other SACs in that cultural differences, such as wearing SA attire, can cause Black and White Christians to question our presence in church. There is cultural dissonance when SACs are seen in church, which further exacerbates our sense of not belonging.

SACs' Engagement with Racial Justice

Given the difficulties of facing either overt or covert racism within wider society, SACs understandably sought, but often did not find, welcome and acceptance within historic denominations. Therefore, many chose to worship with one another, even as recently as 2010, thereby avoiding the need to address the issue.

Also, like other communities, it is likely that some consider it futile to engage with racial justice because they feel that this side of eternity nothing will change; it is best to leave these matters for the Lord to address when he returns.

However, the following exceptions are noteworthy and instructive.

Revd Sudra represented the Alliance of Asian Christians on the "Churches Commission on Racial Justice and brought the subject toward the front of various agendas".[56] South Asian Concern ran "seminars in 1995 and 1996, raising issues about racial tensions", to help people understand how race affected SAs, which later became very apparent during the "2001 riots in Bradford and Oldham".[57]

Revd Frederick George from Sri Lanka served as minister of north London's East Barnet Baptist Church for thirty-eight years. He was a wise and passionate advocate for racial justice within the Baptist family at the regional and national level. He and others called for the London Baptist Association (LBA)[58] to appoint a racial justice coordinator, which encountered opposition but eventually came to pass in 1998.[59]

Revd Dr Inderjit Bhogal is a Methodist minister who consistently and actively advocated for racial justice within Methodism. He describes his ministry as having been lonely, as he is the only Punjabi East African Asian minister, with few other SAs within Methodism. He organized a Black Theology Conference in 1993, a conference for Asian Women Theologians in 2017, and, at the time of writing, for 2023 he is planning an event to mark the thirtieth anniversary of the Black Theology Conference.

Revd Dr Michael Jagessar describes himself as "an Indo-Guyanese-Caribbean in the UK".[60] For twelve years he served as the URC's Secretary for Global and Intercultural Ministries. At his farewell event in February 2020, his work in producing resources for the local church was applauded: "[His] resource production has been second to none. There have been worship resources, not least for Racial Justice Sunday, Bible studies, films, books, and *Better Church Hosting* – a handbook for churches that host migrant communities in a variety of partnerships."[61] Very importantly, he helped the URC to move "from being multicultural to developing intercultural habits that 'ask all to subscribe to a larger view than our own or that of our group'".[62] He shared this insight with me, which I whole heartedly embrace and advocate.

While researching for this essay, my attention has been drawn to Anglican ordinand Niv Lobo of Indian origin who, following Mr George Floyd's murder, wrote an excellent article in *Crossway*, entitled "Racism: Why We Might Miss the Opportunity".[63] Mr Manoj Pujari, a young believer of Hindu background and member of a Baptist Church, has a good grasp of racial justice issues and is emerging as a strong racial justice advocate. It is encouraging to see a new generation of SACs advocating for racial justice, and the hope is that many more will follow.

Personal Reflections and Suggestions

I am a first-generation Indian immigrant who was brought up within a Hindu Brahmin caste home. My experience of unearned caste privilege led me to question and then abandon my Hindu faith in favour of agnosticism/atheism. While studying chemistry at university I concluded that there must be a God and, through the faithful witness of a believer, I accepted Christ as my Saviour and Lord in May 1985. My reflections and suggestions are based on reading, study, personal engagement with a cross section of people, and wide-ranging experience.

Data collection

That none of the historic denominations collect ethnicity data was not surprising, but still disappointing. During my tenure as Regional Minister for Racial Justice with the LBA, I conducted an ethnicity survey in 2003–04. While some were reluctant to complete a detailed form, others regarded it as unnecessarily drawing attention to difference, stating, "We are all one in Christ."

The "one in Christ" argument is often advanced to maintain the status quo, thus perpetuating injustice and exclusion. Well-collated data, by denominations and para-church organizations, is essential to identify the opportunities and challenges that are faced in order to:

- Ensure just and meaningful representation within all sections of local church, denominational structures, and para-church bodies;

- Identify, train, encourage, and equip future leaders to ensure the previous point becomes a reality;
- Devise appropriate strategies for mission and evangelism.

In compliance with GDPR regulations, denominational heads and CEOs of para-church organizations must take the lead in calling for such data collection, articulating the reasons for doing so and encouraging everyone's participation. They must also ensure that data leads to strategic actionable steps, which are regularly monitored for there to be meaningful change.

Welcoming and retaining SAs/SACs

Mr Steve Uppal, Senior Pastor of All Nations Church, Wolverhampton, states, "South Asians are deeply relational/community oriented and so if they attend a Church that doesn't do community well, there are real challenges there."[64] During my tenure at the LBA I suggested to a minister whose fellowship wanted to engage with SAs in their locality that I attend and assess a church service as a mystery worshipper. I wrote a report encouraging positive aspects that I had seen and suggested areas for change. On accepting and implementing the suggestions, the church witnessed an increase in the numbers of SAs/SACs attending and choosing to stay.

Such intentionality and willingness to change are essential within historic and other denominations that want to reach their local SA population.

SACs' unique opportunities to address racial justice

South Asians encompass nine nations, with multiple languages, religions, cultures, and significant intranational differences. Some, like East African or Caribbean Asians, are twice removed from South Asia. Additionally, one must factor in the caste system, which interweaves its way through all these differences. Therefore, as one interviewee rightly observed, there are multiple prejudicial and discriminatory practices among SAs that need to be addressed, which leads to understandable reticence to address racial justice.

From my own spiritual journey, I totally concur with this viewpoint. However, through my study of intersectionality I realize that there is another perspective.[65] Eric Law, a Chinese American Episcopal priest, explains that everyone can find themselves "shifting back and forth between being powerful and powerless depending on the context in which we relate to others."[66] Therefore, while in some SA and SAC spaces I have power and privilege, within the dominant White space not only may I lack power, but I may also experience personal and institutionalized prejudice and discrimination. I believe that my need to face and address my unearned caste privilege does not disqualify me from addressing racism, but by being open about my own journey I have a more credible platform from which to address and challenge racism.

I would encourage other SACs to explore and address their own unearned privileges so that they too can credibly address racial justice, always first advocating for the welfare and wholeness of others.

Insufficient gospel fruit among SAs

Of the various reasons for this, two require constant attention and correction:

- All faiths and cultures seek to assimilate new adherents and arrivals into their mode of being.[67] Therefore, there needs to be a concerted effort to learn and embrace one another's Christ-centred practices and to jettison ungodly aspects of our culture/past faith.[68] (See section on intercultural church for further details.)
- Pastor Uppal observes that, "the amount of "Church splits" that South Asians go through seems disproportionately high".[69]

Pastor Uppal believes that it is a "cultural/class" issue rooted in caste.[70] Among SAs and SACs, caste leads to an idolatrous obsession with status that must be repented of.[71] Pastor Uppal states that this mindset leads too many SACs to think that they too can build and lead their own church, but their ecclesiology of the "Christian holy man who replaces the Hindu/Sikh holy man" will fail.[72]

While Pastor Uppal observes that this a universal issue, as SAC leaders it is incumbent upon us to address and overcome this issue so that we can present Christ with greater credibility to our SA family, friends, and neighbours.

Racial justice is essential for mission and evangelism

During my tenure with the LBA, I often heard the criticism that racial justice is a social gospel agenda that diverts precious resources from mission and evangelism. Yet it is the exact opposite. My Hindu relatives have been quick to point out that the church is riddled with racism and caste prejudice and so we have no right to preach to them. Therefore, I always make the point that racial justice is integral to gospel proclamation because we cannot preach a gospel of reconciliation if we don't take steps to practise it.

In the lights of caste issues cited above, SACs must engage with caste and racial justice issues to share Christ effectively.

The relevance of intercultural church for reaching the SA community

Many western missionaries to SA followed the example of Father Fernandez, who turned "converts as nearly as possible into Portuguese".[73] This practice continues to be followed within the church today when someone from another faith embraces Christ, "as it is a universal phenomenon".[74]

A genuinely intercultural church must not only sing songs and eat foods from different cultures but also examine our cultures through the lens of Scripture to discover what honours God and what does not. I had the opportunity to do just this when in the early 1990s I attended a support group for former Hindus, Sikhs, and Muslims who had embraced Christ. We discovered scriptural affirmation of many aspects of our culture, such as:

- Respect for authority and leadership (Hebrews 13:17);
- Respect, care, and provision for elderly and extended family members (1 Timothy 5:4, 8).

We also explored unbiblical aspects of our culture, such as status and honour referred to above.

To build a genuinely intercultural church, space must be made to explore our culture through Scripture to embrace from each other genuine God- and people-honouring aspects of one another's culture.[75] Pastor Uppal agrees that this must be a multi-way learning process in which we listen to and learn from one another that we may truly honour and glorify God.[76]

Such a church will communicate to SAs that there are aspects of their culture that honour God, and therefore embracing Christ does not entail becoming a "coconut", a derogatory term meaning brown on the outside and white on the inside, because Christianity is the "White" religion. Once they embrace Christ, they can be appropriately discipled to study Scripture so that they can discern the ungodly aspects of their culture that need to be abandoned. But this is an exercise that every other ethnicity and culture needs to undertake, particularly White western Christians who for centuries have assumed that their faith and culture are one and the same.

Youth and young adults – today's and tomorrow's church

Those interviewed within historic denominations who hosted or had close links with language-specific churches mentioned that the place of subsequent generations within church life is a key issue. From personal knowledge, I am aware that some recognize the need for bilingual services, where English is the other language, to keep their young people in church. Others seek to immerse their children and young people in their language and culture to keep them rooted to the older generation. However, since most of their life is spent within British culture, they will become more adept within the majority culture. In some contexts where SAs and SACs are few, young people want to fit in and be accepted within the majority culture rather than adhering to their parents' culture.

Mr Mahesan stated that young SACs are also attracted to churches that fall under the Hillsong or Holy Trinity Brompton umbrella, which will naturally deplete SA churches and cultures.

Within this context Pastor Sanjay Rajo has pioneered Naujavan, meaning "youth" in Hindi, to "inspire, develop, equip and connect young Asian people who feel they don't belong in Church". He states that

231

young people in Asian churches attend "out of dutiful respect, but their faith is non-existent. Some of the services are in Punjabi, Hindi or other Asian languages rather than in English, the mother tongue of many modern young Asians." Naujavan meets three times a year in different locations to "worship, hear the Gospel and get prayed for".[77]

While Naujavan and similar groups for young believers meet an obvious need, Revd Sudra observes that the younger generation are "losing touch with their historical and cultural roots" and that "great[er] integration... has a price and it is greater disintegration of our own ethnic roots!"[78]

I share Revd Sudra's concern, but am also encouraged to hear Pastor Rajo share that Naujavan members "have made lots of our own music that includes more Indian/Asian flavour".[79] He also observes that SA culture's "strong emphasis on family relationships, generosity, hospitality, parties and food... infuses my Christian faith in ways more naturally than standard western culture".[80] These observations are very encouraging because younger SACs must be able to relate to their SA peers with respect to the culture, mindset, and spirituality so that they can meaningfully share Christ with them, particularly as some are strongly reconnecting to their roots.

I would go further in encouraging young SACs to actively invest in learning and reconnecting with their SA culture, language, and God-honouring aspects of their spirituality. Why? Because aspects that are rich, beautiful, and scriptural can enhance our collective walk with Christ and enable us to share Christ with SAs.

I share one example. When my father and other family gave us monetary gifts, they never gave £10, £50 or £100, but always £11, £51 or £101. The additional one signified that there is always more. This for me captures the essence of God our Father, with whom there is always more blessing, favour, and an overflowing cup (Psalm 23:5).

This saying, attributed to Cardinal Basil Hulme, whether apocryphal or not, is salient to this point: "If every person is made in the image and likeness of God, then I must listen to everyone, because they may be saying what only they can say." If we completely lose our family, ethnic, cultural identity, and unthinkingly abandon all aspects of our spiritual heritage, then we rob ourselves and the wider Christian body of enjoying the manifold wisdom of God, which we alone can bring to the table.

Perennial Signs of Hope

"Human proclivity to sin means that the sin of racism will be a perennial issue."[81] I continue to believe this, but there are also perennial signs of hope, which must be affirmed and celebrated. In writing this essay I have observed the following.

- The perennial nature of racism requires new and younger advocates to emerge, who are reflecting on their own and others' experiences and are willing to speak out. Ordinand Lobo and Mr Pujari are picking up the baton. Mr Pujari's answer to my question of whether young SACs have largely assimilated into white British Christianity indicates wider thought, as he has noted that among not only SACs, but also others, there "is a broader acceptance of whiteness". He gives various examples, including how children are given Western/Jewish names, and concludes, "I am not opposed to people freely naming their children. However, the power of words and the significance of names of South Asian culture is being lost."[82] Through writing this piece, I feel admonished to ensure that I pass on my learning and experience to a younger generation.
- The Salvation Army's commitment to identify and address its exclusionary practice of SAs is both courageous and prophetic. In the wake of Mr George Floyd's murder, it is a very timely exercise, which I pray will be fruitful not only for the organization but also for the wider UK Christian family to learn from.
- Mosaic Harrow, led by Revd Mohan Seevaratnam, is seeking to become an intercultural church. "Our aim is for all cultures represented in our community to be expressed in the way we worship and generally 'do church.'"[83]
- All Nations Church, Wolverhampton, led by Pastor Uppal, is deliberately taking steps to be reflective of the picture in Revelation 7:9, where people of every nation, tribe, people, and language are present before God. Pastor Uppal states that he ensures every area of ministry is multi-ethnic and that people of different classes are present. In view of SAs'/SACs' practice and experience of caste and race prejudice, this too is a prophetic lesson.

The UK Christian family must learn from all these prophetic signs of hope. They are indicative of the fact that we serve the true God of hope, who is always at work among his people to lead us into his *shalom*, and we are blessed to have faithful sisters and brothers who have ears to hear and follow him, that all may be blessed. *Shanti!*

> See, I am doing a new thing!
>> Now it springs up; do you not perceive it?
> I am making a way in the wilderness
>> and streams in the wasteland.
> (Isaiah 43:19, NIV)

Notes

1 Nations that form South Asia are Afghanistan, Bangladesh, Bhutan, India, Maldives, Nepal, Pakistan, and Sri Lanka; sometimes Myanmar (Burma) is included.

2 The perception among South Asians is that all White people and Black people are "Christian"; they do not make distinctions about whether someone has a living faith or not.

3 Rozina Visram, *Asians in Britain: 400 Years of History* (London: Pluto Press, 2002), p. 1.

4 Visram, *Asians in Britain*, p. 1.

5 Gary Younge, "Ambalavaner Sivanandan obituary", *The Guardian*, 7 February 2018, www.theguardian.com/world/2018/feb/07/ambalavaner-sivanandan (last viewed 29 April 2022).

6 "Post 1947 Migration to the UK – from India, Bangladesh, Pakistan and Sri Lanka", Striking Women, www.striking-women.org/module/map-major-south-asian-migration-flows/post-1947-migration-uk-india-bangladesh-pakistan-and (last viewed 29 April 2022).

7 "Post 1947 migration to the UK".

8 "Post 1947 migration to the UK".

9 "South Asians Making Britain", Moving People Changing Places, www.movingpeoplechangingplaces.org/migration-histories/south-asians-making-britain.html (last viewed 29 April 2022).

10 "Indentured Labour from South Asia (1834–1917)" Striking Women, www.striking-women.org/module/map-major-south-asian-migration-flows/indentured-labour-south-asia-1834-1917 (last viewed 29 April 2022).

11 Pradip Sudra, "Asian Community", in Michael Mitton (ed.), *The Way of Renewal* (London: Church Publishing House, 1998), p. 126.

12 "Families and Migration: Older People from South Asia", Department for International Development, October 2022, assets.publishing.service. gov.uk/media/57a08d3ced915d3cfd0018dc/R7655GujaratiUKreport.pdf (last viewed 29 April 2022).

13 "New Immigration System: What You Need to Know", HM Government, www.gov.uk/guidance/new-immigration-system-what-you-need-to-know (last viewed 29 April 2022).

14 Desmond Fernandes, "Empty promises: UK fails to protect persecuted Pakistanis, Sri Lankans", *UCA News*, www.ucanews.com/news/empty-promises-uk-fails-to-protect-persecuted-pakistanis-sri-lankans/88927# (last viewed 29 April 2022).

15 Riazat Butt, "Church of England Looks to Attract More Ethnic Minority Christians", *The Guardian*, 30 June 2010, www. theguardian.com/world/2010/jun/30/church-of-england-ethnic-minorities#:~:text=Official%20figures%20show%20that%20 about,who%20live%20in%20the%20UK (last viewed 29 April 2022).

16 Kerala Catholic Association of the UK, www.kcauk.org/index.php/ en (last viewed 29 April 2022); Tamil Catholic Association UK, www. tca-uk.org/#:~:text=The%20Tamil%20Catholic%20Association%20 %28UK%29%20is%20celebrating%20its,all%20the%20needy%20 Tamils%20in%20Srilanka%20whenever%20possible (last viewed 29 April 2022).

17 "Scotland's Census: At a Glance", www.scotlandscensus.gov.uk/ ethnicity-identity-language-and-religion (last viewed 29 April 2022). I am grateful to Revd Mandy Ralph for extracting and sending me the relevant table.

18 While convention is not to use titles for persons within academic papers, I have used titles for those personally known to me. From my cultural perspective it feels uncomfortable not to use titles, particularly for those older than me.

19 Sudra, "Asian Community", p. 126 (italics as original).

20 Sudra, "Asian Community", p. 126.

21 Sudra, "Asian Community", p. 126.

22 Personal communication with Revd Sudra, quoted with permission.

23 "South Asian Forum", Evangelical Alliance, www.eauk.org/what-we-do/ networks/south-asian-forum (last viewed 29 April 2022).

24 NCCUK, nccuk.org (last viewed 29 April 2022).

25 "Bengali Christian Association – BCA, UK", Facebook, www.facebook.

com/pages/category/Community-Organization/Bengali-Christian-Association-BCA-UK-1730514557227078 (last viewed 29 April 2022).

26 British Asian Christian Association, www.britishpakistanichristians. org/ (last viewed 29 April 2022).

27 Material gathered through email exchange with Revd Sudra, which is quoted with his permission, and "Asian Community", his contribution to Michael Mitton (ed.), *The Way of Renewal*.

28 Personal communication with Revd Sudra, quoted with permission.

29 Sudra, "Asian Community", p. 125.

30 Sudra, "Asian Community", p. 126.

31 Sudra, "Asian Community", p. 126.

32 Personal communication with Revd Sudra, quoted with permission.

33 Personal communication with Revd Sudra, quoted with permission.

34 Personal communication with Revd Sudra, quoted with permission.

35 Arif Mohamed with Ram Gidoomal, Robin Thomson, and Raju Abraham, *Diaspora Mission: The Story of South Asian Concern* (Sutton, South Asian Concern, p. 41).

36 Mohamed et al, *Diaspora Mission*, p. 41.

37 Mohamed et al, *Diaspora Mission*, p. 9.

38 Mohamed et al, *Diaspora Mission*, p. 44.

39 Mohamed et al, *Diaspora Mission*, p. 51.

40 Ram Gidoomal, *Sari 'n' Chips* (Oxford: Monarch Books, 1993).

41 Margaret Wardell and Ram Gidoomal, *Chapatis for Tea: Reaching Your Hindu Neighbour: A Practical Guide* (Godalming: Highland Books, 1994).

42 Robin Thomson and C. Rasiah (eds), *Notes for the Journey: Following Jesus, Staying South Asian* (London: South Asian Concern, 2011).

43 Robin Thomson, *Engaging with Hindus: Understanding Their World; Sharing Good News* (Epsom: The Good Book Company, 2014).

44 Mohamed et al, *Diaspora Mission*, pp. 61–62.

45 Mohamed et al, *Diaspora Mission*, pp. 63–65.

46 Personal communication with Mr Robin Thomson, quoted with permission.

47 Mohamed et al, *Diaspora Mission*, p. 101.

48 Mohamed et al, *Diaspora Mission*, p. 102.

49 *Discovering Jesus Through Asian Eyes*, Evangelical Alliance, www.eauk. org/great-commission/resources/discovering-jesus-through-asian-eyes (last viewed 29 April 2022).

50 B. Knell, "Engaging with Other Believers – Establishing Networks", in Bert de Ruiter (ed.), *Engaging with Muslims in Europe* (Nürnberg: VTR Publications, 2014), p. 98.

51 Knell, "Engaging with Other Believers", p. 98.

52 Personal communication with Mr Robin Thomson, quoted with permission.

53 Personal communication with Mr Robin Thomson, quoted with permission.

54 David Wise, "Emergence of Multicultural Congregations in the LBA – Reflection on Greenford Baptist Church 1965–2015", in Faith Bowers, Joe Kapolyo, and Israel Olofinjana (eds), *Encountering London: London Baptists in the 21st Century* (London: London Baptist Association, 2015), p. 218.

55 "Indian Christians Feel Unwelcome in U.K. Churches", *The Hindu*, 29 June 2010, https://www.thehindu.com/news/Indian-Christians-feel-unwelcome-in-U.K.-churches/article16272131.ece (last viewed 29 April 2022).

56 Personal communication with Revd Sudra, quoted with permission.

57 Mohamed et al, *Diaspora Mission*, p. 68.

58 The London Baptist Association (LBA) is now known as London Baptists (LB), but I'll refer to it by its name when I served there.

59 Sivakumar Rajagopalan, "Racial Justice", in *Encountering London*, p. 257.

60 "In Conversation with Rev Dr Michael Jagessar", Council for World Mission, www.cwmission.org/in-conversation-with-rev-dr-michael-jagessar (last viewed 29 April 2022).

61 "United Reformed Church House bids the Revd Dr Michael Jagessar farewell", The Presbyterian Church in Taiwan, 18 February 2020, http://english.pct.org.tw/enNews_ecu.aspx?strBlockID=B00178&strConten tid=C2020021800002&strCTID=&strDesc=Y&strPub=&strASP=en News_ecu (last viewed 17 May 2022).

62 https://urc.org.uk/latest-news/3353-church-house-bids-the-revd-dr-michael-jagessar-farewell.html Accessed 27th February 2021.

63 Niv Lobo, "Racism: Why We Might Miss the Opportunity", Church Society, 8 October 2020, www.churchsociety.org/resource/racism-why-we-might-miss-the-opportunity (last viewed 29 April 2022).

64 Personal communication with Mr Steve Uppal, quoted with permission.

65 Patricia Hill Collins, *Fighting Words: Black Women and the Search for Justice* (Minnesota, University of Minnesota Press, 1998), p. 205.

66 Eric H. F. Law, The Wolf Shall Dwell with the Lamb: A Spirituality for Leadership in a Multicultural Community (St Louis: Chalice Press, 1993), p. 57.

67 Sivakumar Rajagopalan, "My Journey of Faith from Hinduism to Christ to Hindu Yesu Bhakta", in Lucinda Mosher, Andrew Wingate, and Joshva Raja (eds), *Relating with Hindu Diaspora: Anglican & Lutheran Reflections* (London: Anglican Interfaith Networks, Lutheran Porvoo Communion and World Council of Churches, 2015), p. 19.

68 Rajagopalan, "My Journey of Faith", pp. 19–21.

69 Personal communication with Mr Steve Uppal, quoted with permission.

70 Personal communication with Mr Steve Uppal, quoted with permission.

71 Rajagopalan, "My Journey of Faith", p. 20.

72 Personal communication with Mr Steve Uppal, quoted with permission.

73 Stephen Neill, *A History of Christian Missions*, Second Edition (London: Penguin, 1986), p. 156.

74 Kumar Rajagopalan, "My Journey of Faith from Hinduism to Christ to Hindu Yesu Bhakta", in Lucinda Mosher, Andrew Wingate, and Joshva Raja (eds), "Relating with Hindu Diaspora: Anglican & Lutheran Reflections" (Anglican Interfaith Networks, Lutheran Porvoo Communion & World Council of Churches, London, 2015), p. 19.

75 Of course, Scripture itself is culturally located, but within that one can discover what honours God and one another.

76 Personal communication with Mr Steve Uppal, quoted with permission.

77 "Asian Christians in 'Naujavan' uncover their vision", Evangelical Alliance, 19 August 2010, www.eauk.org/church/stories/asian-christians.cfm (last viewed 29 April 2022).

78 Personal communication with Revd Sudra, quoted with permission.

79 Personal communication with Sanjay Rajo, quoted with permission.

80 Personal communication with Sanjay Rajo, quoted with permission.

81 Rajagopalan, "Racial Justice", p. 263.

82 Personal communication with Mr Manoj Pujari, quoted with permission.

83 Mosaic Harrow, mosaicharrow.org.uk (last viewed 29 April 2022).